ISBN 0-8373-1849-1

C-1849    CAREER EXAMINATION SERIES

*This is your*
*PASSBOOK® for...*

# Administrative Assistant II

*Test Preparation Study Guide*

*Questions & Answers*

**NATIONAL LEARNING CORPORATION**

# PASSBOOK®
## NOTICE

This book is SOLELY intended for, is sold ONLY to, and its use is RESTRICTED to *individual*, bona fide applicants or candidates who qualify by virtue of having seriously filed applications for appropriate license, certificate, professional and/or promotional advancement, higher school matriculation, scholarship, or other legitimate requirements of educational and/or governmental authorities.

This book is NOT intended for use, class instruction, tutoring, training, duplication, copying, reprinting, excerption, or adaptation, etc., by:

(1)  Other publishers

(2)  Proprietors and/or Instructors of "Coaching" and/or Preparatory Courses

(3)  Personnel and/or Training Divisions of commercial, industrial, and governmental organizations

(4)  Schools, colleges, or universities and/or their departments and staffs, including teachers and other personnel

(5)  Testing Agencies or Bureaus

(6)  Study groups which seek by the purchase of a single volume to copy and/or duplicate and/or adapt this material for use by the group as a whole without having purchased individual volumes for each of the members of the group

(7)  Et al.

Such persons would be in violation of appropriate Federal and State statutes.

*PROVISION OF LICENSING AGREEMENTS.* — Recognized educational commercial, industrial, and governmental institutions and organizations, and others legitimately engaged in educational pursuits, including training, testing, and measurement activities, may address a request for a licensing agreement to the copyright owners, who will determine whether, and under what conditions, including fees and charges, the materials in this book may be used by them. In other words, a licensing facility exists for the legitimate use of the material in this book on other than an individual basis. However, it is asseverated and affirmed here that the material in this book *CANNOT* be used without the receipt of the express permission of such a licensing agreement from the Publishers.

NATIONAL LEARNING CORPORATION
212 Michael Drive
Syosset, New York  11791

Inquiries re licensing agreements should be addressed to:
The President
National Learning Corporation
212 Michael Drive
Syosset, New York  11791

# PASSBOOK® SERIES

THE *PASSBOOK® SERIES* has been created to prepare applicants and candidates for the ultimate academic battlefield — the examination room.

At some time in our lives, each and every one of us may be required to take an examination — for validation, matriculation, admission, qualification, registration, certification, or licensure.

Based on the assumption that every applicant or candidate has met the basic formal educational standards, has taken the required number of courses, and read the necessary texts, the *PASSBOOK® SERIES* furnishes the one special preparation which may assure passing with confidence, instead of failing with insecurity. Examination questions — together with answers — are furnished as the basic vehicle for study so that the mysteries of the examination and its compounding difficulties may be eliminated or diminished by a sure method.

This book is meant to help you pass your examination provided that you qualify and are serious in your objective.

The entire field is reviewed through the huge store of content information which is succinctly presented through a provocative and challenging approach — the question-and-answer method.

A climate of success is established by furnishing the correct answers at the end of each test.

You soon learn to recognize types of questions, forms of questions, and patterns of questioning. You may even begin to anticipate expected outcomes.

You perceive that many questions are repeated or adapted so that you can gain acute insights, which may enable you to score many sure points.

You learn how to confront new questions, or types of questions, and to attack them confidently and work out the correct answers.

You note objectives and emphases, and recognize pitfalls and dangers, so that you may make positive educational adjustments.

Moreover, you are kept fully informed in relation to new concepts, methods, practices, and directions in the field.

You discover that you are actually taking the examination all the time: you are preparing for the examination by "taking" an examination, not by reading extraneous and/or supererogatory textbooks.

In short, this PASSBOOK®, used directedly, should be an important factor in helping you to pass your test.

# ADMINISTRATIVE ASSISTANT II

## DUTIES

Under general supervision, as a level II assistant to the head of a department or comparable work unit, to be responsible for management of general business activities; to supervise and be responsible for the work of one or more Administrative Assistant I's and/or a group of clerical assistants; perform related work as required.

## EXAMPLES OF TYPICAL TASKS:

In accordance with departmental or divisional policies and procedures, subject to general and specific work assignments with technical phases of the work subject to review on completion, but with considerable responsibility for making recommendations and developing work details, and initiating steps in the procedure; performs a variety of work tasks typified by, but not limited to the following examples:

As an assistant to the head of a relatively small department or a comparable work unit, does administrative, procedural, fiscal, personnel and payroll functions and investigates organizational aspects of the assigned areas of responsibility.

Individually, obtains facts on specific details or organization, work flow, work unit, costs and other management related activities; prepares organization charts and work flow charts; does the more involved and complex tasks of the work unit such as budget development, personnel, and payroll processing, purchasing, financial analysis; complies detailed statements of costs, expenditures, and recommendations; gathers information as to the purpose of existing methods and procedures; analyzes financial, administrative and management implications of proposed changes; determines the effect of recommended change of service, costs, purchasing requirements, personnel, and budget requests; installs approved systems or methods; prepares comprehensive and periodic reports; represents the department in contacts with professional organizations, private concerns and governmental agencies regarding departmental activities.

## SCOPE OF THE WRITTEN TEST

The written test will be designed to test for knowledge, skills, and/or abilities in such areas as:
1. Office management;
2. Supervision;
3. Preparing written material; and
4. Understanding and interpreting written material.

# HOW TO TAKE A TEST

## I. YOU MUST PASS AN EXAMINATION

### A. WHAT EVERY CANDIDATE SHOULD KNOW

Examination applicants often ask us for help in preparing for the written test. What can I study in advance? What kinds of questions will be asked? How will the test be given? How will the papers be graded?

As an applicant for a civil service examination, you may be wondering about some of these things. Our purpose here is to suggest effective methods of advance study and to describe civil service examinations.

Your chances for success on this examination can be increased if you know how to prepare. Those "pre-examination jitters" can be reduced if you know what to expect. You can even experience an adventure in good citizenship if you know why civil service exams are given.

### B. WHY ARE CIVIL SERVICE EXAMINATIONS GIVEN?

Civil service examinations are important to you in two ways. As a citizen, you want public jobs filled by employees who know how to do their work. As a job seeker, you want a fair chance to compete for that job on an equal footing with other candidates. The best-known means of accomplishing this two-fold goal is the competitive examination.

Exams are widely publicized throughout the nation. They may be administered for jobs in federal, state, city, municipal, town or village governments or agencies.

Any citizen may apply, with some limitations, such as the age or residence of applicants. Your experience and education may be reviewed to see whether you meet the requirements for the particular examination. When these requirements exist, they are reasonable and applied consistently to all applicants. Thus, a competitive examination may cause you some uneasiness now, but it is your privilege and safeguard.

### C. HOW ARE CIVIL SERVICE EXAMS DEVELOPED?

Examinations are carefully written by trained technicians who are specialists in the field known as "psychological measurement," in consultation with recognized authorities in the field of work that the test will cover. These experts recommend the subject matter areas or skills to be tested; only those knowledges or skills important to your success on the job are included. The most reliable books and source materials available are used as references. Together, the experts and technicians judge the difficulty level of the questions.

Test technicians know how to phrase questions so that the problem is clearly stated. Their ethics do not permit "trick" or "catch" questions. Questions may have been tried out on sample groups, or subjected to statistical analysis, to determine their usefulness.

Written tests are often used in combination with performance tests, ratings of training and experience, and oral interviews. All of these measures combine to form the best-known means of finding the right person for the right job.

## II. HOW TO PASS THE WRITTEN TEST

### A. *NATURE OF THE EXAMINATION*

To prepare intelligently for civil service examinations, you should know how they differ from school examinations you have taken. In school you were assigned certain definite pages to read or subjects to cover. The examination questions were quite detailed and usually emphasized memory. Civil service exams, on the other hand, try to discover your present ability to perform the duties of a position, plus your potentiality to learn these duties. In other words, a civil service exam attempts to predict how successful you will be. Questions cover such a broad area that they cannot be as minute and detailed as school exam questions.

In the public service similar kinds of work, or positions, are grouped together in one "class." This process is known as *position-classification*. All the positions in a class are paid according to the salary range for that class. One class title covers all of these positions, and they are all tested by the same examination.

### B. *FOUR BASIC STEPS*

#### 1) Study the announcement

How, then, can you know what subjects to study? Our best answer is: "Learn as much as possible about the class of positions for which you've applied." The exam will test the knowledge, skills and abilities needed to do the work.

Your most valuable source of information about the position you want is the official exam announcement. This announcement lists the training and experience qualifications. Check these standards and apply only if you come reasonably close to meeting them.

The brief description of the position in the examination announcement offers some clues to the subjects which will be tested. Think about the job itself. Review the duties in your mind. Can you perform them, or are there some in which you are rusty? Fill in the blank spots in your preparation.

Many jurisdictions preview the written test in the exam announcement by including a section called "Knowledge and Abilities Required," "Scope of the Examination," or some similar heading. Here you will find out specifically what fields will be tested.

#### 2) Review your own background

Once you learn in general what the position is all about, and what you need to know to do the work, ask yourself which subjects you already know fairly well and which need improvement. You may wonder whether to concentrate on improving your strong areas or on building some background in your fields of weakness. When the announcement has specified "some knowledge" or "considerable knowledge," or has used adjectives like "beginning principles of..." or "advanced ... methods," you can get a clue as to the number and difficulty of questions to be asked in any given field. More questions, and hence broader coverage, would be included for those subjects which are more important in the work. Now weigh your strengths and weaknesses against the job requirements and prepare accordingly.

#### 3) Determine the level of the position

Another way to tell how intensively you should prepare is to understand the level of the job for which you are applying. Is it the entering level? In other words, is this the position in which beginners in a field of work are hired? Or is it an intermediate or advanced level? Sometimes this is indicated by such words as "Junior" or "Senior" in the class title. Other jurisdictions use Roman numerals to designate the level – Clerk I, Clerk II, for example. The word "Supervisor" sometimes appears in the title. If the level is not indicated by the title, check the description of duties. Will you be working under very close supervision, or will you have responsibility for independent decisions in this work?

## 4) Choose appropriate study materials

Now that you know the subjects to be examined and the relative amount of each subject to be covered, you can choose suitable study materials. For beginning level jobs, or even advanced ones, if you have a pronounced weakness in some aspect of your training, read a modern, standard textbook in that field. Be sure it is up to date and has general coverage. Such books are normally available at your library, and the librarian will be glad to help you locate one. For entry-level positions, questions of appropriate difficulty are chosen – neither highly advanced questions, nor those too simple. Such questions require careful thought but not advanced training.

If the position for which you are applying is technical or advanced, you will read more advanced, specialized material. If you are already familiar with the basic principles of your field, elementary textbooks would waste your time. Concentrate on advanced textbooks and technical periodicals. Think through the concepts and review difficult problems in your field.

These are all general sources. You can get more ideas on your own initiative, following these leads. For example, training manuals and publications of the government agency which employs workers in your field can be useful, particularly for technical and professional positions. A letter or visit to the government department involved may result in more specific study suggestions, and certainly will provide you with a more definite idea of the exact nature of the position you are seeking.

## III. KINDS OF TESTS

Tests are used for purposes other than measuring knowledge and ability to perform specified duties. For some positions, it is equally important to test ability to make adjustments to new situations or to profit from training. In others, basic mental abilities not dependent on information are essential. Questions which test these things may not appear as pertinent to the duties of the position as those which test for knowledge and information. Yet they are often highly important parts of a fair examination. For very general questions, it is almost impossible to help you direct your study efforts. What we can do is to point out some of the more common of these general abilities needed in public service positions and describe some typical questions.

## 1) General information

Broad, general information has been found useful for predicting job success in some kinds of work. This is tested in a variety of ways, from vocabulary lists to questions about current events. Basic background in some field of work, such as sociology or economics, may be sampled in a group of questions. Often these are principles which have become familiar to most persons through exposure rather than through formal training. It is difficult to advise you how to study for these questions; being alert to the world around you is our best suggestion.

## 2) Verbal ability

An example of an ability needed in many positions is verbal or language ability. Verbal ability is, in brief, the ability to use and understand words. Vocabulary and grammar tests are typical measures of this ability. Reading comprehension or paragraph interpretation questions are common in many kinds of civil service tests. You are given a paragraph of written material and asked to find its central meaning.

## 3) Numerical ability

Number skills can be tested by the familiar arithmetic problem, by checking paired lists of numbers to see which are alike and which are different, or by interpreting charts and graphs. In the latter test, a graph may be printed in the test booklet which you are asked to use as the basis for answering questions.

## 4) Observation

A popular test for law-enforcement positions is the observation test. A picture is shown to you for several minutes, then taken away. Questions about the picture test your ability to observe both details and larger elements.

## 5) Following directions

In many positions in the public service, the employee must be able to carry out written instructions dependably and accurately. You may be given a chart with several columns, each column listing a variety of information. The questions require you to carry out directions involving the information given in the chart.

## 6) Skills and aptitudes

Performance tests effectively measure some manual skills and aptitudes. When the skill is one in which you are trained, such as typing or shorthand, you can practice. These tests are often very much like those given in business school or high school courses. For many of the other skills and aptitudes, however, no short-time preparation can be made. Skills and abilities natural to you or that you have developed throughout your lifetime are being tested.

Many of the general questions just described provide all the data needed to answer the questions and ask you to use your reasoning ability to find the answers. Your best preparation for these tests, as well as for tests of facts and ideas, is to be at your physical and mental best. You, no doubt, have your own methods of getting into an exam-taking mood and keeping "in shape." The next section lists some ideas on this subject.

## IV. KINDS OF QUESTIONS

Only rarely is the "essay" question, which you answer in narrative form, used in civil service tests. Civil service tests are usually of the short-answer type. Full instructions for answering these questions will be given to you at the examination. But in case this is your first experience with short-answer questions and separate answer sheets, here is what you need to know:

## 1) Multiple-choice Questions

Most popular of the short-answer questions is the "multiple choice" or "best answer" question. It can be used, for example, to test for factual knowledge, ability to solve problems or judgment in meeting situations found at work.

A multiple-choice question is normally one of three types—

- It can begin with an incomplete statement followed by several possible endings. You are to find the one ending which *best* completes the statement, although some of the others may not be entirely wrong.
- It can also be a complete statement in the form of a question which is answered by choosing one of the statements listed.
- It can be in the form of a problem – again you select the best answer.

Here is an example of a multiple-choice question with a discussion which should give you some clues as to the method for choosing the right answer:

When an employee has a complaint about his assignment, the action which will *best* help him overcome his difficulty is to
- A. discuss his difficulty with his coworkers
- B. take the problem to the head of the organization
- C. take the problem to the person who gave him the assignment
- D. say nothing to anyone about his complaint

In answering this question, you should study each of the choices to find which is best. Consider choice "A" – Certainly an employee may discuss his complaint with fellow employees, but no change or improvement can result, and the complaint remains unresolved. Choice "B" is a poor choice since the head of the organization probably does not know what assignment you have been given, and taking your problem to him is known as "going over the head" of the supervisor. The supervisor, or person who made the assignment, is the person who can clarify it or correct any injustice. Choice "C" is, therefore, correct. To say nothing, as in choice "D," is unwise. Supervisors have and interest in knowing the problems employees are facing, and the employee is seeking a solution to his problem.

## 2) True/False Questions

The "true/false" or "right/wrong" form of question is sometimes used. Here a complete statement is given. Your job is to decide whether the statement is right or wrong.

SAMPLE: A person-to-person long-distance telephone call costs less than a station-to-station call to the same city.

This statement is wrong, or false, since person-to-person calls are more expensive.

This is not a complete list of all possible question forms, although most of the others are variations of these common types. You will always get complete directions for answering questions. Be sure you understand *how* to mark your answers – ask questions until you do.

## V. RECORDING YOUR ANSWERS

For an examination with very few applicants, you may be told to record your answers in the test booklet itself. Separate answer sheets are much more common. If this separate answer sheet is to be scored by machine – and this is often the case – it is highly important that you mark your answers correctly in order to get credit.

An electric scoring machine is often used in civil service offices because of the speed with which papers can be scored. Machine-scored answer sheets must be marked with a pencil, which will be given to you. This pencil has a high graphite content which responds to the electric scoring machine. As a matter of fact, stray dots may register as answers, so do not let your pencil rest on the answer sheet while you are pondering the correct answer. Also, if your pencil lead breaks or is otherwise defective, ask for another.

Since the answer sheet will be dropped in a slot in the scoring machine, be careful not to bend the corners or get the paper crumpled.

The answer sheet normally has five vertical columns of numbers, with 30 numbers to a column. These numbers correspond to the question numbers in your test booklet. After each number, going across the page are four or five pairs of dotted lines. These short dotted lines have small letters or numbers above them. The first two pairs may also have a "T" or "F" above the letters. This indicates that the first two pairs only are to be used if the questions are of the true-false type. If the questions are multiple choice, disregard the "T" and "F" and pay attention only to the small letters or numbers.

Answer your questions in the manner of the sample that follows:

32. The largest city in the United States is
   A. Washington, D.C.
   B. New York City
   C. Chicago
   D. Detroit
   E. San Francisco

1) Choose the answer you think is best. (New York City is the largest, so "B" is correct.)
2) Find the row of dotted lines numbered the same as the question you are answering. (Find row number 32)
3) Find the pair of dotted lines corresponding to the answer. (Find the pair of lines under the mark "B.")
4) Make a solid black mark between the dotted lines.

## VI. BEFORE THE TEST

Common sense will help you find procedures to follow to get ready for an examination. Too many of us, however, overlook these sensible measures. Indeed, nervousness and fatigue have been found to be the most serious reasons why applicants fail to do their best on civil service tests. Here is a list of reminders:

- Begin your preparation early – Don't wait until the last minute to go scurrying around for books and materials or to find out what the position is all about.
- Prepare continuously – An hour a night for a week is better than an all-night cram session. This has been definitely established. What is more, a night a

6

week for a month will return better dividends than crowding your study into a shorter period of time.

- Locate the place of the exam – You have been sent a notice telling you when and where to report for the examination. If the location is in a different town or otherwise unfamiliar to you, it would be well to inquire the best route and learn something about the building.
- Relax the night before the test – Allow your mind to rest. Do not study at all that night. Plan some mild recreation or diversion; then go to bed early and get a good night's sleep.
- Get up early enough to make a leisurely trip to the place for the test – This way unforeseen events, traffic snarls, unfamiliar buildings, etc. will not upset you.
- Dress comfortably – A written test is not a fashion show. You will be known by number and not by name, so wear something comfortable.
- Leave excess paraphernalia at home – Shopping bags and odd bundles will get in your way. You need bring only the items mentioned in the official notice you received; usually everything you need is provided. Do not bring reference books to the exam. They will only confuse those last minutes and be taken away from you when in the test room.
- Arrive somewhat ahead of time – If because of transportation schedules you must get there very early, bring a newspaper or magazine to take your mind off yourself while waiting.
- Locate the examination room – When you have found the proper room, you will be directed to the seat or part of the room where you will sit. Sometimes you are given a sheet of instructions to read while you are waiting. Do not fill out any forms until you are told to do so; just read them and be prepared.
- Relax and prepare to listen to the instructions
- If you have any physical problem that may keep you from doing your best, be sure to tell the test administrator. If you are sick or in poor health, you really cannot do your best on the exam. You can come back and take the test some other time.


## VII. AT THE TEST

The day of the test is here and you have the test booklet in your hand. The temptation to get going is very strong. Caution! There is more to success than knowing the right answers. You must know how to identify your papers and understand variations in the type of short-answer question used in this particular examination. Follow these suggestions for maximum results from your efforts:

### 1) Cooperate with the monitor

The test administrator has a duty to create a situation in which you can be as much at ease as possible. He will give instructions, tell you when to begin, check to see that you are marking your answer sheet correctly, and so on. He is not there to guard you, although he will see that your competitors do not take unfair advantage. He wants to help you do your best.

### 2) Listen to all instructions

Don't jump the gun! Wait until you understand all directions. In most civil service tests you get more time than you need to answer the questions. So don't be in a hurry.

Read each word of instructions until you clearly understand the meaning. Study the examples, listen to all announcements and follow directions. Ask questions if you do not understand what to do.

### 3) Identify your papers

Civil service exams are usually identified by number only. You will be assigned a number; you must not put your name on your test papers. Be sure to copy your number correctly. Since more than one exam may be given, copy your exact examination title.

### 4) Plan your time

Unless you are told that a test is a "speed" or "rate of work" test, speed itself is usually not important. Time enough to answer all the questions will be provided, but this does not mean that you have all day. An overall time limit has been set. Divide the total time (in minutes) by the number of questions to determine the approximate time you have for each question.

### 5) Do not linger over difficult questions

If you come across a difficult question, mark it with a paper clip (useful to have along) and come back to it when you have been through the booklet. One caution if you do this – be sure to skip a number on your answer sheet as well. Check often to be sure that you have not lost your place and that you are marking in the row numbered the same as the question you are answering.

### 6) Read the questions

Be sure you know what the question asks! Many capable people are unsuccessful because they failed to *read* the questions correctly.

### 7) Answer all questions

Unless you have been instructed that a penalty will be deducted for incorrect answers, it is better to guess than to omit a question.

### 8) Speed tests

It is often better NOT to guess on speed tests. It has been found that on timed tests people are tempted to spend the last few seconds before time is called in marking answers at random – without even reading them – in the hope of picking up a few extra points. To discourage this practice, the instructions may warn you that your score will be "corrected" for guessing. That is, a penalty will be applied. The incorrect answers will be deducted from the correct ones, or some other penalty formula will be used.

### 9) Review your answers

If you finish before time is called, go back to the questions you guessed or omitted to give them further thought. Review other answers if you have time.

### 10) Return your test materials

If you are ready to leave before others have finished or time is called, take ALL your materials to the monitor and leave quietly. Never take any test material with you. The monitor can discover whose papers are not complete, and taking a test booklet may be grounds for disqualification.

## VIII. EXAMINATION TECHNIQUES

1) Read the general instructions carefully. These are usually printed on the first page of the exam booklet. As a rule, these instructions refer to the timing of the examination; the fact that you should not start work until the signal and must stop work at a signal, etc. If there are any *special* instructions, such as a choice of questions to be answered, make sure that you note this instruction carefully.

2) When you are ready to start work on the examination, that is as soon as the signal has been given, read the instructions to each question booklet, underline any key words or phrases, such as *least, best, outline, describe* and the like. In this way you will tend to answer as requested rather than discover on reviewing your paper that you *listed without describing*, that you selected the *worst* choice rather than the *best* choice, etc.

3) If the examination is of the objective or multiple-choice type – that is, each question will also give a series of possible answers: A, B, C or D, and you are called upon to select the best answer and write the letter next to that answer on your answer paper – it is advisable to start answering each question in turn. There may be anywhere from 50 to 100 such questions in the three or four hours allotted and you can see how much time would be taken if you read through all the questions before beginning to answer any. Furthermore, if you come across a question or group of questions which you know would be difficult to answer, it would undoubtedly affect your handling of all the other questions.

4) If the examination is of the essay type and contains but a few questions, it is a moot point as to whether you should read all the questions before starting to answer any one. Of course, if you are given a choice – say five out of seven and the like – then it is essential to read all the questions so you can eliminate the two that are most difficult. If, however, you are asked to answer all the questions, there may be danger in trying to answer the easiest one first because you may find that you will spend too much time on it. The best technique is to answer the first question, then proceed to the second, etc.

5) Time your answers. Before the exam begins, write down the time it started, then add the time allowed for the examination and write down the time it must be completed, then divide the time available somewhat as follows:
   - If 3-1/2 hours are allowed, that would be 210 minutes. If you have 80 objective-type questions, that would be an average of 2-1/2 minutes per question. Allow yourself no more than 2 minutes per question, or a total of 160 minutes, which will permit about 50 minutes to review.
   - If for the time allotment of 210 minutes there are 7 essay questions to answer, that would average about 30 minutes a question. Give yourself only 25 minutes per question so that you have about 35 minutes to review.

6) The most important instruction is to *read each question* and make sure you know what is wanted. The second most important instruction is to *time yourself properly* so that you answer every question. The third most

9

important instruction is to *answer every question*. Guess if you have to but include something for each question. Remember that you will receive no credit for a blank and will probably receive some credit if you write something in answer to an essay question. If you guess a letter – say "B" for a multiple-choice question – you may have guessed right. If you leave a blank as an answer to a multiple-choice question, the examiners may respect your feelings but it will not add a point to your score. Some exams may penalize you for wrong answers, so in such cases *only*, you may not want to guess unless you have some basis for your answer.

7) Suggestions
  a. Objective-type questions
    1. Examine the question booklet for proper sequence of pages and questions
    2. Read all instructions carefully
    3. Skip any question which seems too difficult; return to it after all other questions have been answered
    4. Apportion your time properly; do not spend too much time on any single question or group of questions
    5. Note and underline key words – *all, most, fewest, least, best, worst, same, opposite,* etc.
    6. Pay particular attention to negatives
    7. Note unusual option, e.g., unduly long, short, complex, different or similar in content to the body of the question
    8. Observe the use of "hedging" words – *probably, may, most likely,* etc.
    9. Make sure that your answer is put next to the same number as the question.
    10. Do not second-guess unless you have good reason to believe the second answer is definitely more correct
    11. Cross out original answer if you decide another answer is more accurate; do not erase until you are ready to hand your paper in
    12. Answer all questions; guess unless instructed otherwise
    13. Leave time for review

  b. Essay questions
    1. Read each question carefully
    2. Determine exactly what is wanted. Underline key words or phrases.
    3. Decide on outline or paragraph answer
    4. Include many different points and elements unless asked to develop any one or two points or elements
    5. Show impartiality by giving pros and cons unless directed to select one side only
    6. Make and write down any assumptions you find necessary to answer the questions
    7. Watch your English, grammar, punctuation and choice of words
    8. Time your answers; don't crowd material

8) Answering the essay question

Most essay questions can be answered by framing the specific response around several key words or ideas. Here are a few such key words or ideas:

M's: manpower, materials, methods, money, management
P's: purpose, program, policy, plan, procedure, practice, problems, pitfalls, personnel, public relations

    a. Six basic steps in handling problems:
        1. Preliminary plan and background development
        2. Collect information, data and facts
        3. Analyze and interpret information, data and facts
        4. Analyze and develop solutions as well as make recommendations
        5. Prepare report and sell recommendations
        6. Install recommendations and follow up effectiveness

    b. Pitfalls to avoid
        1. *Taking things for granted* – A statement of the situation does not necessarily imply that each of the elements is necessarily true; for example, a complaint may be invalid and biased so that all that can be taken for granted is that a complaint has been registered
        2. *Considering only one side of a situation* – Wherever possible, indicate several alternatives and then point out the reasons you selected the best one
        3. *Failing to indicate follow up* – Whenever your answer indicates action on your part, make certain that you will take proper follow-up action to see how successful your recommendations, procedures or actions turn out to be
        4. *Taking too long in answering any single question* – Remember to time your answers properly

## IX. AFTER THE TEST

Scoring procedures differ in detail among civil service jurisdictions although the general principles are the same. Whether the papers are hand-scored or graded by machine we have described, they are nearly always graded by number. That is, the person who marks the paper knows only the number – never the name – of the applicant. Not until all the papers have been graded will they be matched with names. If other tests, such as training and experience or oral interview ratings have been given, scores will be combined. Different parts of the examination usually have different weights. For example, the written test might count 60 percent of the final grade, and a rating of training and experience 40 percent. In many jurisdictions, veterans will have a certain number of points added to their grades.

After the final grade has been determined, the names are placed in grade order and an eligible list is established. There are various methods for resolving ties between those who get the same final grade – probably the most common is to place first the name of the person whose application was received first. Job offers are made from the eligible list in the order the names appear on it. You will be notified of your grade and your rank as soon as all these computations have been made. This will be done as rapidly as possible.

People who are found to meet the requirements in the announcement are called "eligibles." Their names are put on a list of eligible candidates. An eligible's chances of getting a job depend on how high he stands on this list and how fast agencies are filling jobs from the list.

When a job is to be filled from a list of eligibles, the agency asks for the names of people on the list of eligibles for that job. When the civil service commission receives this request, it sends to the agency the names of the three people highest on this list. Or, if the job to be filled has specialized requirements, the office sends the agency the names of the top three persons who meet these requirements from the general list.

The appointing officer makes a choice from among the three people whose names were sent to him. If the selected person accepts the appointment, the names of the others are put back on the list to be considered for future openings.

That is the rule in hiring from all kinds of eligible lists, whether they are for typist, carpenter, chemist, or something else. For every vacancy, the appointing officer has his choice of any one of the top three eligibles on the list. This explains why the person whose name is on top of the list sometimes does not get an appointment when some of the persons lower on the list do. If the appointing officer chooses the second or third eligible, the No. 1 eligible does not get a job at once, but stays on the list until he is appointed or the list is terminated.

## X. HOW TO PASS THE INTERVIEW TEST

The examination for which you applied requires an oral interview test. You have already taken the written test and you are now being called for the interview test – the final part of the formal examination.

You may think that it is not possible to prepare for an interview test and that there are no procedures to follow during an interview. Our purpose is to point out some things you can do in advance that will help you and some good rules to follow and pitfalls to avoid while you are being interviewed.

### What is an interview supposed to test?

The written examination is designed to test the technical knowledge and competence of the candidate; the oral is designed to evaluate intangible qualities, not readily measured otherwise, and to establish a list showing the relative fitness of each candidate – as measured against his competitors – for the position sought. Scoring is not on the basis of "right" and "wrong," but on a sliding scale of values ranging from "not passable" to "outstanding." As a matter of fact, it is possible to achieve a relatively low score without a single "incorrect" answer because of evident weakness in the qualities being measured.

Occasionally, an examination may consist entirely of an oral test – either an individual or a group oral. In such cases, information is sought concerning the technical knowledges and abilities of the candidate, since there has been no written examination for this purpose. More commonly, however, an oral test is used to supplement a written examination.

### Who conducts interviews?

The composition of oral boards varies among different jurisdictions. In nearly all, a representative of the personnel department serves as chairman. One of the members of the board may be a representative of the department in which the candidate would work. In some cases, "outside experts" are used, and, frequently, a businessman or some other representative of the general public is asked to serve. Labor and management or other special groups may be represented. The aim is to secure the services of experts in the appropriate field.

However the board is composed, it is a good idea (and not at all improper or unethical) to ascertain in advance of the interview who the members are and what groups they represent. When you are introduced to them, you will have some idea of their backgrounds and interests, and at least you will not stutter and stammer over their names.

*What should be done before the interview?*

While knowledge about the board members is useful and takes some of the surprise element out of the interview, there is other preparation which is more substantive. It *is* possible to prepare for an oral interview – in several ways:

**1) Keep a copy of your application and review it carefully before the interview**

This may be the only document before the oral board, and the starting point of the interview. Know what education and experience you have listed there, and the sequence and dates of all of it. Sometimes the board will ask you to review the highlights of your experience for them; you should not have to hem and haw doing it.

**2) Study the class specification and the examination announcement**

Usually, the oral board has one or both of these to guide them. The qualities, characteristics or knowledges required by the position sought are stated in these documents. They offer valuable clues as to the nature of the oral interview. For example, if the job involves supervisory responsibilities, the announcement will usually indicate that knowledge of modern supervisory methods and the qualifications of the candidate as a supervisor will be tested. If so, you can expect such questions, frequently in the form of a hypothetical situation which you are expected to solve. NEVER go into an oral without knowledge of the duties and responsibilities of the job you seek.

**3) Think through each qualification required**

Try to visualize the kind of questions you would ask if you were a board member. How well could you answer them? Try especially to appraise your own knowledge and background in each area, *measured against the job sought*, and identify any areas in which you are weak. Be critical and realistic – do not flatter yourself.

**4) Do some general reading in areas in which you feel you may be weak**

For example, if the job involves supervision and your past experience has NOT, some general reading in supervisory methods and practices, particularly in the field of human relations, might be useful. Do NOT study agency procedures or detailed manuals. The oral board will be testing your understanding and capacity, not your memory.

**5) Get a good night's sleep and watch your general health and mental attitude**

You will want a clear head at the interview. Take care of a cold or any other minor ailment, and of course, no hangovers.

*What should be done on the day of the interview?*

Now comes the day of the interview itself. Give yourself plenty of time to get there. Plan to arrive somewhat ahead of the scheduled time, particularly if your appointment is in the fore part of the day. If a previous candidate fails to appear, the board might be ready for you a bit early. By early afternoon an oral board is almost invariably behind schedule if there are many candidates, and you may have to wait.

Take along a book or magazine to read, or your application to review, but leave any extraneous material in the waiting room when you go in for your interview. In any event, relax and compose yourself.

The matter of dress is important. The board is forming impressions about you – from your experience, your manners, your attitude, and your appearance. Give your personal appearance careful attention. Dress your best, but not your flashiest. Choose conservative, appropriate clothing, and be sure it is immaculate. This is a business interview, and your appearance should indicate that you regard it as such. Besides, being well groomed and properly dressed will help boost your confidence.

Sooner or later, someone will call your name and escort you into the interview room. *This is it.* From here on you are on your own. It is too late for any more preparation. But remember, you asked for this opportunity to prove your fitness, and you are here because your request was granted.

*What happens when you go in?*

The usual sequence of events will be as follows: The clerk (who is often the board stenographer) will introduce you to the chairman of the oral board, who will introduce you to the other members of the board. Acknowledge the introductions before you sit down. Do not be surprised if you find a microphone facing you or a stenotypist sitting by. Oral interviews are usually recorded in the event of an appeal or other review.

Usually the chairman of the board will open the interview by reviewing the highlights of your education and work experience from your application – primarily for the benefit of the other members of the board, as well as to get the material into the record. Do not interrupt or comment unless there is an error or significant misinterpretation; if that is the case, do not hesitate. But do not quibble about insignificant matters. Also, he will usually ask you some question about your education, experience or your present job – partly to get you to start talking and to establish the interviewing "rapport." He may start the actual questioning, or turn it over to one of the other members. Frequently, each member undertakes the questioning on a particular area, one in which he is perhaps most competent, so you can expect each member to participate in the examination. Because time is limited, you may also expect some rather abrupt switches in the direction the questioning takes, so do not be upset by it. Normally, a board member will not pursue a single line of questioning unless he discovers a particular strength or weakness.

After each member has participated, the chairman will usually ask whether any member has any further questions, then will ask you if you have anything you wish to add. Unless you are expecting this question, it may floor you. Worse, it may start you off on an extended, extemporaneous speech. The board is not usually seeking more information. The question is principally to offer you a last opportunity to present further qualifications or to indicate that you have nothing to add. So, if you feel that a significant qualification or characteristic has been overlooked, it is proper to point it out in a sentence or so. Do not compliment the board on the thoroughness of their examination – they have been sketchy, and you know it. If you wish, merely say, "No thank you, I have nothing further to add." This is a point where you can "talk yourself out" of a good impression or fail to present an important bit of information. Remember, *you close the interview yourself.*

The chairman will then say, "That is all, Mr. _____, thank you." Do not be startled; the interview is over, and quicker than you think. Thank him, gather your belongings and take your leave. Save your sigh of relief for the other side of the door.

*How to put your best foot forward*

Throughout this entire process, you may feel that the board individually and collectively is trying to pierce your defenses, seek out your hidden weaknesses and embarrass and confuse you. Actually, this is not true. They are obliged to make an appraisal of your qualifications for the job you are seeking, and they want to see you in your best light. Remember, they must interview all candidates and a non-cooperative candidate may become a failure in spite of their best efforts to bring out his qualifications. Here are 15 suggestions that will help you:

**1) Be natural – Keep your attitude confident, not cocky**

If you are not confident that you can do the job, do not expect the board to be. Do not apologize for your weaknesses, try to bring out your strong points. The board is interested in a positive, not negative, presentation. Cockiness will antagonize any board member and make him wonder if you are covering up a weakness by a false show of strength.

**2) Get comfortable, but don't lounge or sprawl**

Sit erectly but not stiffly. A careless posture may lead the board to conclude that you are careless in other things, or at least that you are not impressed by the importance of the occasion. Either conclusion is natural, even if incorrect. Do not fuss with your clothing, a pencil or an ashtray. Your hands may occasionally be useful to emphasize a point; do not let them become a point of distraction.

**3) Do not wisecrack or make small talk**

This is a serious situation, and your attitude should show that you consider it as such. Further, the time of the board is limited – they do not want to waste it, and neither should you.

**4) Do not exaggerate your experience or abilities**

In the first place, from information in the application or other interviews and sources, the board may know more about you than you think. Secondly, you probably will not get away with it. An experienced board is rather adept at spotting such a situation, so do not take the chance.

**5) If you know a board member, do not make a point of it, yet do not hide it**

Certainly you are not fooling him, and probably not the other members of the board. Do not try to take advantage of your acquaintanceship – it will probably do you little good.

**6) Do not dominate the interview**

Let the board do that. They will give you the clues – do not assume that you have to do all the talking. Realize that the board has a number of questions to ask you, and do not try to take up all the interview time by showing off your extensive knowledge of the answer to the first one.

**7) Be attentive**

You only have 20 minutes or so, and you should keep your attention at its sharpest throughout. When a member is addressing a problem or question to you, give him your undivided attention. Address your reply principally to him, but do not exclude the other board members.

## 8) Do not interrupt

A board member may be stating a problem for you to analyze. He will ask you a question when the time comes. Let him state the problem, and wait for the question.

## 9) Make sure you understand the question

Do not try to answer until you are sure what the question is. If it is not clear, restate it in your own words or ask the board member to clarify it for you. However, do not haggle about minor elements.

## 10) Reply promptly but not hastily

A common entry on oral board rating sheets is "candidate responded readily," or "candidate hesitated in replies." Respond as promptly and quickly as you can, but do not jump to a hasty, ill-considered answer.

## 11) Do not be peremptory in your answers

A brief answer is proper – but do not fire your answer back. That is a losing game from your point of view. The board member can probably ask questions much faster than you can answer them.

## 12) Do not try to create the answer you think the board member wants

He is interested in what kind of mind you have and how it works – not in playing games. Furthermore, he can usually spot this practice and will actually grade you down on it.

## 13) Do not switch sides in your reply merely to agree with a board member

Frequently, a member will take a contrary position merely to draw you out and to see if you are willing and able to defend your point of view. Do not start a debate, yet do not surrender a good position. If a position is worth taking, it is worth defending.

## 14) Do not be afraid to admit an error in judgment if you are shown to be wrong

The board knows that you are forced to reply without any opportunity for careful consideration. Your answer may be demonstrably wrong. If so, admit it and get on with the interview.

## 15) Do not dwell at length on your present job

The opening question may relate to your present assignment. Answer the question but do not go into an extended discussion. You are being examined for a *new* job, not your present one. As a matter of fact, try to phrase ALL your answers in terms of the job for which you are being examined.

### Basis of Rating

Probably you will forget most of these "do's" and "don'ts" when you walk into the oral interview room. Even remembering them all will not ensure you a passing grade. Perhaps you did not have the qualifications in the first place. But remembering them will help you to put your best foot forward, without treading on the toes of the board members.

Rumor and popular opinion to the contrary notwithstanding, an oral board wants you to make the best appearance possible. They know you are under pressure – but they also want to see how you respond to it as a guide to what your reaction would be under the pressures of the job you seek. They will be influenced by the degree of poise you display, the personal traits you show and the manner in which you respond.

# EXAMINATION SECTION

# EXAMINATION SECTION
# TEST 1

DIRECTIONS: Each question or incomplete statement is followed by several suggested answers or completions. Select the one that *BEST* answers the question or completes the statement. *PRINT THE LETTER OF THE CORRECT ANSWER IN THE SPACE AT THE RIGHT.*

1. It is often desirable for an administrator to consult, during the planning process, the persons to be affected by those plans.
   Of the following, the MAJOR justification for such consultation is that it recognizes the

   A. fact that participating in horizontal planning is almost always more effective than participating in vertical planning
   B. principle of participation and the need for a sense of belonging as a means of decreasing resistance and developing support
   C. principle that lower-level administrators normally are more likely than higher-level administrators to emphasize longer-range goals
   D. fact that final responsibility for the approval of plans should be placed in committees not individuals

   1.____

2. In evaluating performance and, if necessary, correcting what is being done to assure attainment of results according to plan, it is *GENERALLY* best for the administrator to do which one of the following?

   A. Make a continual effort to increase the number of written control reports prepared.
   B. Thoroughly investigate in equal detail all possible deviations indicated by comparison of performance to expectation.
   C. Decentralize, within an operating unit or division, the responsibility for correcting deviations.    -
   D. Concentrate on the exceptions, or outstanding variations, from the expected results or standards

   2.____

3. Generally, changes in the ways in which the supervisors and employees in an organization do things are MORE likely to be welcomed by them when the changes

   A. threaten the security of the supervisors than when they do not
   B. are inaugurated after prior change has been assimilated than when they are inaugurated before other major changes have been assimilated
   C. follow a series of failures in changes when they follow a series of successful changes
   D. are dictated by personal order rather than when they result from an application of previously established impersonal principles

   3.____

4. For sound organizational relationships, of the following, it is generally MOST desirable that

   A. authority and responsibility be segregated from each other, in order to facilitate control
   B. the authority of a manager should be commensurate with his responsibility, and vice versa

   4.____

C. authority be defined as the obligation of an individual to carry out assigned activities to the best of his or her ability

D. clear recognition be given to the fact that delegation of authority benefits only the manager who delegates it

5. In utilizing a checklist of questions for general managerial planning, which one of the following generally isthe FIRST question to be asked and answered?    5.___

    A. Where will it take place?
    B. How will it be done?
    C. Why must it be done?
    D. Who will do it?

6. Of the following, it is USUALLY best to set administrative objectives so that they are    6.___

    A. at a level that is unattainable, so that administrators will continually be strongly motivated
    B. at a level that is attainable, but requires some stretching and reaching by administrators trying to attain them
    C. stated in qualitative rather than quantitative terms whenever a choice between the two is possible
    D. stated in a general and unstructured manner, to permit each administrator maximum freedom in interpreting them

7. In selecting from among administrative alternatives, three general bases for decision are    7.___
open to the manager experience, experimentation, and research and analysis.
Of the following, the best argument AGAINST primary reliance upon experimentation
as the methods of evaluating administrative alternatives is that experimentation is

    A. generally the most expensive of the three techniques
    B. almost always legally prohibited in procedural matters
    C. possible only in areas
    D. where results may be easily duplicated by other experimenters at any time
    E. an approach that requires information on scientific method seldom available to administrators

8. The administrator who utilizes the techniques of operations research, linear programming, and simulation in making an administrative decision should MOST appropriately be considered to be using the techniques of _____ analysis.    8.___

    A. intuitive
    C. nonmathematical
    B. quantitative
    D. qualitative

9. When an additional organizational level is added within a department, that department has MOST directly manifested    9.___

    A. horizontal growth
    C. vertical growth
    B. horizontal shrinkage
    D. vertical shrinkage

10. Of the following, the one which GENERALLY is the most intangible planning factor is     10.____

    A. budget dollars allocated to a function
    B. square feet of space for office use
    C. number of personnel in various clerical titles
    D. emotional impact of a proposed personnel policy among employees

11. Departmentation by function is the same as, or most similar to, departmentation by     11.____

    A. equipment            B. clientele
    C. territory              D. activity

12. Such verifiable factors as turnover, absenteeism, or volume of grievances would gener-     12.____
ally BEST assist in measuring the effectiveness of a program to improve

    A. forms control        B. employee morale
    C. linear programming      D. executive creativit

13. An organization increases the number of subordinates reporting to a manager up to the     13.____
point where incremental savings in costs, better communication and morale, and other
factors equal incremental losses in effectiveness of control, direction, and similar factors.
This action MOST specifically employs the technique of

    A. role playing
    B. queuing theory
    C. marginal analysis
    D. capital standards analysis

14. The term *computer hardware* is MOST likely to refer to     14.____

    A. machines and equipment
    B. programmed instruction texts and compiler decks
    C. training manuals
    D. documentation supporting usage of computing machines

15. Determining what is being accomplished, that is, evaluating the performance and, if nec-     15.____
essary, applying corrective measures so that performance takes place according to plans
is MOST appropriately called management

    A. actuating           B. planning
    C. controlling         D. motivating

16. Of the following, the BEST overall technique for choosing from among several alternative     16.____
public programs proposed to try to achieve the same broad objective generally is

    A. random-sample analysis
    B. input analysis
    C. cost-effectiveness analysis
    D. output analysis

17. When the success of a plan in achieving specific program objectives is measured against     17.____
that plan's costs, the measure obtained is most directly that of the plan's

    A. pervasiveness       B. control potential
    C. primacy           D. efficiency

18. Generally, the degree to which an organization's planning will be coordinated varies      18.___
MOST directly with the degree to which

   A. the individuals charged with executing plans are better compensated than those
charged with developing and evaluating plans
   B. the individuals charged with planning understand and agree to utilize consistent
planning premises
   C. a large number of position classification titles have been established for those individuals charged with organizational planning functions
   D. subordinate unit objectives are allowed to control the overall objectives of the
departments of which such subordinate units are a part

19. The responsibility for specific types of decisions generally is BEST delegated to      19.___

   A. the highest organizational level at which there is an individual possessing the ability, desire, impartiality and access to relevant information needed to make these
decisions
   B. the lowest organizational level at which there is an individual possessing the ability,
desire, impartiality and access to relevant information needed to make these decisions
   C. a group of executives, rather than a single executive, if these decisions deal with an
emergency
   D. The organizational level midway between that which will have to carry out these
decisions and that which will have to authorize the resources for their implementation

20. The process of managing by objectives is MOST likely to lead to a situation in which the      20.___

   A. goal accomplishment objectives of managers tend to have a longer time span as
one goes lower down the line in an organization
   B. establishment of quantitative goals for staff positions is generally easier than the
establishment of quantitative goals for line positions
   C. development of objectives requires the manager to think of the way he will accomplish given results, and of the organization, personnel and resources that he will
need
   D. superiors normally develop and finally approve detailed goals for subordinates
without any prior consultation with either those subordinates or with the top-level
executives responsible for the longer-run objectives of the organization

21. As used with respect to decision making, the application of scientific method to the study      21.___
of alternatives in a problem situation, with a view to providing a quantitative basis for
arriving at an optimum solution in terms of the goals sought is MOST appropriately called

   A. simple number departmentation
   B. geographic decentralization
   C. operations research
   D. trait rating

22. Assume that a bureau head proposes that final responsibility and authority for all plan-      22.___
ning within the bureau is to be delegated to one employee who is to be paid at the level of
an assistant division head in that bureau.
Of the following, the MOST appropriate comment about this proposal is that it is

A. *improper;* mainly because planning does not call for someone at such a high level
B. *improper;* mainly because responsibility for a basic management function such as planning may not properly be delegated as proposed
C. *proper;* mainly because ultimate responsibility for all bureau planning is best placed as proposed
D. *proper;* mainly because every well-managed bureau should have a full-time planning officer

23. Of the following, the MOST important reason that participation has motivating effects is generally that it gives to the individual participating     23._____

    A. a recognition of his desire to feel important and to contribute to achievement of worthwhile goals
    B. an opportunity to participate in work that is beyond the scope of the class specification for his title
    C. a secure knowledge that his organization's top leadership is as efficient as possible considering all major circumstances
    D. the additional information which is likely to be crucial to his promotion

24. Of the following, the MOST essential characteristic of an effective employee suggestion system is that     24._____

    A. suggestions be submitted upward through the chain of command
    B. suggestions be acted upon promptly so that employees may be promptly informed of what happens to their submitted suggestions
    C. suggesters be required to sign their names on the material sent to the actual evaluators for evaluation
    D. suggesters receive at least 25% of the agency's savings during the first two years after their suggestions have been accepted and put into effect by the agency

25. Two organizations have the same basic objectives and the same total number of employees. The span of authority of each intermediate manager is narrower in one organization than it is in the other organization. It is MOST likely that the organization in which each intermediate manager has a narrower span of authority will have     25._____

    A. fewer intermediate managers
    B. more organizational levels
    C. most managers reporting to a larger number of immediate supervisors
    D. more characteristics of a *flat* organizational structure

# KEY (CORRECT ANSWERS)

| | | | | |
|---|---|---|---|---|
| 1. | B | | 11. | D |
| 2. | D | | 12. | B |
| 3. | B | | 13. | C |
| 4. | B | | 14. | A |
| 5. | C | | 15. | C |
| | | | | |
| 6. | B | | 16. | C |
| 7. | A | | 17. | D |
| 8. | B | | 18. | B |
| 9. | C | | 19. | B |
| 10. | D | | 20. | C |

| | |
|---|---|
| 21. | C |
| 22. | B |
| 23. | A |
| 24. | B |
| 25. | B |

———

# TEST 2

DIRECTIONS: Each question or incomplete statement is followed by several suggested answers or completions. Select the one that *BEST* answers the question or completes the statement. *PRINT THE LETTER OF THE CORRECT ANSWER IN THE SPACE AT THE RIGHT.*

1. Which one of the following BEST expresses the essence of the merit idea or system in public employment?

    A. A person's worth to the organization–the merit of his attributes and capacities–is the governing factor in his selection, assignment, pay, recognition, advancement and retention.

    B. Written tests of the objective type are the only fair way to select on a merit basis from among candidates for open-competitive appointment to positions within the merit system.

    C. Employees who have qualified for civil service positions shall have life-time tenure during good behavior in those positions regardless of changes in public programs.

    D. Periodic examinations with set date limits within which all persons desiring to demonstrate their merit may apply, shall be publicly advertised and held for all promotional titles.

1.\_\_\_\_

2. Of the following, the promotion selection policy generally considered MOST antithetical to the merit concept is the promotion selection policy which

    A. is based solely on objective tests of competence

    B. is based solely on seniority

    C. may require a manager to lose his best employee to another part of the organization

    D. permits operating managers collectively to play a significant role in promotion decisions

2.\_\_\_\_

3. Of the following, the problems encountered by government establishments which are MOST likely to make extensive delegation of authority difficult to effectuate tend to be problems of

    A. accountability and insuring uniform administration

    B. line and staff relationships within field offices

    C. generally employee opposition to such delegation of authority and to the subsequent record-keeping activities

    D. use of the management-by-objectives approach

3.\_\_\_\_

4. The major decisions as to which jobs shall be created and who shall carry which responsibilities should GENERALLY be made by

    A. budgetary advisers

    B. line managers

    C. classification specialists

    D. peer-level rating committees

4.\_\_\_\_

5. The ultimate controlling factor in structuring positions in the public service, MOST generally, should be the

5.\_\_\_\_

A.  possibility of providing upgrading for highly productive employees
B.  collective bargaining demands initially made by established public employee unions
C.  positive motivational effects upon productivity resulting from an inverted pyramid job structure
D.  effectivenss of the structuring in serving the mission of the organization

6.  Of the following, the most usual reason for UNSATISFACTORY line-staff relationships is          6.____

A.  inept use of the abilities of staff personnel by line management
B.  the higher salaries paid to line officials
C.  excessive consultation between line officials and staff officials at the same organizational level
D.  a feeling among the staff members thatv only lower-level line members appreciate their work

7.  Generally, an employee receiving new information from a fellow employee is MOST likely          7.____
to

A.  forget the new information if it is consistent with his existing beliefs much more easily than he forgets the new information if it is inconsistent with his existing beliefs
B.  accept the validity of the new information if it is consistent with his existing beliefs more readily than he accepts the validity of the new information if it is inconsistent with his existing beliefs
C.  have a less accurate memory of the new information if it is consistent with his existing beliefs than he has of the new information if it is inconsistent with his existing beliefs.
D.  ignore the new information if it is consistent with his existing beliefs more often than he ignores the new information if it is inconsistent with his existing beliefs

8.  Virtually all of us use this principle in our human communications -- perhaps without realizing it. In casual conversations, we are alert for cues to whether we are understood (e.g., attentive nods from the other person). Similarly, an instructor is always interested in reactions among those to whom he is giving instruction. The effective administrator is equally conscious of the need to determine his subordinates' reactions to what he is trying to communicate.          8.____
The principle referred to in the above selection is MOST appropriately called

A.  cognitive dissonance                    B.  feedback
C.  negative reinforcement                  D.  noise transmission

9.  Of the following, the PRINCIPAL function of an *ombudsman* generally is to          9.____

A.  review departmental requests for new data processing equipment so as to reduce duplication
B.  receive and investigate complaints from citizens who are displeased with the actions or non-actions of administrative officials and try to effectuate warranted remedies
C.  review proposed departmental reorganizations in order to advise the chief executive whether or not they are in accordance with the latest principles of proper management structuring
D.  presiding over courts of the judiciary convened to try *sitting* judges

10. Of the following, the MOST valid reason for recruiting an intermediate-level administrator from outside an agency, rather than from within the agency, normally is to    10.____

   A. improve the public image of the agency as a desirable place in which to be employed
   B. reduce the number of potential administrators who must be evaluated prior to filling the position
   C. minimize the morale problems arising from frequent internal staff upgradings
   D. obtain fresh ideas and a fresh viewpoint on agency problems

11. A group of positions that are sufficiently similar in nature and level of duties, responsibilities, and qualifications required to warrant similar treatment for purposes of recruitment, examination, and pay, is MOST appropriately called a(n)    11.____

   A. grade                  B. pay range
   C. class                  D. occupational group

12. Governmental personnel testing, MOST generally, has done which one of the following?    12.____

   A. Shown greater precision in testing for creativity and courage than in testing for intelligence and achievement
   B. Developed more useful tests of intelligence, aptitude and achievement than of creativity, courage, and commitment
   C. Failed in the attempt to develop any testing mechanisms in the areas of aptitude or achievement to the point where they are of any use in eliminating extraneous, prejudicial factors in the selection process
   D. Made more use of previous employment records in selecting novices from the outside for junior positions than it has in selecting persons from the outside to fill more senior positions

13. Of the following, the MAJOR objective of government managers in most job restructuring generally should be to    13.____

   A. reduce the percentage that lower-level employees in the government service constitute of the total
   B. reduce the percentage range of the salaries paid within each classified title
   C. concentrate as much of the higher-skill duties in as few of the jobs as possible
   D. package duties into job combinations that are the same as the job combinations traditionally used by lower-paying private employers in the surrounding geographical area

14. Which one of the following statements is MOST generally supported by modern industrial and behavioral research?    14.____

   A. High productivity and high quality each show a substantial negative correlation with high morale.
   B. Where professional employees participate in defining how much and what caliber of their service should be considered acceptable, they generally will set both types of goals substantially below those which management alone would have set.
   C. Professional employees get greater satisfaction out of work that challenges them to exert their capacities fully.
   D. The participative approach to management relieves the manager of the need to be a decision-maker.

15. The term *PPBS* relates MOST directly to one of the systems principally designed to do   15.___
which one of the following?

    A. Reduce the number of mistakes resulting in spoilage and wasted effort to zero
    B. Obtain greater cost effectiveness
    C. Assure that all operations are performed at the highest quality level that is techni-
       cally attainable at the present time
    D. Assure that all output units are fully verified prior to being sent out

16. Assume that you are working with a computer programmer to solve a complex problem.   16.___
Together, you have defined your problem in everyday English clearly enough to proceed.
In the next step, you both start breaking down the information in the definition so that you
both can decide on the operations needed for programming the problem. This next step
of getting from the definition *to* the problem to the point where you can begin laying out
the steps actually to be taken in solving the problem is MOST appropriately called

    A. completing the documentation
    B. implementing the solution
    C. identifying the problem statement
    D. analyzing the problem

17. Assume that during the fiscal year 2006-2007, a bureau produced 20% more work units   17.___
than it produced in the fiscal year 2005-2006. Also, assume that during the fiscal year
2006-2007 that bureau's staff was 20% SMALLER than it was in the fiscal year 2005-
2006.
On the basis of this information, it would be most proper to conclude that the number
of work units produced per staff member in that bureau in the fiscal year 2006-2007
exceeded the number of work units produced per staff member in that bureau in the
fiscal year 2005-2006 by which one of the following percentages?

    A. 20%         B. 25%         C. 40%         D. 50%

18. Assume that during the following five fiscal years (FY), a bureau has received the follow-   18.___
ing appropriations:
    FY 1997-1998 - $200,000: FY 1998-1999 - $240,000
    FY 1999-2000 - $280,000: FY 2000-2001 - $390,000
    FY 2001-2002 - $505,000
The bureau's appropriation for which one of the following fiscal years showed the
LARGEST percentage of increase over the bureau's appropriation for the immediately
previous fiscal year?

    A. FY 1998-1999               B. FY 1999-2000
    C. FY 2000-2001               D. FY 2001-2002

19. A bureau has a very large number of clerical personnel engaged in very similar duties,   19.___
and only a limited portion can be absent at any one time if the workload is to be handled
properly.
Which one of the following would generally be the bureau head's BEST approach
toward scheduling the annual leave time (vacations, etc.) to be taken by the employees
of that bureau? The bureau head

A. personally receives from each employee his preferred schedule of annual leave time, personally decides on when the employee can most conveniently be spared from the Viewpoint of the office workload, and issues his decisions to all concerned in the form of a binding memorandum.

B. advises his subordinate supervisors and employees of the parameters and constraints in time and numbers upon annual leave. The employees and subordinate supervisors prepare a proposed annual leave schedule within those limitations and submit it to the bureau head for approval or modification, and for promulgation.

C. initially asks his subordinate supervisors to prepare a proposed annual leave schedule for employees with a minimum of consultation with the employees. He then circulates this schedule to the employees over his signature as a proposed schedule and invites reaction directly to him.

D. asks employee or union representatives to prepare a proposed schedule with all leave to be taken spread evenly over the entire vacation period. He personally reviews and accepts or modifies this proposal.

20. An agency head desires to have an estimate of the *potential* of a middle-level administrative employee for development for higher-level administrative positions. He also desires to try to minimize possible errors or capriciousness which might creep into that estimate. Of the following, it would generally be MOST desirable to have the estimate

20._____

A. result from the pooled judgment of three or more past or present substantial-level supervisors of the subject employee and of persons with lateral or service contracts with the subject employee

B. made solely by substantial-level executives outside the past or present direct line of supervision above the subject employee

C. result from the pooled judgment of substantial level personnel staff members rather than line executives

D. made solely by the present immediate line supervisor of the subject employee

21. Which one of the following generally BEST characterizes the basic nature of budget making and budget administration from a managerial viewpoint?

21._____

A. Budget administration is control, while budget making is planning.
B. Budget administration is planning, while budget making is control.
C. Both budget making and budget administration are only control functions; neither is a planning function.
D. Both budget making and budget administration are only planning functions; neither is a control function.

22. In preparing his annual budget request for a large bureau with both substantial continuing and anticipated new activities, the bureau head must consider various factors (e.g., retaining credibility and obtaining required funds). Of the following, the BEST long-range budgeting strategy would NORMALLY be for the bureau head to request

22._____

A. twice what is actually needed on the assumption that higher authorities will generally cut the requested amount in half

B. ten per cent less than he actually estimates to be needed and to submit a supplementary request later for that ten per cent

C. what is needed for the continuing activities plus twenty-five per cent to allow some slack funds

D.   what he estimates is needed to continue existing essential programs and to fund needed new activities

23.   If we total all of the occasions in which all governmental positions are filled with new faces (persons who did not occupy those specific positions previously), we generally would find that a GREATER number will result from

A.   new accessions from the outside than from movement of personnel within the organization
B.   movement of personnel within the organization than from new accessions from the outside
C.   promotion of staff personnel to higher staff jobs than from promotion of line personnel to higher line jobs
D.   filling of Exempt and Non-Competitive Class positions than from filling of Competitive Class positions

23.____

24.   Listed immediately below are four measures to be utilized to try to achieve a major personnel goal:
   (1)   Diversifying tasks in any one unit as much as feasible
   (2)   Delegating authority to each layer in the hierarchy to the maximum extent cosistent with the clarity of policy guides, training of staff, and the effectiveness of post-audit procedures
   (3)   Assigning whole integrals of functions to individuals or units instead of splitting them into fine specializations with separate employees or groups concentrating on each
   (4)   Permitting workers to follow through on tasks or projects from start to finish rather than carry out single segments of the process
The major personnel goal which all of the above measures, taken together, may BEST be expected to serve is

A.   increasing job simplification
B.   promoting E.E.O. affirmative action
C.   making and keeping jobs as meaningful as they can practically be
D.   increasing the number of promotional levels available so as to maximize advancement opportunities as much as possible

24.____

25.   Which one of the following is generally the BEST criterion for determining the classification title to which a position should be allocated?
The

A.   personal qualifications possessed by the present or expected appointee to the position
B.   consequences of the work of the position or the responsibility it carries
C.   number of work units required to be produced or completed in the position
D.   consequences of inadequate overall governmental pay scales upon recruitment of outstanding personnel

25.____

———————

# KEY (CORRECT ANSWERS)

| | | | | |
|---|---|---|---|---|
| 1. | A | | 11. | C |
| 2. | B | | 12. | B |
| 3. | A | | 13. | C |
| 4. | B | | 14. | C |
| 5. | D | | 15. | B |
| 6. | A | | 16. | D |
| 7. | B | | 17. | D |
| 8. | B | | 18. | C |
| 9. | B | | 19. | B |
| 10. | D | | 20. | A |

| | |
|---|---|
| 21. | A |
| 22. | D |
| 23. | B |
| 24. | C |
| 25. | B |

———

# EXAMINATION SECTION
## TEST 1

DIRECTIONS: Each question or incomplete statement is followed by several suggested answers or completions. Select the one that BEST answers the question or completes the statement. *PRINT THE LETTER OF THE CORRECT ANSWER IN THE SPACE AT THE RIGHT.*

1. An administrator in a department should be thoroughly familiar with modern methods of personnel administration. This statement is          1.____

   A. true, because this familiarity will help him in performing the normal functions of his office
   B. false, because personnel administration is not a departmental matter, but is centralized in the Civil Service Commission
   C. *true,* because this knowledge will insure the elimination of personnel problems in the department
   D. *false,* because departmental problems of a minor character are handled by the personnel representative, while major problems are the responsibility of the commissioner

2. The LEAST true of the following is that an administrative assistant in a department          2.____

   A. executes the policy laid down by the commissioner or his deputies
   B. in the main, carries out the policies of the commissioner but with some leeway where his own frame of reference is determinative
   C. is never required to formulate policy
   D. is responsible for the successful accomplishment of a section of the department's program

3. If a representative committee of employees in a large department is to meet with an administrative officer for the purpose of improving staff relations and of handling grievances, it is BEST that these meetings be held          3.____

   A. at regular intervals
   B. whenever requested by an aggrieved employee
   C. at the discretion of the administrative officer
   D. whenever the need arises

4. In the theory and practice of public administration, the one of the following which is LEAST generally regarded as a staff function is          4.____

   A. budgeting                    B. fire fighting
   C. purchasing                   D. research and information

5. The LEAST essential factor in the successful application of a service rating system is          5.____

   A. careful training of reporting officers
   B. provision for self–rating
   C. statistical analysis to check reliability
   D. utilization of objective standards of performance

6. Of the following, the one which is NOT an aim of service rating plans is 6.____

    A. establishment of a fair method of measuring employee value to the employer
    B. application of a uniform measurement to employees of the same class and grade performing similar functions
    C. application of a uniform measurement to employees of the same class and grade however different their assignments may be
    D. establishment of a scientific duties plan

7. A rule or regulation relating to the internal management of a department becomes effec- 7.____
tive

    A. only after it is filed in the office of the clerk
    B. as soon as issued by the department head
    C. only after it has been published officially
    D. when approved by the mayor

8. Of the following, the one MOST generally regarded as an *administrative* power is the 8.____

    A. veto power               B. message power
    C. power of pardon         D. rule making power

9. In public administration functional allocation involves 9.____

    A. integration and the assignment of administrative power
    B. the assignment of a single power to a single administrative level
    C. the distribution of a number of subsidiary responsibilities among all levels of government
    D. decentralization of administrative responsibilities

10. In the field of public administration, the LEAST general result of coordination is the 10.____

    A. performance of a well–rounded job
    B. elimination of jurisdictional overlapping
    C. performance of functions otherwise neglected
    D. elimination of duplication of work

11. Of the following, the MOST complicated and difficult problem confronting the reorganizer 11.____
in the field of public administration is

    A. ridding the government of graft
    B. ridding the government of crude incompetence
    C. ridding the government of excessive decentralization
    D. conditioning organization to modern social and economic life

12. The *most accurate* description of the process of integration in the field of public adminis- 12.____
tration is

    A. transfer of administrative authority from a lower to a higher level of government
    B. transfer of administrative authority from a higher to a lower level of government
    C. concentration of administrative authority within one level of government
    D. formal cooperation between city and state governments to administer a function

13. The one of the following who was *most closely* allied with *scientific management* is      13.____

    A.  Mosher       B.  Probst       C.  Taylor       D.  White

14. Of the following wall colors, the one which will reflect the GREATEST amount of light,      14.____
other things being equal, is

    A.  buff       B.  light gray       C.  light blue       D.  brown

15. Natural illumination is LEAST necessary in a(n)      15.____

    A.  executive office                B.  reception room
    C.  central stenographic bureau    D.  conference room

16. The MOST desirable relative humidity in an office is      16.____

    A.  30%       B.  50%       C.  70%       D.  90%

17. When several pieces of correspondence are filed in the same folder they are *usually*      17.____
arranged

    A.  according to subject           B.  numerically
    C.  in the order in which they are received  D.  alphabetically

18. Eliminating slack in work assignments is      18.____

    A.  speed-up       B.  time study       C.  motion study
    D.  efficient managment

19. *Time studies* examine and measure      19.____

    A.  past performance           B.  present performance
    C.  long-run effect              D.  influence of change

20. In making a position analysis for a duties classification, the one of the following factors      20.____
which must be considered is the

    A.  capabilities of the incumbent
    B.  qualifications of the incumbent
    C.  efficiency attained by the incumbent
    D.  responsibility assigned to the incumbent

21. The MAXIMUM number of subordinates who can be effectively supervised by one      21.____
administrative assistant is BEST considered as

    A.  determined by the law of *span of control*
    B.  determined by the law of *span of attention*
    C.  determined by the type of work supervised
    D.  fixed at not more than six

22. Of the following devices used in personnel administration, the MOST basic is      22.____

    A.  classification           B.  service rating
    C.  appeals               D.  in-service training

23. Of the following, the LEAST important factor for sound organization is the     23.\_\_\_\_

    A. individual and his position
    B. hierarchical form of organization
    C. location and delegation of authority
    D. standardization of salary schedules

24. *Stretch–out* is a term that originated with the     24.\_\_\_\_

    A. imposition of a furlough
    B. system of semi–monthly relief payments
    C. development of labor technology
    D. irregular development of low–cost housing projects

25. The one of the following which is LEAST generally true of a personnel division in a large     25.\_\_\_ department is that it is

    A. concerned with having a certain point of view on personnel permeate the executive staff
    B. charged with aiding operating executives with auxiliary staff service, assistance and advice
    C. charged to administer a certain few operating duties of its own
    D. charged with the basic responsibility for the efficient operation of the entire depart- ment

———

# KEY (CORRECT ANSWERS)

| | | | |
|---|---|---|---|
| 1. A | | 11. D | |
| 2. C | | 12. C | |
| 3. A | | 13. C | |
| 4. B | | 14. A | |
| 5. B | | 15. B | |
| 6. D | | 16. A | |
| 7. B | | 17. C | |
| 8. D | | 18. D | |
| 9. C | | 19. B | |
| 10. C | | 20. D | |

21. C
22. A
23. D
24. C
25. D

———

# TEST 2

DIRECTIONS: Below are ten words numbered 1 through 10 and twenty other words divided into four groups - Group A, Group B, Group C and Group D. For each of the ten numbered words, select the word in one of the four groups which is MOST NEARLY the same in meaning. The letter of that group is the answer for the item. *PRINT THE LETTER OF THE CORRECT ANSWER IN THE SPACE AT THE RIGHT.*

| | | | | |
|---|---|---|---|---|
| 1. abnegation | GROUP A | GROUP B | GROUP C | 1._____ |
| 2. calumnious | articulation | bituminous | assumption | 2._____ |
| | fusion | deductive | forecast | |
| 3. purview | catastrophic | repudiation | terse | 3._____ |
| | inductive | doleful | insolence | |
| 4. lugubrious | leadership | prolonged | panorama | 4._____ |
| 5. hegemony | | | | 5._____ |
| 6. arrogation | | GROUP D | | 6._____ |
| 7. coalescence | | scope | | 7._____ |
| | | vindication | | |
| 8. prolix | | amortization | | 8._____ |
| | | productive | | |
| 9. syllogistic | | slanderous | | 9._____ |
| 10. contumely | | | | 10._____ |

Questions 11-25.

DIRECTIONS: Each question or incomplete statement is followed by several suggested answers or completions. Select the one that BEST answers the question or completes the statement.

11. In large cities the total cost of government is of course *greater* than in small cities but    11._____

    A. this is accompanied by a decrease in per capita cost
    D. the per capita cost is also greater
    C. the per capita cost is approximately the same
    D. the per capita cost is considerably less in approximately 50% of the cases

12. The one of the following which is LEAST characteristic of governmental reorganizations    12._____
is the

    A. saving of large sums of money
    B. problem of morale and personnel
    C. task of logic and management
    D. engineering approach

13. The LEAST accurate of the following statements about graphic presentation is     13.____

    A. it is desirable to show as many coordinate lines as possible in a finished diagram
    B. the horizontal scale should read from left to right and the vertical scale from top to bottom
    C. when two or more curves are represented for comparison on the same chart, their zero lines should coincide
    D. a percentage curve should not be used when the purpose is to show the actual amounts of increase or decrease

14. Grouping of figures in a frequency distribution results in a *loss* of     14.____

    A. linearity        B. significance        C. detail        D. coherence

15. The true financial condition of a city is BEST reflected when its accounting system is placed upon a(n)     15.____

    A. cash basis                B. accrual basis
    C. fiscal basis              D. warrant basis

16. When the discrepancy between the totals of a trial balance is $36, the LEAST probable cause of the error is     16.____

    A. omission of an item
    B. entering of an item on the wrong side of the ledger
    C. a mistake in addition or subtraction
    D. transposition of digits

17. For the *most effective* administrative management, appropriations should be     17.____

    A. itemized        B. lump sum        C. annual        D. bi-annual

18. Of the following types of expenditure control in the practice of fiscal management, the one which is LEAST important is that which relates to     18.____

    A. past policy affecting expenditures
    B. future policy affecting expenditures
    C. prevention of improper use of funds
    D. prevention of overdraft

19. The sinking fund method of retiring bonds does NOT     19.____

    A. permit investment in a new issue of city bonds when the general market is unsatisfactory
    B. cause irreparable injury to the city's credit when the city is unable to make a scheduled contribution
    C. require periodic actuarial computations
    D. cost as much to administer as the serial bond method

20. Of the following, the statement that is FALSE is:    20.____

    A. Non-profit hospitalization plans are based on underlying principles similar to those which underlie mutual insurance
    B. Federal, state and local governments pay for more than half of the medical care received by more than half of the population of the country
    C. In addition to non-profit hospitalization, non-profit organizations providing reimbursement for medical and nursing care are now being organized in this state
    D. Voluntary health insurance must be depended on since a state system of health insurance is unconstitutional

21. The *most accurate* of the following statements concerning birth and death rates is:    21.____

    A. A high birth rate is usually accompanied by a relatively high death rate
    B. A high birth rate is usually accompanied by a relatively low death rate
    C. The rate of increase in population for a given area may be obtained by subtracting the death rate from the birth rate
    D. The rate of increase in population for a given area may be obtained by subtracting the birth rate from the death rate

22. Empirical reasoning is based upon    22.____

    A. experience and observation
    B. *a priori* propositions
    C. application of an established generalization
    D. logical deduction

23. 45% of the employees of a certain department are enrolled in in-service training courses and 35% are registered in college courses.    23.____
The percentage of employees NOT enrolled in either of these types of courses is

    A. 20%    B. at least 20% and not more than 55%
    C. approximately 40%    D. none of these

24. A typist can address approximately R envelopes in a 7-hour day. A list containing S addresses is submitted with a request that all envelopes be typed within T hours.    24.____
The number of typists needed to complete this task would be

    A. $\dfrac{7RS}{T}$    B. $\dfrac{S}{7RT}$    C. $\dfrac{R}{7ST}$    D. $\dfrac{7S}{RT}$

25. Bank X allows a customer to write without charge five checks per month for each $100     25.___
on deposit, but a check deposited or a cash deposit counts the same as a check written.
Bank Y charges ten cents for every check written, requires no minimum balance and
allows deposit of cash or of checks made out to customer free. A man receives two salary checks and, on the average, five other checks each month. He pays, on the average,
twelve bills a month, five of which are for amounts between $5 and $10, five for amounts
between $10 and $20, two for about $30. Assume that he pays these bills either by check
or by Post Office money order (the charges for money orders are: $3.01 to $10–11¢;
$10.01 to $20–13¢; $20.01 to $40–15¢) and that he has a savings account paying 2%.
Assume also that if he has an account at Bank X, he keeps a balance sufficient to avoid
any service charges. Of the following statements in relation to this man, the one that is
TRUE is that

   A. the monthly cost of an account at Bank Y is approximately as great as the cost of
an account at Bank X and also the account is more convenient
   B. to use an account at Bank Y costs more than the use of money orders, but this disadvantage is offset by the fact that cancelled checks act as receipts for bills paid
   C. money orders are cheapest but this advantage is offset by the fact that one must
go to the Post Office for each order
   D. an account at Bank X is least expensive and has the advantage that checks
endorsed to the customer may be deposited in it

———

# KEY (CORRECT ANSWERS)

| | | | | |
|---|---|---|---|---|
| 1. | B | | 11. | B |
| 2. | D | | 12. | A |
| 3. | D | | 13. | A |
| 4. | B | | 14. | C |
| 5. | A | | 15. | B |
| | | | | |
| 6. | C | | 16. | C |
| 7. | A | | 17. | B |
| 8. | B | | 18. | A |
| 9. | B | | 19. | B |
| 10. | C | | 20. | D |

| | |
|---|---|
| 21. | A |
| 22. | A |
| 23. | B |
| 24. | D |
| 25. | D |

———

# EXAMINATION SECTION
## TEST 1

DIRECTIONS: Each question or incomplete statement is followed by several suggested answers or completions. Select the one that BEST answers the question or completes the statement. *PRINT THE LETTER OF THE CORRECT ANSWER IN THE SPACE AT THE RIGHT.*

1. The new head of a central filing unit, after studying a procedure in use, decided that it was unsatisfactory.
He thereupon drew up an entirely new procedure which made no use of and ignored the existing procedure.
This plan of action is, in general,

    A. *satisfactory;* a new broom sweeps clean
    B. *unsatisfactory;* any plan should use available resources to the utmost before resorting to new creation
    C. *satisfactory;* in general, use of part of an old procedure and part of a new procedure results in an unworkable patchwork arrangement
    D. *unsatisfactory; before* deciding that the existing procedure was unusable he should have requested that an independent, unbiased agency study the problem
    E. *satisfactory;* it is usually less time consuming to construct a new plan than to remedy an old one

1.\_\_\_\_

2. Assume that you have broken a complex job into simpler and smaller components. After you have assigned a component to each employee, should you proceed to teach each employee a number of alternative methods for doing his job?

    A. *Yes;* the more methods for performing a job an employee knows, the more chance there is that he will choose the one best suited to his abilities
    B. *No;* experienced employees should be permitted to decide how to perform the jobs assigned to them
    C. *Yes;* if several different methods are available a desirable flexibility of operation results
    D. *No;* a single method for each job should be decided upon and taught
    E. *Yes;* the employees will have greater interest in their jobs

2.\_\_\_\_

3. Assume that you are the head of a major staff unit and that a line unit has requested from your unit a special report to be completed in one day. After reviewing the request you decide that much time would be saved if two items which you know are superfluous are omitted from the report. You discuss the matter with the head of the other unit and he still insists that the two items are essential for his purposes.
The one of the following actions which you should take at this stage is to

    A. plan to complete the report, including the two items, as expeditiously as possible
    B. write a memorandum to the department head giving both opinions fairly and asking for a decision
    C. plan to complete the report without the two items, as expeditiously as possible
    D. devise a plan for preparing the report without the two items which will permit you to add them later if they prove necessary although some time may be lost
    E. again review the report with the line unit showing them why the two items are unnecessary

3.\_\_\_\_

4. The one of the following functions of a supervisor which can be MOST successfully dele-     4.___
gated is

    A. responsibility for accomplishing the unit's mission
    B. handling discipline
    C. checking completed work
    D. reporting to the bureau chief
    E. placing subordinates in the proper job

5. It is a standard operating procedure in an office which receives several thousand forms     5.___
each week to have the file on clerk accumulate a week's receipts before filing them.
The forms will not be examined for a period of one month after receipt.
In comparison with daily filing, this procedure is, in general,

    A. *less satisfactory;* it keeps the files unnecessarily incomplete
    B. *more satisfactory;* it tends to reduce filing time
    C. *less satisfactory;* all information should be placed in a safe storage place as soon
        as possible
    D. *more satisfactory;* it tends to eliminate the prefiling period
    E. *less satisfactory;* it tends to build up an unncessary backlog of work

6. Some organizations attempt to keep a constant backlog of work. This procedure is usu-     6.___
ally

    A. *undesirable;* reports are not ready when they are needed
    B. *desirable;* it tends to insure continuity of work flow
    C. *undesirable;* production records are too difficult to keep
    D. *desirable;* it tends to keep the employees under constant pressure
    E. *undesirable;* it tends to keep the employees under constant pressure

7. The first few times a procedure is carried through, a close check should be kept of all     7.___
work times.
The PRIMARY reason for this is to

    A. be able to present a clear picture of the situation
    B. determine if the employees understand the procedure
    C. evaluate the problems which may have been presented by the new procedure
    D. determine the efficiency of the employees
    E. permit revision of schedules

8. The one of the following pieces of information which is of LEAST importance is setting up     8.___
the schedule for a given job is the time

    A. which is required to perform each component of the job
    B. when the source material will be available
    C. the job will take under adverse conditions
    D. by which the job must be completed
    E. employees will be available

9. Every employee should have a thorough knowledge of the organization of which he is a part.
Of the following, the BEST justification for the above opinion is that

    A.  the feeling of being a member of a team develops a responsible attitude toward one's everyday duties
    B.  in an emergency, an employee may be called upon to perform duties other than his own
    C.  the intricate details of an organization as complicated as a city department cannot easily be reduced to an organization chart
    D.  an understanding of the different specialized units in an organization is often necessary to achieve the organization's given objective
    E.  may city jobs are technical; thus, each employee should be trained to have more than a single narrow skill

9._____

10. The one of the following which is NOT a good rule in administering discipline is for you as a supervisor to

    A.  reprimand the employee in private even though the fault was committed before others
    B.  allow the employee a chance to reply to your criticism if he wishes
    C.  be as specific as possible in criticizing the employee for his faults
    D.  be sure you have all the facts before you reprimand an employee for an error he has committed
    E.  allow an extended period to elapse after an error has been committed before reprimanding an employee

10._____

11. After you have submitted your annual evaluations of the work of your subordinates, one of them whose work has not been satisfactory complains to you that your evaluation was unjustified. For you to avoid discussing the evaluation but to point out two or three specific instances where the employee's work was below standard is

    A.  *desirable;* an employee should be told what aspects of his work are unsatisfactory
    B.  *undesirable; once* the evaluation has been submitted there is no point in reconsidering it
    C.  *desirable;* once the evaluation has been submitted there is no point in reconsidering it but a discussion of the employee's weaknesses may help
    D.  *undesirable;* it would have been better to explain how you arrived at your evaluation
    E.  *desirable;* entering into a general argument is bad for the discipline of an organization

11._____

12. The chief of a central files bureau which has 50 employees, customarily spends a consid-    12.____
erable portion of his time in spot-checking the files, reviewing material being transferred
from active to inactive files and similar activities.
From the viewpoint of the department top management, the MOST pertinent evaluation which can be made on the basis of this information is that the

   A. supervisor is conscientious and hardworking
   B. bureau may need additional staff
   C. supervisor has not made a sufficient delegation of authority and responsibility
   D. bureau needs an in-service training course as the work of its employees requires
      an abnormal amount of review
   E. filing system employed may be inadequate

13. Assume that you are in charge of a unit with 40 employees.    13.____
The department head requests immediate preparation of a special and rather complicated report which will take about a day to complete if everyone in your unit works on
it.
After breaking the job into simple components and assigning each component to an
employee, should more than one person be instructed on the procedure to be followed
on each component?

   A. *No;* the procedure would be a waste of time in this instance
   B. *Yes;* it is always desirable to have a replacement available in the event of illness or
      any other emergency
   C. *No;* in general, as long as an employee's job performance is satisfactory, there is
      no need to train an alternate
   D. *Yes;* the presence of more than one person in a unit who can perform a given task
      tends to prevent the formation of a bottleneck
   E. *No;* there is, in general, no need to train more than one employee in the perfor-
      mance of a special job

14. A new employee who has shown that she is capable of performing superior work during    14.____
the first month of her employment falls far below this standard after the first month.
For the supervisor to wait until the end of the probationary period and then recommend
that she be discharged if her work is still unsatisfactory is

   A. *undesirable;* she should have been discharged when her work became unsatisfac-
      tory
   B. *desirable;* there is no place in the civil service for unsatisfactory emploees
   C. *undesirable;* he should immediately attempt to determine the cause of the poor
      performance
   D. *desirable;* the employee is entitled to an opportunity to prove herself
   E. *undesirable;* the employee is obviously capable of performing good work and sim-
      ply requires some guidance from the supervisor

15. In order to make sure that work is completed on time, the unit supervisor should    15.____

   A. use the linear method of delegating responsibility
   B. pitch in and do as much of the work himself as he can
   C. schedule the work and keep himself informed of its progress
   D. not assign more than one person to any one task
   E. know the capabilities of his subordinates

16. One of the more effective ways to obtain optimum performance from employees is to keep them off balance by not letting them feel secure in the job; to permit an employee to feel secure is to invite him to settle into a comfortable rut.
The point of view expressed in this statement is

    A. *correct;* studies have shown that the degree of effort put forth on a job generally varies directly with the degree of job insecurity
    B. *incorrect;* studies have shown that a relatively high degree of security is conducive to best job performance
    C. *correct;* while studies have shown that there is little relationship between security and job performance, what tendencies are present support the point of view expressed
    D. *incorrect;* studies have shown that there is little relationship between security and job performance and what tendencies are present are opposed to the point of view expressed
    E. *correct;* while no specific studies have been made in this field, analogous studies made in similar fields show that permitting a feeling of security to develop results in decreased job performance

16._____

Questions 17-19.

DIRECTIONS: Answer questions 17 through 19 on the basis of the following:
    The supervisor of a large clerical and statistical division has assigned to one of the units under his supervision the preparation of a special statistical report required by the department head. The unit accepted the assignment without comment but soon ran into considerable difficulty because no one in his unit had had any statistical training.

17. If a result of this lack of training is that the report is not completed on time, although everyone has done all that could be expected, the responsibility for the failure rests with

    A. the department head    B. the supervisor
    C. the unit head    D. the employees in the unit
    E. no one

17._____

18. This incident indicates that the supervisory staff has insufficient knowledge of employee

    A. capabilities    B. reaction to increased demands
    C. on-the-job training needs    D. work habits
    E. ability to perform ordinary assignments

18._____

19. After working on the report for two days, the unit head notifies the supervisor that he will not be able to get the report out in the required time. He states that his staff will be completely trained in another day or two and that after that preparing the report will be a simple matter. At this stage the supervisor decides to have the statistical unit prepare the report.
This action on the part of the supervisor is

    A. *undesirable;* the unit head should be given an incentive to continue with his training program which may produce good results
    B. *desirable;* it is the most effective way in which the supervisor can show his displeasure with the unit head's failure
    C. *undesirable;* it may adversely affect the morale of the unit
    D. *desirable;* it will generally result in a better report completed in a shorter time
    E. *undesirable;* the time spent training the unit will be completely wasted

19._____

20. A supervisor criticizes a subordinate's work by telling him that he is disappointed with it.    20.___
The supervisor states that the work is completely unsatisfactory, shows where it is bad
and says that improvement is expected.
This approach is usually

    A. *good;* the employee knows just where he stands
    B. *poor;* some favorable comment should be made at the same time if possible
    C. *good;* it is good policy to keep this type of interview as short as possible
    D. *poor;* the employee should be asked to explain why his work is poor
    E. *good;* the supervisor did not criticize the subordinate in front of other employees

Questions 21-25

DIRECTIONS:   COLUMN I below lists five kinds of statistical data which are to be transformed
into a chart or a graph for incorporation into the department annual report.
COLUMN II lists nine different kinds of graphs or charts. For each type of information listed in COLUMN I, select the chart or graph from COLUMN II by
means of which it should be demonstrated.

<u>COLUMN I</u>                                       <u>COLUMN II</u>

21. The relationship between employees'
occupational classification and their sala-   A.
ries, for all employees by occupational
classification, showing minimum, maximum and average salary in each group.

21.___

22. A comparison of the number of employees in the department, the departmental-
budget the number of employees in the
operating divisions and the operating   B.
division budget for each year over a ten-
year period.

22.___

23. The amount of money spent for each of
the department's 10 most important functions during the past year.

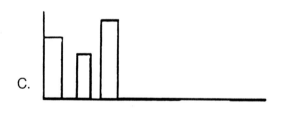

C.

23.___

24. The percentage of the department's budget spent for each of the department's
activities for each year over a ten-year
period.   D.

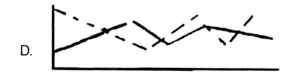

24.___

COLUMN I (cont'd)                    COLUMN II

25. The number of each kind of employee
employed in the department over a
period of twenty years and the total number of employees in the department for
each of these periods.

25.____

E.

F.

G.

H.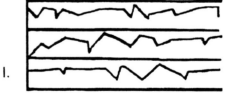

I.

# KEY (CORRECT ANSWERS)

| | | | |
|---|---|---|---|
| 1. | B | 11. | D |
| 2. | D | 12. | C |
| 3. | A | 13. | A |
| 4. | C | 14. | C |
| 5. | B | 15. | C |
| 6. | B | 16. | B |
| 7. | E | 17. | B |
| 8. | C | 18. | A |
| 9. | A | 19. | D |
| 10. | E | 20. | B |

| | |
|---|---|
| 21. | F |
| 22. | D |
| 23. | C |
| 24. | H |
| 25. | G |

———

# TEST 2

1. The report of the head of Unit Y to his bureau chief on the performance of a new clerical employee indicates that the performance is not up to the expected standard. After reading the report, the bureau chief transferred the employee to Unit X.
   This action on the part of the bureau chief was                                        1.\_\_\_\_

   A. in line with good personnel practice; an employee who does poorly in one place may do better in another
   B. *premature;* an attempt to discover the cause of the poor performance should be made first
   C. *desirable;* personnel reports become meaningless unless acted upon at once
   D. *undesirable;* unsatisfactory employees should be dismissed and not transferred from unit to unit
   E. in the best interests of the organization; whenever a supervisor cannot get along with a subordinate for whatever reason, it is desirable to transfer the subordinate

2. Suppose that you have been consulted by a department head who wishes to initiate an in-service training course in his department. The department head suggests that, as a first step, a training course be initiated for supervisors in the department.
   This suggestion is BEST characterized as                                               2.\_\_\_\_

   A. *undesirable;* the supervisors are generally the persons least in need of work incentives
   B. *desirable;* it is generally cheaper and more effective to train a few supervisors than a large number of employees
   C. *undesirable;* supervisors may be held up to ridicule if they are isolated for training
   D. *desirable;* trained supervisors are needed to train employees
   E. *undesirable;* employees should be trained before supervisors

3. Any person thoroughly familiar with the specific steps in a particular class of work is well qualified to serve as a training course instructor in that work.
   This statement is erroneous CHIEFLY because                                           3.\_\_\_\_

   A. it is practically impossible for any instructor to be acquainted with all the specific steps in a particular class of work
   B. what is true of one class of work is not necessarily true of other types of work
   C. a qualified instructor cannot be expected to have detailed information about many specific fields
   D. the steps in any type of work are usually interrelated and not independent or unique
   E. the quantity of information possessed by an instructor does not bear a direct relationship to the quality of instruction

4. Of the following, the MOST significant argument against making it compulsory for civil     4.___
   service employees to attend a training course is that

   A. unwilling trainees will be penalized in any event by non-promotion
   B. most training requires additional time and expense on the part of the trainee
   C. training is highly desirable but not absolutely essential for adequate job perfor-
      mance
   D. incompetent work is generally reflected in poor service ratings
   E. trainees must be receptive if training is to be successful

5. There are four basic systems of job evaluation which have been extensively used by gov-     5.___
   ernment and industry.
   The one of the following which is NOT one of these is the _____ system.

   A. Benchmark          B. Factor Comparison      C. Point
   D. Job Classification  E. Ranking

6. Of the following, the CHIEF advantage derived by filling all vacancies in an organization     6.___
   by promotion from below rather than from outside the organization is that such a procedure

   A. fills existing vacancies from the widest possible recruitment base
   B. stimulates individual employees to improve their work habits
   C. avoids personality difficulties likely to arise when an employee is assigned to
      supervise former colleagues
   D. indirectly coordinates the work of different units by interchange of personnel
   E. encourages reorientation and review of administrative procedures

7. Of the following, the CHIEF justification for a periodic classification audit is that     7.___

   A. salaries should be readjusted at frequent intervals
   B. some degree of personnel turnover should always be expected
   C. a career service requires regular promotion opportunities
   D. employees require frequent stimulation and encouragement
   E. positions frequently change over a period of time

8. A classification analyst sorts jobs horizontally and vertically.     8.___
   Of the following, the LEAST important job factor to be considered with respect to vertical placement is

   A. independence of action and decision
   B. consequence of errors
   C. kind and character of work performed
   D. degree of supervision received
   E. determination of policy

9. Assume that you have been assigned to prepare a plan for conducting a large scale job     9._____
   classification survey.
   Of the following, the BEST suggestion for reducing the number of appeals from the
   final allocations likely to be received after the classification study has been completed
   is to

   A. have supervisors check statements of employees on classification questionnaires
   B. allocate present positions to proposed classes according to jurisdictional assign-
      ments
   C. adjust salary to present level of work performed by employees
   D. allow employee participation throughout the classification process
   E. postpone controversial problems until simpler problems have been solved and a
      general blueprint laid down

10. A comment made by an employee about a training couse was, *"Oh, I suppose it's impor-*    10._____
    *tant for the job but it's a waste of time for me just to sit in that course and yawn while the*
    *instructor rambles on."*
    The fundamental error in training methodology, to which this criticism points, is failure
    to provide

    A. goals for the students
    B. for individual differences
    C. connecting links beteeen new and old material
    D. for student participation
    E. motivation for the subject matter of the course

11. You are preparing a long report addressed to your superior on a study which you have    11._____
    conducted for him.
    The one of the following sections which should come first in the report is a

    A. description of the working procedure utilized in the study
    B. description of the situation which exists
    C. summary of the conclusions of the survey
    D. discussion of possible objections to the report and their refutation
    E. description of the method of installing the recommendations

12. While setting up a reporting system to help the department planning section, an adminis-   12._____
    trator proposed the policy that no overlap or duplication be permitted even if it meant that
    some minor areas were left uncovered.
    This policy is

    A. *undesirable;* overlap is frequently necessary
    B. *desirable;* the presence of overlap and duplication indicates defective planning
    C. *undesirable;* setting up general policy in advance of the specific reporting system
       may lead to inflexibility
    D. *desirable;* it is not necessary to get complete coverage in order to be able to plan
       operations
    E. *undesirable;* duplication is preferable to leaving any area uncovered

Questions 13-15

DIRECTIONS: Questions 13 through 15 are based on the following:

Prior to revising its child care program, a department feels that it is necessary to get some information from the mothers served by the existing program in order to determine where changes are required. A questionnaire is to be constructed to obtain this information.

13. Of the following points which can be taken into consideration in the construction of the questionnaire, the one which is of LEAST importance is

    A. that the data are to be put into punch cards
    B. the aspects of the program which seem to be in need of change
    C. the type of person who will fill out the questionnaire
    D. testing the questionnaire for ambiguity in advance of general distribution
    E. setting up a control group so that answers received can be compared to a standard.

14. To discuss this questionnaire with all mothers who have been asked to answer it, before they actually fill it out, is

    A. *desirable;* the mothers may be able to offer valuable suggestions for changes in the form of the questionnaire
    B. *undesirable;* it is of some value but consumes too much valuable time
    C. *desirable;* cooperation and uniform interpretation will tend to be achieved
    D. *undesirable;* it may cause the answers to be biased
    E. *desirable;* the group will tend to support the program

15. Of the following items included in the questionnaire, the one which will be of LEAST assistance for comparing attitudes toward the program among different kinds of persons, is

    A. name     B. address     C. age     D. place of birth   E. education

16. You have been asked, to prepare for public distribution a statement dealing with a controversial matter.
Of the following approaches, the one which would USUALLY be MOST effective is to present your department's point of view

    A. as tersely as possible with no reference to any other matters
    B. developed from ideas and facts well known to most readers
    C. and show all the statistical data and techniques which were used in arriving at it
    D. in such a way that the controversial parts are omitted
    E. substantiated by supporting quotations from persons in the specialized field even if they are not well known

17. During a conference of administrative staff personnel, the department head discussing       17._____
the letter prepared for his signature stated, *"Use no more words than are necessary to express your meaning."*
Following this rule in letter writing is, in general,

   A. *desirable;* considerable time will be saved in the preparation of correspondence
   B. *undesirable;* it is frequently necessary to elaborate on an explanation in order to make certain that the reader will understand
   C. *desirable;* terse statements give government letters a business-like air which impresses readers favorably
   D. *undesirable;* terse statements are generally cold and formal and produce an unfavorable reaction in the reader
   E. *desirable;* the use of more words than are necessary is likely to obscure the meaning and tire the reader

18. While you are designing the layout for a departmental procedure manual, it is suggested       18._____
that you carefully arrange your reading material so that there will be a minimum amount of blank space on the page.
Of the following judgments of this suggestion, the one which is the MOST valid basis for action is that it is

   A. *bad;* readability and ease of reference will be decreased
   B. *good;* the cost of production can be decreased considerably without any great disadvantage
   C. of little or no importance; more or less blank space on the page will not affect the value of the manual
   D. *good;* it will make for a smaller, easier to handle book
   E. *bad;* replacement of out-dated pages is made more difficult by having more material on a page

19. After the planning of an employees procedure manual had been completed, the suggestion was made that the manual should be prepared and arranged so that changes could       19._____
be made readily. Of the following decisions with respect to this suggestion, the one which is MOST desirable from the viewpoint of good administration is that the suggestions should

   A. not be considered as it is generally impossible to prepare a satisfactory manual which will take everything into consideration
   B. be followed only if it does not conflict with the planned layout
   C. be used even if it is somewhat more costly than the planned layout
   D. be noted and acted upon at the next revision of the manual
   E. not be considered as this type of manual is more difficult to maintain properly

20. Assume that you are in charge of preparing a procedure manual of about 100 pages for       20._____
a large clerical unit. After you have decided to use a looseleaf format, one of your subordinates proposes that only one side of the page be printed.
This proposal is

   A. *good;* replacement of obsolete pages is made easier
   B. *poor;* cost is increased
   C. *good;* provision is automatically made for employee's notes
   D. *poor;* it will increase the size of the manual, making it more difficult to use
   E. *good;* indexing will be made easier

21. It may be assumed that if all departments had qualified personnel officers, not all depart-   21.___
ments would be lacking adequate training programs. However, the most cursory examination of the situation will show that some departments do not have adequate training
programs. Thus we must conclude that some of them lack qualified personnel officers.
The argument presented in the report is

   A. *correct;* the conclusion follows logically from the assumption and the facts
   B. *not correct;* what can be concluded is that no department has a qualified personnel
   officer
   C. *not correct;* no conclusion with respect to the presence of personnel officers in
   departments can be drawn from the information
   D. *not correct;* what can be concluded is that the absence of an adequate training pro-
   gram in a department implies the absence of a. personnel officer
   E. *correct;* but the conclusion is false as the hypothesis is not true

22. In a study of the relationship between a fixed discipline policy and the incidence of late-   22.___
ness, it would be MOST in formative to have data proving the statement:

   A. In those organizations in which there is no fixed discipline policy, the incidence of
   lateness is variable.
   B. The incidence of lateness has not decreased in those organizations where fixed
   discipline policies have been abandoned.
   C. The incidence of lateness and the discipline policy vary from organization to orga-
   nization.
   D. Discipline policies sometimes ignore the problem of lateness.
   E. In organizations with a fixed discipline policy, the incidence of lateness is variable.

23. The data prove that an increase in the number of clerks performing filing work results in   23.___
an increased cost per item filed.
On the basis of these data, we can be certain that

   A. if filing costs per item filed increase, it is caused by an increase in the number of
   clerks filing
   B. if filing costs per item filed decrease, the number of clerks filing cannot be increas-
   ing
   C. if the number of clerks filing is changed, the unit cost per filing will change
   D. if the number of clerks filing is not increased, the cost per unit filed will not increase
   E. if the number of clerks filing is decreased, the cost per item filed will decrease

24. Each unit either has sufficient space assigned to it or it has not. No unit which has insuf-   24.___
ficient space assigned to it has neglected to ask for additional space.
From these data we can state

   A. units with sufficient space have not asked for additional space
   B. only units which have sufficient space have not asked for additional space
   C. nothing about the relationship between the need for additional space and requests
   made for additional space
   D. all units which have requested additional space have in sufficient space
   E. no units which have requested additional space have sufficient space

25. One argument which is presented against a strict career system in the civil service is as follows:

    25._____

    The employees who are recruited today for low-level jobs become the administrators of tomorrow. At the present time the employees we are attracting for the low-level jobs are untrained and poorly educated. Thus it follows that the administrators of tomorrow will be untrained and poorly educated.

    The one of the following which is a CORRECT criticism of the reasoning is that

    A. the argument is logically correct but the conclusion is false as the hypothesis that we are attracting untrained and poorly educated people for our low level jobs is false
    B. the conclusion does not follow logically from hypotheses
    C. the argument is logically correct, but the conclusion is false because it is a false hypothesis that tomorrow's administrators will come from employees who hold low level jobs
    D. the argument is logically correct and the conclusion is correct
    E. while the argument is logically correct and the hypotheses are not demonstrably false, the argument ignores the realities of the case that those who are untrained today may be trained tomorrow

---

# KEY (CORRECT ANSWERS)

| | | | | |
|---|---|---|---|---|
| 1. | B | | 11. | C |
| 2. | D | | 12. | E |
| 3. | E | | 13. | E |
| 4. | E | | 14. | C |
| 5. | A | | 15. | A |
| 6. | B | | 16. | B |
| 7. | E | | 17. | E |
| 8. | C | | 18. | A |
| 9. | D | | 19. | C |
| 10. | D | | 20. | A |

| | |
|---|---|
| 21. | C |
| 22. | B |
| 23. | B |
| 24. | B |
| 25. | B |

---

# TEST 3

DIRECTIONS: Each question or incomplete statement is followed by several suggested answers or completions. Select the one that BEST answers the question or completes the statement. *PRINT THE LETTER OF THE CORRECT ANSWER IN THE SPACE AT THE RIGHT.*

1. Surveying modern administration, it becomes clear that there is GREATEST need at present for administrators with

    A. a good knowledge of personnel administration
    B. the ability to write good reports
    C. a working knowledge of modern methods analysis
    D. a broad rather than specialized viewpoint
    E. the ability to analyze complicated fiscal programs

1.__

2. The one of the following which is a fundamental obstacle to effective planning in MOST governmental agencies is

    A. inadequate staff or resources
    B. the absence of the properly centralized administration
    C. the absence of clearly defined objective and constituent programs
    D. the neglect of analysis of ways and means
    E. the absence of functional boundaries for units and individuals

2.__

3. A department consists of several independent bureaus each responsible to the commissioner for its own planning, operation and reporting, a central personnel unit and the commissioner's office consisting of a secretary and several clerks to handle public relations.
The one of the following UNDESIRABLE characteristics which is MOST likely to arise in this organization is

    A. absence of planning
    B. weak and ineffectual leadership
    C. failure to have employees properly trained
    D. a lack of an easily understandable goal
    E. duplication of work

3.__

4. The one of the following practices which is MOST likely to lead to confusion, recrimination and jurisdictional conflict among the bureaus of a department is the failure to

    A. make clear and unambiguous assignments
    B. systematically subdivide the work
    C. explain general policy to those responsible for its achievement
    D. allocate equitably available resources
    E. set up uniform operating procedures for all units

4.__

5. The one of the following which is MOST likely to occur in an over-specialized administrative set-up is

    A. inability to recruit proper personnel to fill over-specialized positions
    B. improper supervision
    C. failure of employees to realize the broad implications of their work
    D. lack of proper decentralization of authority, as emphasis on specialization goes hand-in-hand with over-centralization
    E. inability to solve technical problems which are not entirely in one specialty

5.__

6. Of the following, the LEAST valid reason for a department head continuing to require that     6._____
a weekly report be forwarded to him, is that the report forms a basis for

    A. measuring performance
    B. making decisions
    C. revising policy
    D. the execution of the mission of the unit which receives it
    E. the operation of the unit which is required to prepare it

7. Administrators must learn not to farm out essential functions to unintegrated agencies,     7._____
but to organize all responsibilities in unified but decentralized hierarchies.
A problem which an administrator may be expected to face if he has not learned this is
that

    A. the organization fails to develop administrators capable of independent action
    B. issues will not be posed at the level where decisions should be made
    C. relationships with the public will not be satisfactory
    D. it will be difficult to achieve administrative control or get agreement on departmen-
tal action
    E. individual agencies will be unable to complete the work scheduled

8. The central staff planning unit within any organization includes in its functions helping to     8._____
plan policy at one extreme and planning detailed execution at the other extreme.
With respect to the actual execution, the planning activity should

    A. have no concern with it
    B. simply forward and explain new plans
    C. have only the responsibility of explaining in the form of plans the objectives of top
management
    D. keep track of how the plans are working out but make no attempt to supervise their
execution
    E. supervise the execution of new plans

9. The head of a department assigned final responsibility for the training function to the per-     9._____
sonnel office.
This assignment was

    A. *undesirable;* this type of centralization prevents a staff organization from carrying
out staff functions
    B. *desirable;* experience has shown that centralization of this type results in more effi-
cient and economic operation
    C. *undesirable;* the personnel office usually does not have the technical "know how"
to carry this responsibility
    D. *desirable;* if training is left to the line officials, it never is accomplished
    E. *undesirable;* this responsibility must rest with the supervisor

10. A department head insisted that operating officials participate in the development of new    10.___
procedures along with the planning section.
Participation of this type is, on the whole

    A. *desirable;* operating realities are more likely to be considered
    B. *undesirable;* the inclusion of conflicting views before the plan is drawn may result in
       no plan
    C. *desirable;* plans will be more flexible and objectives more clearly defined
    D. *undesirable;* the operating officials should decide to what extent they wish to partic-
       ipate with no pressure from the top
    E. *desirable;* to back down on a procedure once it has been decided upon is a sign of
       weakness

11. Much of the current criticism of the administration of large organizations is basically a    11.___
criticism of our failure to place the same emphasis on accountability that we do on
authority and responsibility.
The one of the following acts which is MOST likely to insure accountability for the discharge of responsibilities inherent in the delegation of authority is the

    A. establishment of appropriate reports and controls
    B. organization of a methods analysis section
    C. delegation of authority so made as to support functional or homogeneous activities
    D. delegation of authority so made as to preserve unity of command
    E. decentralization of responsibility and authority

12. This statement has been made:    12.___

        A man who is a top-notch executive in one organization would make a top-notch
    executive in any other organization, even if the organizations are as diverse as a sales agency
    and a research foundation.

    This statement is, in general,

    A. *correct;* the characteristics required for a good executive are invariant with respect
       to organization
    B. *incorrect;* there is no way of predicting how a good executive in one organization
       would be in any other
    C. *correct;* while the characteristics required for a good executive vary from organiza-
       tion to organization, the common core requirements are great enough to insure
       similar performance
    D. *incorrect;* although some prediction can be made, different types of organizations
       require different types of executives
    E. *correct;* success as an executive does not depend upon "characteristics" but on the
       man; if he is able to direct and execute in one organization he will be able to do so
       in any other

13. Reported information is not needed at levels higher than those at which decisions are made on the basis of the information reported.
This statement is, in general,

    A. *correct; if* no action is to be taken on the basis of the information, the information is unnecessary
    B. *incorrect;* all information is of importance in arriving at a sound decision
    C. correct; levels below the one at which the decision is made have need of the information
    D. incorrect; levels below the one at which the decision is made do not have need of the information
    E. *correct; decisions* should be made on the basis of information reported

14. Of the following, the characteristic of an organization which BEST shows that the organizational hierarchy is effective is that

    A. the department head commands the respect of the employees
    B. the organization is sufficiently flexible to assume functions in fields not related to its major field of endeavor
    C. responsibility has been appropriately delegated throughout the organization
    D. the department continues to function effectively even though there is continual turnover in the higher supervisory ranks
    E. no employee in the organization is subject to orders from more than one source

15. It is only because the primary purpose of traditional discipline has been to preserve the structure of command that a need has arisen for ameliorative safeguards such as a formal statement of 'cause', right of hearing and right of appeal. The BEST current practice with respect to discipline is that

    A. few ameliorative safeguards of the kind enumerated are desirable as their presence hurts the public service
    B. discipline is a means of controlling deviations from established authority
    C. the safeguards enumerated are not sufficient for the protection of the employee
    D. discipline should be based upon education, persuasion and consultation
    E. unquestioned obedience to each order should not be expected but that a supervisor should be, prepared at all times to demonstrate the reasonablenes, of his requests

16. Of the following types of work, the one for which a manual process is MOST usually to be preferred over a mechanized process is one in which the transactions are very

    A. numerous    B. similar    C. dissimilar
    D. predictable    E. unpredictable

17. Work flow charts are used in an organization PRIMARILY because they

    A. indicate present and future objectives clearly
    B. are frequently used records
    C. clearly indicate when each operation will be performed
    D. summarize the work procedures of the organization
    E. tend to clarify thinking by presenting certain facts clearly

18. With respect to a report prepared by an IBM installation, the one of the following changes    18.___
which is LEAST likely to cause a change in the procedure for preparing the report is a
change in the

    A.  volume of work               B.  source documents
    C.  final report                    D.  employees assigned
    E.  time allowed for the preparation of the report

19. The one of the following which is NOT necessarily a characteristic of a good buying pro-    19.___
cedure is that it

    A.  provides for proper analysis of purchases made
    B.  is simple
    C.  makes provision for substitutions where possible and necessary
    D.  makes sealed bids mandatory
    E.  recruits many bidders

20. Data relating to the operation of any unit should be accumulated and periodically sum-    20.___
marized and analyzed, PRIMARILY in order to

    A.  point out the most efficient and least efficient workers
    B.  determine the relative value of each procedure
    C.  locate the elements of an operation which are unusually efficient or inefficient
    D.  evaluate the importance of maintaining operating records and quotas
    E.  compare the work performed by comparable units

21. Of the following, the MAJOR function of an administrative planning and research staff    21.___
unit is to

    A.  investigate trouble points in the organization
    B.  reorganize inefficient units
    C.  assist the executive to plan future operations
    D.  conduct continuous investigations and planning
    E.  write the necessary operation and procedure manuals

22. The one of the following which does NOT require definition when setting up a work mea-    22.___
surement system is the

    A.  level of work accomplishment at which to measure
    B.  work unit in which to measure
    C.  time unit by which to measure
    D.  acceptable quota for each activity
    E.  reporting system to be used

23. During a discussion of the time unit that would be appropriate to measure employee-time     23.____
in a work measurement program in a public agency, the man-day was suggested.
This unit is

    A. *satisfactory;* record keeping will be kept to a minimum
    B. *unsatisfactory;* it will be difficult to verify the unit against official time records
    C. *satisfactory;* it will be easy to verify the unit against official time records
    D. *unsatisfactory;* its use will unnecessarily complicate record keeping
    E. *satisfactory;* it permits more meaningful comparisons to be made between equal
       periods of time

24. As part of a space layout survey, an administrator instructed his subordinates to study     24.____
the flow of work and sequence of operating procedures.
His MAJOR purpose in doing this was to determine

    A. the physical distribution and movement of personnel, material and equipment
    B. the amount of space which is available and the amount of space which will be
       required
    C. the order in which the component steps in the different procedures are performed
    D. what future requirements will be, based on observable present trends
    E. how the distribution of personnel to various organization units is related to their
       space requirements

25. Before discussing a proposed office layout, the administrative officer stated, *"We intend*     25.____
*to have a minimum number of private offices. We will assign private offices only where*
*quiet is deemed essential or confidential conferences are required."*
The one of the following which is usually the MOST valid reason for this rule is that it

    A. permits proper placing of employees who deal with the public
    B. makes it easier to locate supervisors near the units they control
    C. tends to ensure that the work of each unit will flow continually forward within itself
    D. allows placing complementary units close together
    E. makes clerical supervision easier

# KEY (CORRECT ANSWERS)

| | | | | |
|---|---|---|---|---|
| 1. | D | | 11. | A |
| 2. | C | | 12. | D |
| 3. | E | | 13. | A |
| 4. | A | | 14. | C |
| 5. | C | | 15. | D |
| | | | | |
| 6. | E | | 16. | C |
| 7. | D | | 17. | E |
| 8. | D | | 18. | D |
| 9. | E | | 19. | D |
| 10. | A | | 20. | C |

| | |
|---|---|
| 21. | D |
| 22. | D |
| 23. | D |
| 24. | A |
| 25. | E |

———————

# EXAMINATION SECTION
## TEST 1

DIRECTIONS: Each question or incomplete statement is followed by several suggested answers or completions. Select the one that BEST answers the question or completes the statement. *PRINT THE LETTER OF THE CORRECT ANSWER IN THE SPACE AT THE RIGHT.*

1. The one of the following which has had GREATEST effect upon size of the budget of large cities in the last twenty years is   1.\_\_\_\_

    A. change in the organization of the city resulting from new charters
    B. increase in services rendered by the city
    C. development of independent authorities
    D. increase in the city's ability to borrow money
    E. increase in the size of the city

2. The one of the following services for which cities receive the LEAST amount of direct financial assistance from state governments is   2.\_\_\_\_

    A. education    B. welfare    C. housing    D. roads    E. museums

3. Major problems which face most large cities, including New York, arise from the vertical sandwiching of governments in a single area and from the many independent governments that crowd the boundaries of the central city.
Of the following methods of solving these problems, the one which has been MOST successful in the past has been to   3.\_\_\_\_

    A. decentralize the administration of the central city
    B. create various supra-municipal authorities which tend to integrate the activities of the metropolitan area
    C. bring the metropolitan population under a single local government
    D. set up intermunicipal coordinating agencies to solve area administrative and economic problems
    E. allow each government element in the metropolitan area to work out its own solution

4. By means of the *debt limit* the states regulate many facets of the debt of the cities.
The one of the following factors which is NOT regulated in this manner is the   4.\_\_\_\_

    A. purpose for which the debt is incurred
    B. amount of debt which may be incurred
    C. terms of the notes or bonds issued by the city
    D. forms of debts which may be incurred
    E. source from which the money may be borrowed

5. The one of the following which is a characteristic of NEITHER the state nor the Federal governments, but which is a characteristic of the government of cities is that the latter   5.\_\_\_\_

    A. is not sovereign but an agent
    B. does not have the power to raise taxes
    C. cannot enter into contracts
    D. may not make treaties with foreign countries
    E. may not coin money

Questions 6-8.

DIRECTIONS:   Questions 6 through 8 are based on the following paragraph:

*The regressive uses of discipline are ubiquitous. Administrative architects who seek the optimum balance between structure and morale must accordingly look toward the identification and isolation of disciplinary elements. The whole range of disciplinary sanctions, from the reprimand to the dismissal, presents opportunities for reciprocity and accommodation of institutional interests. When rightly seized upon, these opportunities may provide the moment and the means for fruitful exercise of leadership and collaboration.*

6.   The one of the following ways of reworking the ideas presented in this paragraph in order      6.
to be BEST suited for presentation in an in-service training course in supervision is:

   A.   When one of your men does something wrong, talk it over with him. Tell him what
he should have done. This is a chance for you to show the man that you are on his
side and that you would welcome him on your side.
   B.   It is not necessary to reprimand or to dismiss an employee because he needs disciplining. The alert foreman will lead and collaborate with his subordinates making
discipline unnecessary.
   C.   A good way to lead the men you supervise is to take those opportunities which
present themselves to use the whole range of disciplinary sanctions from reprimand to dismissal as a means for enforcing collaboration.
   D.   Chances to punish a man in your squad should be welcomed as opportunities to
show that you are a '*good guy*' who does not bear a grudge.
   E.   Before you talk to a man or have him report to the office for something he has done
wrong, attempt to lead him and get him to work with you. Tell him that his actions
were wrong, that you expect him not to repeat the same wrong act, and that you
will take a firmer stand if the act is repeated.

7.   Of the following, the PRINCIPAL point made in the paragraph is that      7.

   A.   discipline is frequently used improperly
   B.   it is possible to isolate the factors entering into a disciplinary situation
   C.   identification of the disciplinary elements is desirable
   D.   disciplinary situations may be used to the advantage of the organization
   E.   obtaining the best relationship between organizational form and spirit, depends
upon the ability to label disciplinary elements

8.   The MOST novel idea presented in the paragraph is that      8

   A.   discipline is rarely necessary
   B.   discipline may be a joint action of man and supervisor
   C.   there are disciplinary elements which may be identified
   D.   a range of disciplinary sanctions exists
   E.   it is desirable to seek for balance between structure and morale

9. When, in the process of developing a classification plan, it has been decided that certain      9.____
positions all have distinguishing characteristics sufficiently similar to justify treating them
alike in the process of selecting appointees and establishing pay rates or scales, then the
kind of employment represented by such positions will be called a 'class'.
According to this paragraph, a group of positions is called a class if they

    A. have distinguishing characteristics
    B. represent a kind of employment
    C. can be treated in the same mannner for some functions
    D. all have the same pay rates
    E. are treated in the same manner in the development of a classification plan

Questions 10–12.

DIRECTIONS:   Questions 10 through 12 are based on the following paragraph:

*The fundamental characteristic of the type of remote control which management needs
to bridge the gap between itself and actual operations is the more effective use of records
and reports—more specifically, the gathering and interpretation of the facts contained in
records and reports. Facts, for management purposes, are those data (narrative and quantitative) which express in simple terms the current standing of the agency's program, work
and resources in relation to the plans and policies formulated by management. They are
those facts or measures (1) which permit management to compare current status with past
performance and with its forecasts for the immediate future, and (2) which provide management with a reliable basis for long–range forecasting.*

10. According to the above statement, a characteristic of a type of management control      10.____

    A. is the kind of facts contained in records and reports
    B. is narrative and quantitative data
    C. is its remoteness from actual operations
    D. is the use of records
    E. which expresses in simple terms the current standing of the agency's program,
       provides management with a reliable basis for long-range forecasting

11. For management purposes, facts are, according to the paragraph      11.____

    A. forecasts which can be compared to current status
    B. data which can be used for certain control purposes
    C. a fundamental characteristic of a type of remote control
    D. the data contained in records and reports
    E. data (narrative and quantitative) which describe the plans and policies formulated
       by management

12. An inference which can be drawn from this statement is that

    A. management which has a reliable basis for long–range forecasting has at its disposal a type of remote control which is needed to bridge the gap between itself and actual operations
    B. data which do not express in simple terms the current standing of the agency's program, work and resources in relationship to the plans and policies formulated by management, may still be facts for management purposes
    C. data which express relationships among the agency's program, work and resources are management facts
    D. the gap between management and actual operations can only be bridged by characteristics which are fundamentally a type of remote control
    E. management compares current status with past performance in order to obtain a reliable basis for long–range forecasting

Questions 13–14.

DIRECTIONS: Questions 13 and 14 are based on the following paragraph:

*People must be selected to do the tasks involved and must be placed on a payroll in jobs fairly priced. Each of these people must be assigned those tasks which he can perform best; the work of each must be appraised, and good and poor work singled out appropriately. Skill in performing assigned tasks must be developed, and the total work situation must be conducive to sustained high performance. Finally, employees must be separated from the work force either voluntarily or involuntarily because of inefficient or unsatisfactory performance or because of curtailment of organizational activities.*

13. A personnel function which is NOT included in the above description is

    A. classification    B. training    C. placement
    D. severance    E. service rating

14. The underlying implied purpose of the policy enunciated in the above paragraph is

    A. to plan for the curtailment of the organizational program when it becomes necessary
    B. to single out appropriate skill in performing assigned tasks
    C. to develop and maintain a high level of performance by employees
    D. that training employees in relation to the total work situation is essential if good and poor work are to be singled out
    E. that equal money for equal work results in a total work situation which insures proper appraisal

15. Changes in program must be quickly and effectively translated into organizational adjust-    15._____
ments if the administrative machinery is to be fully adapted to current operating needs.
Continuous administrative planning is indispensable to the successful and expeditious
accomplishment of such organization changes.
According to this statement,

    A.  the absence of continuous administrative planning must result in out–moded
administrative machinery
    B.  continuous administrative planning is necessary for changes in program
    C.  if changes in program are quickly and effectively translated into organizational
adjustments, the administrative machinery is fully adapted to current operating
needs
    D.  continuous administrative planning results in successful and expeditious accom-
plishment of organization changes
    E.  if administrative machinery is not fully adapted to current operating needs, then
continuous administrative planning is absent

16. The first line supervisor executes policy as elsewhere formulated. He does not make pol-    16._____
icy. He is the element of the administrative structure closest to the employee group.
From this point of view, it follows that a MAJOR function of the first line supervisor is to

    A.  suggest desirable changes in procedure to top management
    B.  prepare time schedules showing when his unit will complete a piece of work so that
it will dovetail with the requirements of other units
    C.  humanize policy so as to respect employee needs and interests
    D.  report danger points to top management in order to forestall possible bottlenecks
    E.  discipline employees who continuously break departmental rules

17. During a supervisory staff meeting, the department head said to the first line supervisors,    17._____
*"The most important job you have is to get across to the employees in your units the
desirability of achieving our department's aims and the importance of the jobs they are
performing toward reaching our goals."*
In general, adoption of this point of view would tend to result in an organization

    A.  in which supervisors would be faced by many disciplinary problems caused by
employee reaction to the program
    B.  in which less supervision is required of the work of the average employee
    C.  having more clearly defined avenues of communication
    D.  lacking definition; supervisors would tend to forget their primary mission of getting
the assigned work completed as efficiently as possible
    E.  in which most employees would be capable of taking over a supervisory position
when necessary

18. A supervisor, in assigning a man to a job, generally followed the policy of fitting the man    18._____
to the job.
This procedure is

    A.  *undesirable;* the job should be fitted to the man
    B.  *desirable;* primary emplasis should be on the work to be accomplished
    C.  *undesirable;* the policy does not consider human values
    D.  *desirable;* setting up a definite policy and following it permits careful analysis
    E.  *undesirable;* it is not always possible to fit the available man to the job

19. Assume that one of the units under your jurisdiction has 40 typists. Their skill ranges     19.__
from 15 to 80 words a minute. The MOST feasible of the following methods to increase
the typing output of this unit is to

   A. study the various typing jobs to determine the skill requirements for each type of
   work and assign to each typist tasks commensurate with her skill
   B. assign the slow typists to clerical work and hire new typists
   C. assign such tasks as typing straight copy to the slower typists
   D. reduce the skill requirements necessary to produce a satisfactory quantity of work
   E. simplify procedures and keep reports, memoranda and letters short and concise

20. In a division of a department, private secretaries were assigned to members of the tech-     20.__
nical staff since each required a secretary who was familiar with his particular field and
who could handle various routine matters without referring to anyone. Other members of
the staff depended for their dictation and typing work upon a small pool consisting of two
stenographers and two typists. Because of turnover and the difficulty of recruiting new
stenographers and typists, the pool had to be discontinued.
Of the following, the MOST satisfactory way to provide stenographic and typing service
for the division is to

   A. organize the private secretaries into a decentralized pool under the direction of a
   supervisor to whom nontechnical staff members would send requests for stenographic and typing assistance
   B. organize the private secretaries into a central pool under the direction of a supervisor to whom all staff members would send requests for stenographic and typing
   assistance
   C. train clerks as typists and typists as stenographers
   D. relieve stenographers and typists of jobs that can be done by messengers or clerks
   E. conserve time by using such devices as indicating minor corrections on a final draft
   in such a way that they can be erased and by using duplicating machines to eliminate typing many copies

21. Even under perfect organizational conditions, the relationships between the line units     21.__
and the units charged with budget planning and personnel management may be precari-
ous at times.
The one of the following which is a MAJOR reason for this is that

   A. service units assist the head of the agency in formulating and executing policies
   B. line units frequently find lines of communication to the agency head blocked by ser-
   vice units
   C. there is a natural antagonism between planners and doers
   D. service units tend to become line in attitude and emphasis, and to conflict with
   operating units
   E. service units tend to function apart from the operating units

22. The one of the following which is the CHIEF reason for training supervisors is that          22.____

    A.  untrained supervisors find it difficult to train their subordinates
    B.  most persons do not start as supervisors and consequently are in need of supervisory training
    C.  training permits a higher degree of decentralization of the decision–making process
    D.  training permits a higher degree of centralization of the decision–making process
    E.  coordinated actions on the part of many persons pre–supposes familiarity with the procedures to be employed

23. The problem of determining the type of organization which should exist is inextricably          23.____
interwoven with the problem of recruitment. In general, this statement is

    A.  *correct;* since organizations are man–made they can be changed
    B.  *incorrect;* the organizational form which is most desirable is independent of the persons involved
    C.  *correct;* the problem of organization cannot be considered apart from employee qualifications
    D.  *incorrect;* organizational problems can be separated into many parts and recruitment is important in only few of these
    E.  *correct; a* good recruitment program will reduce the problems of organization

24. The conference as an administrative tool is MOST valuable for solving problems which          24.____

    A.  are simple and within a familiar frame of reference
    B.  are of long standing
    C.  are novel and complex
    D.  are not solvable
    E.  require immediate solution

25. Of the following, a recognized procedure for avoiding conflicts in the delegation of author-          25.____
ity is to

    A.  delegate authority so as to preserve control by top management
    B.  provide for a workable span of control
    C.  preview all assignments periodically
    D.  assign all related work to the same control
    E.  use the linear method of assignment

# KEY (CORRECT ANSWERS)

| | | | |
|---|---|---|---|
| 1. | B | 11. | B |
| 2. | E | 12. | A |
| 3. | C | 13. | A |
| 4. | E | 14. | C |
| 5. | A | 15. | A |
| 6. | A | 16. | C |
| 7. | D | 17. | B |
| 8. | B | 18. | B |
| 9. | C | 19. | A |
| 10. | D | 20. | A |

| | |
|---|---|
| 21. | D |
| 22. | C |
| 23. | C |
| 24. | C |
| 25. | D |

# TEST 2

DIRECTIONS: Each question or incomplete statement is followed by several suggested answers or completions. Select the one that BEST answers the question or completes the statement. *PRINT THE LETTER OF THE CORRECT ANSWER IN THE SPACE AT THE RIGHT.*

1. A danger which exists in any organization as complex as that required for administration of a large city is that each department comes to believe that it exists for its own sake. The one of the following which has been attempted in some organizations as a cure for this condition is to

    A.  build up the departmental esprit de corps
    B.  expand the functions and jurisdictions of the various departments so that better integration is possible
    C.  develop a body of specialists in the various subject matter fields which cut across departmental lines
    D.  delegate authority to the lowest possible echelon
    E.  systematically transfer administrative personnel from one department to another

1.\_\_\_\_

2. At best, the organization chart is ordinarily and necessarily an idealized picture of the intent of top management, a reflection of hopes and aims rather than a photograph of the operating facts within the organization.
The one of the following which is the BASIC reason for this is that the organization chart

    A.  does not show the flow of work within the organization
    B.  speaks in terms of positions rather than of live employees
    C.  frequently contains unresolved internal ambiguities
    D.  is a record of past organization or of proposed future organization and never a photograph of the living organization
    E.  does not label the jurisdiction assigned to each component unit

2.\_\_\_\_

3. The drag of inadequacy is always downward. The need in administration is always for the reverse; for a department head to project his thinking to the city level, for the unit chief to try to see the problems of the department.
The inability of a city administration to recruit administrators who can satisfy this need usually results in departments characterized by

    A.  disorganization           B.  poor supervision
    C.  circumscribed viewpoints     D.  poor public relations
    E.  a lack of programs

3.\_\_\_\_

4. When as a result of a shift in public sentiment, the elective officers of a city are changed, is it desirable for career administrators to shift ground without performing any illegal or dishonest act in order to conform to the policies of the new elective officers?

    A.  *No;* the opinions and beliefs of the career officials are the result of long experience in administration and are more reliable than those of politicians
    B.  *Yes;* only in this way can citizens, political officials and career administrators alike have confidence in the performance of their respective functions

4.\_\_\_\_

C. *No;* a top career official who is so spineless as to change his views or procedures as a result of public opinion is of little value to the public service
D. *Yes;* legal or illegal, it is necessary that a city employee carry out the orders of his superior officers
E. *No;* shifting ground with every change in administration will preclude the use of a constant overall policy

5. Participation in developing plans which will affect levels in the organization in addition to his own, will contribute to an individual's understanding of the entire system. When possible, this should be encouraged.
This policy is, in general,

A. *desirable;* the maintenance of any organization depends upon individual understanding
B. *undesirable;* employees should participate only in those activities which affect their own level, otherwise conflicts in authority may arise
C. *desirable;* an employee's will to contribute to the maintenance of an organization depends to a great extent on the level which he occupies
D. *undesirable;* employees can be trained more efficiently and economically in an organized training program than by participating in plan development
E. *desirable;* it will enable the employee to make intelligent suggestions for adjustment of the plan in the future

6. Constant study should be made of the information contained in reports to isolate those elements of experience which are static, those which are variable and repetitive, and those which are variable and due to chance.
Knowledge of those elements of experience in his organization which are static or constant will enable the operating official to

A. fix responsibility for their supervision at a lower level
B. revise the procedure in order to make the elements variable
C. arrange for follow–up and periodic adjustment
D. bring related data together
E. provide a frame of reference within which detailed standards for measurement can be installed

7. A chief staff officer, serving as one of the immediate advisors to the department head, has demonstrated a special capacity for achieving internal agreements and for sound judgment. As a result he has been used more and more as a source of counsel and assistance by the department head. Other staff officers and line officials as well have discovered that it is wise for them to check with this colleague in advance on all problematical matters handed up to the department head.
Developments such as this are

A. *undesirable;* they disrupt the normal lines for flow of work in an organization
B. *desirable;* they allow an organization to make the most of its strength wherever such strength resides
C. *undesirable;* they tend to undermine the authority of the department head and put it in the hands of a staff officer who does not have the responsibility
D. *desirable;* they tend to resolve internal ambiguities in organization
E. *undesirable;* they make for bad morale by causing *cut throat* competition

8.  A common difference among executives is that some are not content unless they are out        8.\_\_\_\_
    in front in everything that concerns their organization, while others prefer to run things by
    pulling strings, by putting others out in front and by stepping into the breach only when
    necessary.
    Generally speaking, an advantage this latter method of operation has over the former
    is that it

    A.  results in a higher level of morale over a sustained period of time
    B.  gets results by exhortation and direct stimulus
    C.  makes it unnecessary to calculate integrated moves
    D.  makes the personality of the executive felt further down the line
    E.  results in the executive getting the reputation for being a good fellow

9.  Administrators frequently have to get facts by interviewing people. Although the interview       9.\_\_\_\_
    is a legitimate fact gathering technique, it has definite limitations which should not be
    overlooked.
    The one of the following which is an important limitation is that

    A.  people who are interviewed frequently answer questions with guesses rather than
        admit their ignorance
    B.  it is a poor way to discover the general attitude and thinking of supervisors inter-
        viewed
    C.  people sometimes hesitate to give information during an interview which they will
        submit in written form
    D.  it is a poor way to discover how well employees understand departmental policies
    E.  the material obtained from the interview can usually be obtained at lower cost from
        existing records

10. It is desirable and advantageous to leave a maximum measure of planning responsibility        10.\_\_\_\_
    to operating agencies or units, rather than to remove the responsibility to a central plan-
    ning staff agency.
    Adoption of the former policy (decentralized planning) would lead to

    A.  *less* effective planning; operating personnel do not have the time to make long–
        term plans
    B.  *more* effective planning; operating units are usually better equipped technically
        than any staff agency and consequently are in a better position to set up valid
        plans
    C.  *less* effective planning; a central planning agency has a more objective point of
        view than any operating agency can achieve
    D.  *more* effective planning; plans are conceived in terms of the existing situation and
        their execution is carried out with the will to succeed
    E.  *less* effective planning; there is little or no opportunity to check deviation from plans
        in the proposed set-up

Questions 11–15.

DIRECTIONS:   The following sections appeared in a report on the work production of two
              bureaus of a department.

Base your answer to questions 11 through 15 on this information.

Throughout the report, assume that each month has 4 weeks.

Each of the two bureaus maintains a chronological file. In Bureau A, every 9 months on the average, this material fills a standard legal size file cabinet sufficient for 12,000 work units. In Bureau B, the same type of cabinet is filled in 18 months. Each bureau maintains three complete years of information plus a current file. When the current file cabinet is filled, the cabinet containing the oldest material is emptied, the contents disposed of and the cabinet used for current material. The similarity of these operations makes it possible to consolidate these files with little effort.

Study of the practice of using typists as filing clerks for periods when there is no typing work showed (1) Bureau A has for the past 6 months completed a total of 1500 filing work units a week using on the average 200 man–hours of trained file clerk time and 20 man–hours of typist time (2) Bureau B has in the same period completed a total of 2000 filing work units a week using on the average 125 man–hours of trained file clerk time and 60 hours of typist time. This includes all work in chronological files. Assuming that all clerks work at the same speed and that all typists work at the same speed, this indicates that work other than filing should be found for typists or that they should be given some training in the filing procedures used... It should be noted that Bureau A has not been producing the 1,600 units of technical (not filing) work per 30 day period required by Schedule K, but is at present 200 units behind. The Bureau should be allowed 3 working days to get on schedule.

11. What percentage (approximate) of the total number of filing work units completed in both units consists of the work involved in the maintenance of the chronological files?   11.__

   A. 5%      B. 10%      C. 15%      D. 20%      E. 25%

12. If the two chronological files are consolidated, the number of months which should be allowed for filling a cabinet is   12.__

   A. 2      B. 4      C. 6      D. 8      E. 14

13. The MAXIMUM number of file cabinets which can be released for other uses as a result of the consolidation recommended is   13.__

   A. 0      B. 1      C. 2      D. 3
   E. not determinable on the basis of the data given

14. If all the filing work for both units is consolidated without any diminution in the amount to be done and all filing work is done by trained file clerks, the number of clerks required (35–hour work week) is   14.__

   A. 4      B. 5      C. 6      D. 7      E. 8

15. In order to comply with the recommendation with respect to Schedule K, the present work production of Bureau A must be increased by   15.__

   A. 50%      B. 100%      C. 150%      D. 200%
   E. an amount which is not determinable on the basis of the data given

16. A certain training program during World War II resulted in training of thousands of super-    16.____
visors in industry. The methods of this program were later successfully applied in various
governmental agencies. The program was based upon the assumption that there is an
irreducible minimum of three supervisory skills.
The one of these skills among the following is

   A. to know how to perform the job at hand well
   B. to be able to deal personally with workers, especially face to face
   C. to be able to imbue workers with the will to perform the job well
   D. to know the kind of work that is done by one's unit and the policies and procedures
      of one's agency
   E. the "know-how" of administrative and supervisory processes

17. A comment made by an employee about a training course was, *We never have any idea*    17.____
*how we are getting along in that course.*The fundamental error in training methods to
which this criticism points is

   A. insufficient student participation
   B. failure to develop a feeling of need or active want for the material being presented
   C. the training sessions may be too long
   D. no attempt may have been made to connect the new material with what was
      already known
   E. no goals have been set for the students

18. Assume that you are attending a departmental conference on efficiency ratings at which    18.____
it is proposed that a man–to–man rating scale be introduced.
You should point out that, of the following, the CHIEF weakness of the man–to–man
rating scale is that

   A. it involves abstract numbers rather than concrete employee characteristics
   B. judges are unable to select their own standards for comparison
   C. the standard for comparison shifts from man to man for each person rated
   D. not every person rated is given the opportunity to serve as a standard for compari-
      son
   E. standards for comparison will vary from judge to judge

19. Assume that you are conferring with a supervisor who has assigned to his subordinates    19.____
efficiency ratings which you believe to be generally too low. The supervisor argues that
his ratings are generally low because his subordinates are generally inferior.
Of the following, the evidence MOST relevant to the point at issue can be secured by
comparing efficiency ratings assigned by this supervisor

   A. with ratings assigned by other supervisors in the same agency
   B. this year with ratings assigned by him in previous years
   C. to men recently transferred to his unit with ratings previously earned by these men
   D. with the general city average of ratings assigned by all supervisors to all employ-
      ees
   E. with the relative order of merit of his employees as determined independently by
      promotion test marks

20. The one of the following which is NOT among the most common of the compensable fac-    20.___
tors used in wage evaluation studies is

    A. initiative and ingenuity required
    B. physical demand
    C. responsibility for the safety of others
    D. working conditions
    E. presence of avoidable hazards

21. If independent functions are separated, there is an immediate gain in conserving special    21.___
skills. If we are to make optimum use of the abilities of our employees, these skills must
be conserved.
Assuming the correctness of this statement, it follows that

    A. if we are not making optimum use of employee abilities, independent functions
       have not been separated
    B. we are making optimum use of employee abilities if we conserve special skills
    C. we are making optimum use of employee abilities if independent functions have
       been separated
    D. we are not making optimum use of employee abilities if we do not conserve special
       skills
    E. if special skills are being conserved, independent functions need not be separated

22. A reorganization of the bureau to provide for a stenographic pool instead of individual    22.___
unit stenographers will result in more stenographic help being available to each unit
when it is required, and consequently will result in greater productivity for each unit. An
analysis of the space requirements shows that setting up a stenographic pool will require
a minimum of 400 square feet of good space. In order to obtain this space, it will be necessary to reduce the space available for technical personnel, resulting in lesser productivity for each unit.
On the basis of the above discussion, it can be stated that in order to obtain greater
productivity for each unit

    A. a stenographic pool should be set up
    B. further analysis of the space requirement should be made
    C. it is not certain as to whether or not a stenographic pool should be set up
    D. the space available for each technician should be increased in order to compen-
       sate for the absence of a stenographic pool
    E. a stenographic pool should not be set up

23. The adoption of a single consolidated form will mean that most of the form will not be    23.___
used in any one operation. This would create waste and confusion.
This conclusion is based upon the unstated hypothesis that

    A. if waste and confusion are to be avoided, a single consolidated form should be
       used
    B. if a single consolidated form is constructed, most of it can be used in each opera-
       tion
    C. if waste and confusion are to be avoided, most of the form employed should be
       used
    D. most of a single consolidated form is not used
    E. a single consolidated form should not be used

24. Assume that you are studying the results of mechanizing several hand operations. The type of data which would be MOST useful in proving that an increase in mechanization is followed by a lower cost of operation is data which show that in    24._____

    A. some cases a lower cost of operation was not preceded by an increase in mechanization
    B. no case was a higher cost of operation preceded by a decrease in mechanization
    C. some cases a lower cost of operation was preceded by a decrease in mechanization
    D. no case was a higher cost of operation preced by an increase in mechanization
    E. some cases an increase in mechanization was followed by a decrease in cost of operation

25. The type of data which would be MOST useful in determining if an increase in the length of rest periods is followed by an increased rate of production is data which would indicate that    25._____

    A. *decrease* in the total production never follows an increase in the length of the rest period
    B. *increase* in the total production never follows an increase in the length of the rest period
    C. *increase* in the rate of production never follows a decrease in the length of the rest period
    D. *decrease* in the total production may follow a decrease in the length of the rest period
    E. *increase* in the total production sometimes follows an increase in the length of the rest period

# KEY (CORRECT ANSWERS)

| | | | | |
|---|---|---|---|---|
| 1. | E | | 11. | C |
| 2. | B | | 12. | C |
| 3. | C | | 13. | B |
| 4. | B | | 14. | D |
| 5. | E | | 15. | E |
| | | | | |
| 6. | A | | 16. | B |
| 7. | B | | 17. | E |
| 8. | A | | 18. | E |
| 9. | A | | 19. | C |
| 10. | D | | 20. | E |

| | |
|---|---|
| 21. | D |
| 22. | C |
| 23. | C |
| 24. | D |
| 25. | A |

————

# TEST 3

DIRECTIONS:  Each question or incomplete statement is followed by several suggested answers or completions. Select the one that BEST answers the question or completes the statement. *PRINT THE LETTER OF THE CORRECT ANSWER IN THE SPACE AT THE RIGHT.*

1.  You have been asked to answer a request from a citizen of the city. After giving the request careful consideration you find that it cannot be granted.
    In answering the letter, you should begin by

    A.  saying that the request cannot be granted
    B.  discussing in detail the consideration you gave to the request
    C.  quoting the laws relating to the request
    D.  explaining in detail why the request cannot be granted
    E.  indicating an alternative method of achieving the end desired

    1.____

2.  Reports submitted to the department head should be complete to the last detail. As far as possible, summaries should be avoided.
    This statement is, in general,

    A.  *correct;* only on the basis of complete information can a proper decision be reached
    B.  *incorrect;* if all reports submitted were of this character a department head would never complete his work
    C.  *correct;* the decision as to what is important and what is not can only be made by the person who is responsible for the action
    D.  *incorrect;* preliminary reports, obviously, cannot be complete to the last detail
    E.  *correct;* summaries tend to conceal the actual state of affairs and to encourage generalizations which would not be made if the details were known; consequently they should be avoided if possible

    2.____

3.  The supervisor of a large bureau, who was required in the course of business to answer a large number of letters from the public, completely formalized his responses, that is, the form and vocabulary of every letter he prepared were the same as far as possible. This method of solving the problem of how to handle correspondence is, in general,

    A.  *good;* it reduces the time and thought necessary for a response
    B.  *bad;* the time required to develop a satisfactory standard form and vocabulary is usually not available in an active organization
    C.  *good;* the use of standard forms causes similar requests to be answered in a similar way
    D.  *bad;* the use of standard forms and vocabulary to the extent indicated results in letters in *officialese* hindering unambiguous explanation and clear understanding
    E.  *good;* if this method were applied to an entire department, the answering of letters could be left to clerks and the administrators would be free for more constructive work

    3.____

4.  Of the following systems of designating the pages in a loose–leaf manual subject to constant revision and addition, the MOST practicable one is to use

    A.  decimals for main divisions and integers for subdivisions
    B.  integers for main divisions and letters for subdivisions
    C.  integers for main divisions and decimals for subdivisions
    D.  letters for main divisions and integers for subdivisions
    E.  intergers for main divisions and integers for subdivisions

    4.____

5. A subordinate submits a proposed draft of a form which is being revised to facilitate filling    5.__
   in the form on a typewriter. The draft shows that the captions for each space will be
   printed below the space to be filled in.
   This proposal is

   A. *undesirable;* it decreases visibility
   B. *desirable;* it makes the form easy to understand
   C. *undesirable;* it makes the form more difficult to understand
   D. *desirable;* it increases visibility
   E. *undesirable;* it is less compact than other layouts

6. The one of the following which is NOT an essential element of an integrated reporting    6.__
   system for work–measurement is a

   A. uniform record form for accumulating data and instructions for its maintenance
   B. procedure for routing reports upward through the organization and routing summa-
      ries downward
   C. standard report form for summarizing basic records and instructions for its prepa-
      ration
   D. method for summarizing, analyzing and presenting data from several reports
   E. looseleaf revisable manual which contains all procedural materials that are reason-
      ably permanent and have a substantial reference value

7. Forms control only accomplishes the elimination, consolidation and simplifcation of    7.__
   forms. It constributes little to the elimination, consolidation and simplification of pro–
   cedures .
   This statement is

   A. *correct;* the form is static while the procedure is dynamic; consequently control of
      one does not necessarily result in control of the other
   B. *incorrect;* forms frequently dictate the way work is laid out; consequently control of
      one frequently results in control of the other
   C. *correct;* the procedure is primary and the form secondary; consequently control of
      procedure will also control form
   D. *incorrect;* the form and procedure are identical from the viewpoint of work control;
      consequently control of one means control of the other
   E. *correct;* the assurance that forms are produced and distributed economically has
      little relationship to the consolidation and simplification of procedures

8. Governmental agencies frequently attempt to avoid special interest group pressures by    8.
   referring them to the predetermined legislative policy, or to the necessity for rules and
   regulations applying generally to all groups and situations.
   Of the following, the MOST important weakness of this formally correct position is that

   A. it is not tenable in the face of determined opposition
   B. it tends to legalize and formalize the informal relationships between citizen groups
      and the government
   C. the achievement of an agency's aims is in large measure dependent upon its ability
      to secure the cooperation and support of special interest groups
   D. independent groups which participate in the formulation of policy in their sphere of
      interest tend to criticize openly and to press for changes in the direction of their pol-
      icy
   E. agencies following this policy find it difficult to decentralize their public relation
      activities as subdivisions can only refer to the agency's overall policy

9. One of the primary purposes of the performance budget is to improve the ability to examine budgetary requirement by groups who have not been engaged in the construction of the budget. This is acomplished by

    A. making line by line appropriations
    B. making lump sum appropriations by department
    C. enumerating authorization for all expenditures
    D. standardizing the language used and the kinds of authorizations permitted
    E. permitting examination on the level of accomplishment

9.\_\_\_\_

10. When engaged in budget construction or budget analysis, there is no point in trying to determine the total or average benefits to be obtained from total expenditures for a particular commodity or function.
The validity of this argument is USUALLY based upon the

    A. viewpoint that it is not possible to construct a functional budget
    B. theory (or phenomenon) of diminishing utility
    C. hypothesis that as governmental budgets provide in theory for minimum requirements, there is no need to determine total benefits
    D. assumption that such determinations are not possible
    E. false hypothesis that a comparison between expected and achieved results does not aid in budget construction

10.\_\_\_\_

Questions 11-12.

DIRECTIONS: Answer questions 11 and 12 on the basis of the following paragraph.
    Production planning is mainly a process of synthesis. As a basis for the positive act of bringing complex production elements properly together, however, analysis is necessary, especially if improvement is to be made in an existing organization. The necessary analysis requires customary means of orientation and preliminary fact gathering with emphasis, however, on the recognition of administrative goals and of the relationship among work steps.

11. The entire process described is PRIMARILY one of

    A. taking apart, examining and recombining
    B. deciding what changes are necessary, making the changes and checking on their value
    C. fact finding so as to provide the necessary orientation
    D. discovering just where the emphasis in production should be placed and then modifying the existing procedure so that it is placed properly
    E. recognizing administrative goals and the relationship among work steps

11.\_\_\_\_

12.  In production planning according to the above paragraph, analysis is used PRIMARILY     12.___
     as

    A.  a means of making important changes in an organization
    B.  the customary means of orientation and preliminary fact finding
    C.  a development of the relationship among work steps
    D.  a means for holding the entire process intact by providing a logical basis
    E.  a method to obtain the facts upon which a theory can be built

Questions 13-15.

DIRECTIONS:   Answer questions 13 through 15 on the basis of the following paragraph.


    Public administration is policy–making.  But it is not autonomous, exclusive or isolated policy–making.  It is policy–making on a field where mighty forces contend, forces engendered in and by society. It is policy-making subject to still other and various policy makers. Public administration is one of a number of basic political processes by which these people achieves and controls government.

13.  From the point of view expressed in this paragraph, public administration is     13.___

    A.  becoming a technical field with completely objective processes
    B.  the primary force in modern society
    C.  a technical field which should be divorced from the actual decision–making func-
        tion
    D.  basically anti–democratic
    E.  intimately related to politics -

14.  According to the paragraph, public administration is NOT entirely     14.___

    A.  a force generated in and by society
    B.  subject at times to controlling influences
    C.  a social process
    D.  policy–making relating to administrative practices
    E.  related to policy–making at lower levels

15.  The paragraph asserts that public administration     15___

    A.  develops the basic and controlling policies
    B.  is the result of policies made by many different forces
    C.  should attempt to break through its isolated policy–making and engage on a
        broader field
    D.  is a means of directing government
    E.  is subject to the political processes by which acts are controlled

Questions 16-18.

DIRECTIONS: Answer questions 16 through 18 on the basis of the following paragraph.
    In order to understand completely the source of an employee's insecurity on his job, it is necessary to understand how he came to be, who he is and what kind of a person he is away from his job. This would necessitate an understanding of those personal assets and liabilities which the employee brings to the job situation. These arise from his individual characteristics and his past experiences and established patterns of interpersonal relations. This whole area is of tremendous scope, encompassing everything included within the study of psychiatry and interpersonal relations. Therefore, it has been impracticable to consider it in detail. Attention has been focused on the relatively circumscribed area of the actual occupational situation. The factors considered those which the employee brings to the job situation and which arise from his individual characteristics and his past experience and established patterns of interpersonal relations are: intellectual–level or capacity, specific aptitudes, education, work experience, health, social and economic background, patterns of interpersonal relations and resultant personality characteristics.

16. According to the above paragraph, the one of the following I fields of study which would     16.____
    be of LEAST importance in the study of the problem is the

    A.  relationships existing among employees
    B.  causes of employee insecurity in the job situation
    C.  conflict, if it exists, between intellectual level and work experience
    D.  distribution of intellectual achievement
    E.  relationship between employee characteristics and the established pattern of inter-
        personal relations in the work situation

17. According to the above paragraph, in order to make a thoroughgoing and comprehensive    17.____
    study of the sources of employee insecurity, the field of study should include

    A.  only such circumscribed areas as are involved in extra–occupational situations
    B.  a study of the dominant mores of the period
    C.  all branches of the science of psychology
    D.  a determination of the characteristics, such as intellectual capacity, which an
        employee should bring to the job situation
    E.  employee personality characteristics arising from previous relationships with other
        people

18. It is implied by this paragraph that it would be of GREATEST advantage to bring to this   18.____
    problem a comprehensive knowledge of

    A.  all established patterns of interpersonal relations
    B.  the milieu in which the employee group is located
    C.  what assets and liabilities are presented in the job situation
    D.  methods of focusing attention on relatively circumscribed regions
    E.  the sources of an employee's insecurity on his job

Questions 19–20.

DIRECTIONS:   Answer questions 19 and 20 on the basis of the following paragraph.

If, during a study, some hundreds of values of a variable (such as annual number of late-nesses for each employee in a department) have been noted merely in the arbitrary order in which they happen to occur, the mind cannot properly grasp the significance of the record; the observations must be ranked or classified in some way before the characteristics of the series can be comprehended, and those comparisons, on which arguments as to causation depend, can be made with other series. A dichotomous classification is too crude; if the val-ues are merely classified according to whether they exceed or fall short of some fixed value, a large part of the information given by the original record is lost. Numerical measurements lend themselves with peculiar readiness to a manifold classification.

19.   According to the above statement, if the values of a variable which are gathered during a       19
      study are classified in a few subdivisions, the MOST likely result will be

      A.   an inability to grasp the significance of the record
      B.   an inability to relate the series with other series
      C.   a loss of much of the information in the original data
      D.   a loss of the readiness with which numerical measurements lend themselves to a
           manifold classification
      E.   that the order in which they happen to occur will be arbitrary

20.   The above statement advocates, with respect to numerical data, the use of                       20

      A.   arbitrary order
      B.   comparisons with other series
      C.   a two value classification
      D.   a many value classification
      E.   all values of a variable

Questions 21–25.

DIRECTIONS:   Answer questions 21 trough 25 on the basis of the following chart.

DEPARTMENT X
WORKLOAD AND LABOR FORCE
2000-2009

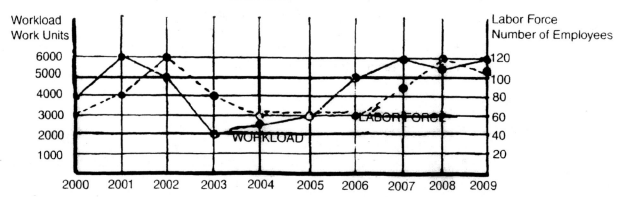

21. The one of the following years for which average employee production was LOWEST was 
    21.____

    A.  2001     B.  2003     C.  2005     D.  2007     E.  2009

22. The average annual employee production for the ten–year period was, in terms of work units, MOST NEARLY 
    22.____

    A.  30     B.  50     C.  70     D.  80     E.  90

23. On the basis of the chart, it can be deduced that personnel needs for the coming year are budgeted on the basis of 
    23.____

    A.  workload for the current year
    B.  expected workload for the coming year
    C.  no set plan
    D.  average workload over the five years immediately preceding the period
    E.  expected workload for the five coming years

24. The chart indicates that the operation is carefully programmed and that the labor force has been used properly.
This opinion is 
    24.____

    A.  *supported* by the chart; the organization has been able to meet emergency situations requiring much additional work without commensurate increases in staff
    B.  *not supported* by the chart; the irregular work load shows a complete absence of planning
    C.  *supported* by the chart; the similar shapes; of the workload and labor force curves show that these important factors are closely related ⁻
    D.  *not supported* by the chart; poor planning with respect to labor requirements is obvious from the chart
    E.  *supported* by the chart; the average number of units of work performed in any 5–year period during the 10 years shows sufficient regularity to indicate a definite trend

25. The chart indicates that the department may be organized in such a way as to require a permanent minimum staff which is too large for the type of operation indicated.
This opinion is 
    25.____

    A.  *supported* by the chart; there is indication that the operation calls for an irreducible minimum number of employees and application of the most favorable work production records show this to be too high for normal operation
    B.  *not supported* by the chart; the absence of any sort of regularity makes it impossible to express any opinion with any degree of certainty
    C.  *supported* by the chart; the expected close relationship between workload and labor force is displaced somewhat, a phenomenon which usually occurs as a result of a fixed minimum requirement
    D.  *not supported* by the chart; the violent movement of the labor force curve makes it evident that no minimum requirements are in effect
    E.  *supported* by the chart; calculation shows that the average number of employees was 84 with an average variation of 17.8, thus indicating that the minimum number of 60 persons was too high for efficient operation

# KEY (CORRECT ANSWERS)

| 1. | A | | 11. | A |
|----|---|--|-----|---|
| 2. | B | | 12. | E |
| 3. | D | | 13. | E |
| 4. | C | | 14. | D |
| 5. | A | | 15. | D |
| 6. | E | | 16. | D |
| 7. | B | | 17. | E |
| 8. | C | | 18. | B |
| 9. | E | | 19. | C |
| 10. | B | | 20. | D |

| 21. | B |
|-----|---|
| 22. | B |
| 23. | A |
| 24. | D |
| 25. | A |

# EXAMINATION SECTION
## TEST 1

DIRECTIONS: Each question or incomplete statement is followed by several suggested answers or completions. Select the one that BEST answers the question or completes the statement. *PRINT THE LETTER OF THE CORRECT ANSWER IN THE SPACE AT THE RIGHT.*

1. In discussing with a subordinate the assignment which you are giving him, it is MOST important that you place greatest stress on

    A. the immediate job to be done
    B. what was accomplished in the past
    C. the long-term goals of the organization
    D. what others have accomplished

1._____

2. Personal friendship and intimacy exhibited by the administrative assistant toward his subordinates should ALWAYS be

    A. kept to a bare minimum
    B. free and unrestricted
    C. in accordance with the personal qualities of each individual subordinate
    D. tempered by the need for objectivity

2._____

3. Assume that one of the office assistants under your supervision approaches you and asks if you would give her advice on some problems that she is having with her husband. Of the following, the MOST appropriate action for you to take is to

    A. tell her that she would be making a mistake in discussing it with you
    B. listen briefly to her problem and then suggest how she might get help in solving it
    C. give her whatever advice she needs based on your knowledge or experience in this area
    D. refer her to a lawyer specializing in marital problems

3._____

4. When you return from lunch one day, you find Miss P, one of your subordinates, in your office crying uncontrollably. When she calms down, she tells you that Mr. T, another subordinate, insulted her but she would prefer not to give details because they are very personal.
Your IMMEDIATE reaction should be to

    A. reprimand Mr. T for his callousness
    B. reprimand the worker in your office for not controlling herself
    C. get as much information as possible about exactly what happened
    D. tell Miss P that she will have to take care of her own affairs

4._____

5. If one of the office assistants under your supervision does not seem to be able to get along well with the other employees, the FIRST step that you should take in such a situation should be to try to find out

    A. more about the background of the office assistant
    B. the reason the office assistant has difficulty in getting along
    C. if another department would be interested in employing the office assistant
    D. the procedures required for dismissal of the office assistant

5._____

6. Suppose that you expect that your department will send two of your subordinates for out-   6.___
side training on the use of new office equipment while others will be trained on the job.
When preparing a yearly budget and schedule for the personnel that you supervise,
training costs to be paid for by the department should be

    A.   excluded and treated separately as a special request when the specific training
        need arises
    B.   estimated and included in the budget and manpower schedules
    C.   left out of the schedule since personnel are thoroughly trained before assignment
        to a position
    D.   considered only if training involves time away from the job

7. There is a rumor going around your department that one of the administrative assistants   7.___
is going to resign.
Since it is not true, the BEST action to take would be to

    A.   find the person starting the rumor, and advise him that disciplinary action will follow
        if the rumors do not stop
    B.   disregard the rumor since the grapevine is always inaccurate
    C.   tell the truth about the situation to those concerned
    D.   start another rumor yourself that contradicts this rumor

8. Suppose a student is concerned over the possibility of failing a course and losing matric-   8.___
ulated status. He comes to you for advice.
The BEST thing for you to do is to

    A.   tell the student it is not your function to discuss student problems
    B.   impress the student with the importance of academic performance and suggest
        that more study is necessary
    C.   send the student to a career counselor for testing
    D.   suggest that he see the instructor or appropriate faculty advisor depending on the
        cause of the problem

9. A member of the faculty had requested that an overhead projector be reserved for a   9.___
seminar. At the time of the seminar, the projector has not been placed in the room, and
you find that one of your office assistants forgot to send the request to the building staff.
Of the following possible actions, which one should be taken FIRST?

    A.   See to it that the projector is moved to the seminar room immediately.
    B.   Personally reprimand the subordinate responsible.
    C.   Suggest rescheduling the seminar.
    D.   Tell the faculty member that the problem was caused by a fault in the machine.

10. Assume that you have to give work assignments to a male office assistant and a female   10.___
office assistant. It would be BEST to

    A.   allow the woman to have first choice of assignments
    B.   give the female preference in assignments requiring patience
    C.   give the male preference in assignments requiring physical action
    D.   make assignments to each on the basis of demonstrated ability and interest

11. In the *initial* phase of training a new employee to perform his job, which of the following approaches is MOST desirable?

    A. Have him read the office manual
    B. Tell him to watch the other employees
    C. Give him simple tasks to perform
    D. Have him do exactly what everyone else is doing

11.____

12. Assume that one of the employees under your supervision performs her work adequately, but you feel that she might be more productive if she changed some of her methods.
You should

    A. discuss with her those changes which you think would be helpful
    B. refrain from saying anything since her work is adequate
    C. suggest that she might be helped by talking to a guidance counselor
    D. assign her to another job

12.____

13. One of the office assistants under your supervision complains to you that the report which you assigned her to prepare is monotonous work and unnecessary. The report is a monthly compilation of figures which you submit to your superior.
Of the following, the *best* action to take FIRST is to

    A. ask her why she feels the work is unnecessary
    B. tell her that she is employed to do whatever work is assigned to her
    C. have her do other work at the same time to provide more interest
    D. assign the report to another subordinate

13.____

14. Of the following, the GREATEST advantage of keeping records of the quantity of work produced by the office assistants under your supervision is to

    A. have the statistics available in case they are required
    B. enable you to take appropriate action in case of increase, decrease, or other variation in output
    C. provide a basis for promotion or other personnel action
    D. give you a basis for requesting additional employees

14.____

15. It is not possible to achieve maximum productivity from your subordinates *unless* they are told

    A. what the rewards are for their performance
    B. how they will be punished for failure
    C. what it is they are expected to do
    D. that they must work hard if they are to succeed

15.____

16. Suppose that you observe that one of the assistants on your staff is involved with an extremely belligerent student who is demanding information that is not readily available in your department. One staff member is becoming visibly upset and is apparently about to lose his temper.
Under these circumstances, it would be BEST for you to

16.____

A. leave the room and let the situation work itself out
B. let the assistant lose his temper, then intervene and calm both parties at the same time
C. step in immediately and try to calm the student in order to suggest more expedient ways of getting the information
D. tell the student to come back and discuss the situation when he can do it calmly

17. Suppose you have explained an assignment to a newly appointed clerk and the clerk has demonstrated her ability to do the work. After a short period of time, the clerk tells you that she is afraid of incorrectly completing the assignment.
Of the following, the BEST course of action for you to take is to

17.___

A. tell her to observe another clerk who is doing the same type of work
B. explain to her the importance of the assignment and tell her not to be nervous
C. assign her another task which is easier to perform
D. try to allay her fears and encourage her to try to do the work

Questions 18-22.

DIRECTIONS:   Questions 18 through 22 consist of the names of students who have applied for a certain college program and are to be classified according to the criteria described below.

The following table gives pertinent data for 6 different applicants with regard to:
Grade averages, which are expressed on a scale running from
    0 (low) to 4 (high);
Scores on qualifying test, which run from 200 (low) to 800 (high); Related work experience, which is expressed in number of months; Personal references, which are rated from 1 (low) to 5 (high).

| Applicant | Grade Average | Test Score | Work Experience | Reference |
|---|---|---|---|---|
| Jones | 2.2 | 620 | 24 | 3 |
| Perez | 3.5 | 650 | 0 | 5 |
| Lowitz | 3.2 | 420 | 2 | 4 |
| Uncker | 2.1 | 710 | 15 | 2 |
| Farrow | 2.8 | 560 | 0 | 3 |
| Shapiro | 3.0 | 560 | 12 | 4 |

An administrative assistant is in charge of the initial screening process for the program. This process requires classifying applicants into the following four groups:

A. SUPERIOR CANDIDATES. Unless the personal reference rating is lower than 3, all applicants with grade averages of 3.0 or higher and test scores of 600 or higher are classified as superior candidates.
B. GOOD CANDIDATES. Unless the personal reference rating is lower than 3, all applicants with one of the following combinations of grade averages and test scores are classified as good candidates: (1) grade average of 2.5 to 2.9 and test score of 600 or higher; (2) grade average of 3.0 or higher and test score of 550 to 599.
C. POSSIBLE CANDIDATES. Applicants with one of the following combinations of qualifications are classified as possible candidates: (1) grade average of 2.5 to 2.9 and test score of 550 to 599 and a personal reference rating of 3 or higher; (2) grade average of 2.0 to 2.4 and test score of 500 or higher and at least 21 months' work experience and a personal reference rating of 3 or higher; (3) a combination

of grade average and test score that would otherwise qualify as *superior* or *good* but a personal reference score lower than 3.

D. REJECTED CANDIDATES. Applicants who do not fall in any of the above groups are to be rejected.

## EXAMPLE

Jones' grade average of 2.2 does not meet the standard for either a superior candidate (grade average must be 3.0 or higher) or a good candidate (grade average must be 2.5 to 2.9). Grade average of 2.2 does not qualify Jones as a possible candidate if Jones has a test score of 500 or higher, at least 21 months' work experience, and a personal reference rating of 3 or higher. Since Jones has a test score of 620, 24 months' work experience, and a reference rating of 3, Jones is a possible candidate. The answer is C.

Answer Questions 18 through 22 as explained above, indicating for each whether the applicant should be classified as a

A. superior candidate
C. possible candidate

B. good candidate
D. rejected candidate

18. Perez 18._____

19. Lowitz 19._____

20. Uncker 20._____

21. Farrow 21._____

22. Shapiro 22._____

23. A new training program is being set up for which certain new forms will be needed. You have been asked to design these forms. 23._____
Of the following, the FIRST step you should take in planning the forms is

A. finding out the exact purpose for which each form will be used
B. deciding what size of paper should be used for each form
C. determining whether multiple copies will be needed for any of the forms
D. setting up a new filing system to handle the new forms

24. You have been asked to write a report on methods of hiring and training new employees. Your report is going to be about ten pages long. 24._____
For the convenience of your readers, a brief summary of your findings should

A. appear at the beginning of your report
B. be appended to the report as a postscript
C. be circulated in a separate memo
D. be inserted in tabular form in the middle of your report

25. Assume that your department is being moved to new and larger quarters, and that you have been asked to suggest an office layout for the central clerical office. Of the following, your FIRST step in planning the new layout should ordinarily be to 25._____

A. find out how much money has been budgeted for furniture and equipment
B. make out work-flow and traffic-flow charts for the clerical operations
C. measure each piece of furniture and equipment that is presently in use
D. determine which files should be moved to a storage area or destroyed

# KEY (CORRECT ANSWERS)

| | | | | |
|---|---|---|---|---|
| 1. | A | | 11. | C |
| 2. | D | | 12. | A |
| 3. | B | | 13. | A |
| 4. | C | | 14. | B |
| 5. | B | | 15. | C |
| 6. | B | | 16. | C |
| 7. | C | | 17. | D |
| 8. | D | | 18. | A |
| 9. | A | | 19. | D |
| 10. | D | | 20. | D |

21. C
22. B
23. A
24. A
25. B

# TEST 2

DIRECTIONS: Each question or incomplete statement is followed by several suggested answers or completions. Select the one that BEST answers the question or completes the statement. *PRINT THE LETTER OF THE CORRECT ANSWER IN THE SPACE AT THE RIGHT.*

1. In modern office layouts, screens and dividers are often used instead of walls to set off working groups. Advantages given for this approach have included all of the following EXCEPT

    A. more frequent communication between different working groups
    B. reduction in general noise level
    C. fewer objections from employees who are transferred to different groups
    D. cost savings from increased sharing of office equipment

1.\_\_\_\_\_

2. Of the following, the CHIEF reason for moving less active material from active to inactive files is to

    A. dispose of material that no longer has any use
    B. keep the active files down to a manageable size
    C. make sure that no material over a year old remains in active files
    D. separate temporary records from permanent records

2.\_\_\_\_\_

3. The use of a microfiche system for information storage and retrieval would make MOST sense in an office where

    A. a great number of documents must be kept available for permanent reference
    B. documents are ordinarily kept on file for less than six months
    C. filing is a minor and unimportant part of office work
    D. most of the records on file are working forms on which additional entries are frequently made

3.\_\_\_\_\_

4. The work loads in different offices fluctuate greatly over the course of a year. Ordinarily, the MOST economical way of handling a peak load in a specific office is to

    A. hire temporary help from an outside agency
    B. require regular employees to put in overtime
    C. use employees from other offices that are not busy
    D. buy special equipment for operations that can be automated

4.\_\_\_\_\_

5. A faculty member has given you a long list of student grades to be typed. Since your typed list will be the basis for permanent records, it is essential that it contain no errors. The BEST way of checking this typed list is to

    A. ask the faculty member to glance over the typed version and have him correct any mistakes
    B. have someone read the handwritten list aloud, while you check the typed list as each item is read
    C. read the typed list yourself to see that it makes good sense and that there are no omissions or duplications
    D. make a spot-check by comparing several entries in the typed list against the original entries on the handwritten list

5.\_\_\_\_\_

6. It is necessary to purchase a machine for your department which will be used to make single copies of documents and to make copies of memos that are distributed to as many as 150 people.
Of the following kinds of machines, which one is BEST suited for your department's purposes?
A(n)

    A. laser copier        B. fax machine
    C. inkjet printer        D. multipage scanner

6.__

7. Suppose that faculty members have fallen into the habit of asking clerical employees in your department to perform messenger service between your building and other parts of the school. Such demands are becoming increasingly common, and you feel that the two or three man-hours per day involved is too much. Furthermore, these assignments disrupt the work of the department.
Of the following solutions, which one is most likely to result in the GREATEST efficiency?

    A. Hire a full-time messenger whose only job will be to run intra-school errands
    B. Establish a rule that no employees in your department will act as messengers under any circumstances, and that all materials must be sent by ordinary interoffice mail
    C. Notify other departments that from now on they must use their own employees for messenger service to or from your building
    D. Allow the clerical employees to perform messenger service only in cases of urgent need, and have interoffice mail used in all other cases

7.__

8. A new employee is trying to file records for three different students whose names are Robinson, John L., Robinson, John, and Robinson, John Leonard. The employee does not know in what order the records should be filed.
You should

    A. tell the employee to use whatever order seems most convenient
    B. suggest that all the records be put in one folder and arranged chronologically according to date of enrollment
    C. explain that, by the *nothing-before-something* principle, John comes first, John L. second, and John Leonard last
    D. instruct the employee to keep them together but arrange them chronologically according to date of birth

8.__

9. An *out card* or *out guide* should be placed in a file drawer to mark the location of material that

    A. has not yet been received
    B. should be transferred to an inactive file
    C. has been temporarily removed
    D. is no longer needed

9.__

10. Assume that your office does not presently have a formal records-retention program. Your supervisor has suggested that such a program be set up, and has asked you to make a study and submit your recommendations.
The FIRST step in your study should be to

10.__

A. find out how long it has been since the files were last cleaned out
B. take an inventory of the types of materials now in the files
C. learn how much storage space you can obtain for old records
D. decide which files should be thrown out instead of being stored

11. In an organization where a great deal of time and money is spent on information management, it often makes sense to use a *systems analysis* approach in reviewing operations and deciding how they can be carried out more efficiently.
Of the following, the FIRST question that a *systems analysis* should ask about any
procedure is

    11.\_\_\_\_

A. whether the procedure can be handled by automatic data-processing equipment
B. exactly how the procedure is meshed with other existing procedures used in the
organization
C. how many employees should be hired to carry out the present procedure
D. what is the end result that the use of the procedure is supposed to achieve

12. You have been notified that a *work simplification* study is going to be carried out in your
department.
The one of the following which is MOST likely to be the purpose of this study is to

    12.\_\_\_\_

A. increase the productivity of the office by eliminating unnecessary procedures and
irrelevant record keeping
B. produce a new office manual that explains current procedures in a simple and easily understandable way
C. determine whether there are any procedures so simple that they can be handled
by untrained workers
D. substitute computer processing for all operations that are now performed manually

13. Suppose that a cost study has been made of various clerical procedures carried out in
your college, and that the study shows that the average cost of a dictated business letter
is over $5.00 per letter.
Of the following cost factors that go into making up this total cost, the LARGEST *single*
factor is certain to be the cost of

    13.\_\_\_\_

A. stationery and postage
C. labor
B. office machinery
D. office rental

14. Which of the following software programs is BEST for collecting and sorting data,
creating graphs and preparing spreadsheets?

    14.\_\_\_\_

A. Microsoft Excel
C. Microsoft Powerpoint
B. Microsoft Word
D. QuarkXPress

15. Which of the following software programs is BEST for creating visual presentations
containing text, photos and charts?

    15.\_\_\_\_

A. Microsoft Excel
C. Microsoft Powerpoint
B. Microsoft Outlook
D. Adobe Photoshop

16. A supervisor asks you to e-mail a file that has been saved on your computer as a photograph. Since you do not remember the file name, you must search by file type. Which of the following file extensions should you run a search for?

   A.  .html         B.  .pdf         C.  .jpg         D.  .doc

16.___

17. In records management, the term *vital records* refers generally to papers that

   A.  are essential to life
   B.  are needed for an office to continue operating after fire or other disaster
   C.  contain statistics about birth and death
   D.  can be easily replaced

17.___

18. A city agency maintains a complete set of records on its clients on a central computer. A branch office finds that it frequently needs access to this data.
A computer output device which could be installed in the branch office to provide the data is called a

   A.  sorter                        B.  tabulator
   C.  card punch               D.  terminal

18.___

19. A certain employee is paid at the rate of $9.10 per hour, with time-and-a-half for overtime. Hours in excess of 40 hours a week count as overtime. During the past week the employee put in 44 working hours.
The employee's gross wages for the week are MOST NEARLY

   A.  $368         B.  $396         C.  $414         D.  $444

19.___

20. You are making a report on the number of inside and outside calls handled by a particular switchboard. Over a 5-day period, the total number of all inside and outside calls handled by the switchboard was 2,314. The average number of inside calls per day was 274. You cannot find one day's tally of outside calls, but the total number of outside calls for the other four days was 776.
Fron this information, how many outside calls must have been reported on the missing tally?

   A.  168         B.  190         C.  194         D.  274

20.___

21. One typist can type 100 address labels in 1 hour. Another typist can type 100 address labels in 1 hour and 15 minutes. If there are 450 address labels to be typed and both typists are put to work on the job, how soon can they be expected to finish the work?
In _____ hours.

   A.  $2\frac{1}{4}$         B.  $2\frac{1}{2}$         C.  $4\frac{1}{2}$         D.  5

21.___

22. A floor plan has been prepared for a new building, drawn to a scale of $\frac{1}{2}$ inch = 1 foot. A 

    certain area is drawn 1 foot long and $7\frac{1}{2}$ inches wide on the floor plan.

    The actual dimensions of this area in the new building are _____ feet long and _____ feet wide.

    A. $6; 3\frac{1}{4}$    B. $12; 7\frac{1}{2}$    C. 20; 15    D. 24; 15

23. In recent years a certain college has admitted a number of students with high school grades of C-plus or lower. It has usually turned out that an average of *65%* of these students completed their freshman year. Last year 340 such students were admitted. By the end of the year, 102 of these students were no longer in college, but the others completed successfully.
    How many MORE students completed the year than would have been expected, based on the average results of previous years?

    A. 14    B. 17    C. 39    D. 119

24. The morale of employees is an important factor in the maintenance of job interest. Which of the following is generally LEAST valuable in strengthening morale?

    A. Attempting to take a personal interest in one's subordinates
    B. Encouraging employees to speak openly about their opinions and suggestions
    C. Fostering a feeling of group spirit among the workers
    D. Having all employees work at the same rate

25. Of the following, the BEST way for a supervisor to determine when *further* on-the-job training in a particular work area is needed is by

    A. asking the employees
    B. evaluating the employees' work performance
    C. determining the ratio of idle time to total work time
    D. classifying the jobs in the work area

———————

# KEY (CORRECT ANSWERS)

| | |
|---|---|
| 1. B | 11. D |
| 2. B | 12. A |
| 3. A | 13. C |
| 4. C | 14. A |
| 5. B | 15. C |
| 6. A | 16. C |
| 7. D | 17. B |
| 8. C | 18. D |
| 9. C | 19. C |
| 10. B | 20. A |

| |
|---|
| 21. B |
| 22. D |
| 23. B |
| 24. D |
| 25. B |

———

# EXAMINATION SECTION
## TEST 1

DIRECTIONS: Each question or incomplete statement is followed by several suggested answers or completions. Select the one that BEST answers the question or completes the statement. *PRINT THE LETTER OF THE CORRECT ANSWER IN THE SPACE AT THE RIGHT.*

1.  One of the things that can ruin morale in a work group is the failure to exercise judgment in the assignment of overtime work to your subordinates.
    Of the following, the MOST desirable supervisory practice in assigning overtime work is to

    A.  *rotate* overtime on a uniform basis among all your subordinates
    B.  *assign* overtime to those who are *moonlighting* after regular work hours
    C.  *rotate* overtime as much as possible among employees willing to work additional hours
    D.  *assign* overtime to those employees who take frequent long weekend vacations

    1.____

2.  The consistent delegation of authority by you to experienced and reliable subordinates in your work group is generally considered

    A.  *undesirable,* because your authority in the group may be threatened by an unscrupulous subordinate
    B.  *undesirable,* because it demonstrates that you cannot handle your own workload
    C.  *desirable,* because it shows that you believe that you have been accepted by your subordinates
    D.  *desirable,* because the development of subordinates creates opportunities for assuming broader responsibilities yourself

    2.____

3.  The MOST effective way for you to deal with a false rumor circulating among your subordinates is to

    A.  have a trusted subordinate state a counter-rumor
    B.  recommend disciplinary action against the *rumor mongers*
    C.  point out to your subordinates that rumors degrade both listener and initiator
    D.  furnish your subordinates with sufficient authentic information

    3.____

4.  Two of your subordinates tell you about a mistake they made in a report that has already been sent the top management.
    Which of the following questions is *most likely* to elicit the MOST valuable information from your subordinates?

    A.  Who is responsible?
    B.  How can we explain this to top management?
    C.  How did it happen?
    D.  Why weren't you more careful?

    4.____

5.  Assume that you are responsible for implementing major changes in work flow patterns and personnel assignments in the unit of which you are in charge.
    The *one* of the following actions which is *most likely* to secure the willing cooperation of those persons who will have to change their assignmentsis

    5.____

A. having the top administrators of the agency urge their cooperation at a group meeting
B. issuing very detailed and carefully planned instructions to the affected employees regarding the changes
C. integrating employee participation into the planning of the changes
D. reminding the affected employees that career advancement depends upon compliance with organizational objectives

6. Of the following, the BEST reason for using face-to-face communication *instead of* written communication is that face-to-face communication

    A. allows for immediate feedback
    B. is more credible
    C. enables greater use of detail and illustration
    D. is more polite

6.___

7. Of the following, the *most likely* DISADVANTAGE of giving detailed instructions when assigning a task to a subordinate is that such instructions may

    A. conflict with the subordinate's ideas of how the task should be done
    B. reduce standardization of work performance
    C. cause confusion in the mind of the subordinate
    D. inhibit the development of new procedures by the subordinate

7.___

8. Assume that you are a supervisor of a unit consisting of a number of subordinates and that one subordinate, whose work is otherwise acceptable, keeps on making errors in one particular task assigned to him in rotation. This task consists of routine duties which all your subordinates should be able to perform.
Of the following, the BEST way for you to handle this situation is to

    A. do the task yourself when the erring employee is scheduled to perform it and assign this employee other duties
    B. reorganize work assignments so that the task in question is no longer performed in rotation but assigned full-time to your most capable subordinate
    C. find out why this subordinate keeps on making the errors in question and see that he learns how to do the task properly
    D. maintain a well-documented record of such errors and, when the evidence is overwhelming, recommend appropriate disciplinary action

8.___

9. In the past, Mr. T, one of your subordinates, had been generally withdrawn and suspicious of others, but he had produced acceptable work. However, Mr. T has lately started to get into arguments with his fellow workers during which he displays intense rage. Friction between this subordinate and the others in your unit is mounting and the unit's work is suffering.
Of the following, which would be the BEST way for you to handle this situation?

    A. Rearrange work schedules and assignments so as to give Mr. T no cause for complaint
    B. Instruct the other workers to avoid Mr. T and not to respond to any abuse
    C. Hold a unit meeting and appeal for harmony and submergence of individual differences in the interest of work
    D. Maintain a record of incidents and explore with Mr. T the possibility of seeking professional help

9.___

10. You are responsible for seeing to it that your unit is functioning properly in the accomplishment of its budgeted goals.
    Which of the following will provide the LEAST information on how well you are accomplishing such goals?

    A. Measurement of employee performance
    B. Identification of alternative goals
    C. Detection of employee errors
    D. Preparation of unit reports

10.\_\_\_\_

11. Some employees see an agency training program as a threat. Of the following, the *most likely* reason for such an employee attitude toward training is that the employee involved feel that

    A. some trainers are incompetent
    B. training rarely solves real work-a-day problems
    C. training may attempt to change comfortable behavior patterns
    D. training sessions are boring

11.\_\_\_\_

12. Of the following, the CHIEF characteristic which distinguishes a *good* supervisor from a *poor* supervisor is the *good* supervisor's

    A. ability to favorably impress others
    B. unwillingness to accept monotony or routine
    C. ability to deal constructively with problem situations
    D. strong drive to overcome opposition

12.\_\_\_\_

13. Of the following, the MAIN disadvantage of on-the-job training is that, *generally,*

    A. special equipment may be needed
    B. production may be slowed down
    C. the instructor must maintain an individual relationship with the trainee
    D. the on-the-job instructor must be better qualified than the classroom instructor

13.\_\_\_\_

14. All of the following are *correct* methods for a supervisor to use in connection with employee discipline EXCEPT

    A. trying not to be too lenient or too harsh
    B. informing employees of the rules and the penalties for violations of the rules
    C. imposing discipline immediately after the violation is discovered
    D. making sure, when you apply discipline, that the employee understands that you do not want to do it

14.\_\_\_\_

15. Of the following, the MAIN reason for a supervisor to establish standard procedures for his unit is to

    A. increase the motivation for his subordinates
    B. make it easier for the subordinates to submit to authority
    C. reduce the number of times that his subordinates have to consult him
    D. reduce the number of mistakes that his subordinates will make

15.\_\_\_\_

16. Of the following, the BEST reason for using form letters in correspondence is that they are

    A. concise and businesslike
    B. impersonal in tone
    C. uniform in appearance
    D. economical for large mailings

16.\_\_

17. The use of loose-leaf office manuals for the guidance of employees on office policy, organization, and office procedures has won wide acceptance.
The MAIN advantage of the loose-leaf format is that it

    A. allows speedy reference
    B. facilitates revisions and changes
    C. includes a complete index
    D. presents a professional appearance

17.\_\_

18. Office forms sometimes consist of several copies, each of a different color.
The MAIN reason for using *different* colors is to

    A. make a favorable impression on the users of the form
    B. distinguish each copy from the others
    C. facilitate the preparation of legible carbon copies
    D. reduce cost, since using colored stock permits recycling of paper

18.\_\_

19. Which of the following is the BEST justification for obtaining a photocopying machine for the office?

    A. A photocopying machine can produce an unlimited number of copies at a low fixed cost per copy.
    B. Employees need little training in operating a photocopying machine.
    C. Office costs will be reduced and efficiency increased.
    D. The legibility of a photocopy generally is superior to copy produced by any other office duplicating device.

19.\_\_

20. Which one of the following should be the most IMPORTANT overall consideration when preparing a recommendation to automate a large-scale office activity?
The

    A. number of models of automated equipment available
    B. benefits and costs of automation
    C. fears and resistance of affected employees
    D. experience of offices which have automated similar activities

20.\_\_

21. A tickler file is MOST appropriate for filing materials

    A. chronologically according to date they were received
    B. alphabetically by name
    C. alphabetically by subject
    D. chronologically according to date they should be followed up

21.\_\_

22. Which of the following is the BEST reason for decentralizing rather than centralizing the use of duplicating machines?    22.____

    A. Developing and retaining efficient deplicating machine operators
    B. Facilitating supervision of duplicating services
    C. Motivating employees to produce legible duplicated copies
    D. Placing the duplicating machines where they are most convenient and most frequently used

23. Window envelopes are sometimes considered preferable to individually addressed envelopes PRIMARILY because    23.____

    A. window envelopes are available in standard sizes for all purposes
    B. window envelopes are more attractive and official-looking
    C. the use of window envelopes eliminates the risk of inserting a letter in the wrong envelope
    D. the use of window envelopes requires neater typing

24. In planning the layout of a new office, the utilization of space and the arrangement of staff, furnishings and equipment should *usually* be MOST influenced by the    24.____

    A. gross square footage
    B. status differences in the chain of command
    C. framework of informal relationships among employees
    D. activities to be performed

25. When delegating responsibility for an assignment to a subordinate, it is MOST important that you    25.____

    A. retain all authority necessary to complete the assignment
    B. make your self generally available for consultation with the subordinate
    C. inform your superiors that you are no longer responsible for the assignment
    D. decrease the number of subordinates whom you have to supervise

---

# KEY (CORRECT ANSWERS)

| | | | | | |
|---|---|---|---|---|---|
| 1. | C | 11. | C | 21. | D |
| 2. | D | 12. | C | 22. | D |
| 3. | D | 13. | B | 23. | C |
| 4. | D | 14. | D | 24. | D |
| 5. | C | 15. | C | 25. | B |
| 6. | A | 16. | D | | |
| 7. | D | 17. | B | | |
| 8. | C | 18. | B | | |
| 9. | D | 19. | C | | |
| 10. | B | 20. | B | | |

---

# TEST 2

Questions 1-5.

DIRECTIONS: Answer Questions 1 through 5 on the basis of the following passage.

The most effective control mechanism to prevent gross incompetence on the part of public employees is a good personnel program. The personnel officer in the line departments and the central personnel agency should exert positive leadership to raise levels of performance. Although the key factor is the quality of the personnel recruited, staff members other than personnel officers can make important contributions to efficiency. Administrative analysts, now employed in many agencies, make detailed studies of organization and procedures, with the purpose of eliminating delays, waste, and other inefficiencies. Efficiency is, however, more than a question of good organization and procedures; it is also the product of the attitudes and values of the public employees. Personal motivation can provide the will to be efficient. The best management studies will not result in substantial improvement of the performance of those employees who feel no great urge to work up to their abilities.

1. The passage indicates that the *key* factor in preventing gross incompetence of public employees is the
   A. hiring of administrative analysts to assist personnel people
   B. utilization of effective management studies
   C. overlapping of responsibility
   D. quality of the employees hired

   1.__

2. According to the above passage, the central personnel agency staff *should*
   A. work more closely with administrative analysts in the line departments than with personnel afficers
   B. make a serious effort to avoid jurisdictional conflicts with personnel officers in line departments
   C. contribute to improving the quality of work of public employees
   D. engage in a comprehensive program to change the public's negative image of public employees

   2.__

3. The passage indicates that efficiency in an organization can BEST be brought about by
   A. eliminating ineffective control mechanisms
   B. instituting sound organizational procedures
   C. promoting competent personnel
   D. recruiting people with desire to do good work

   3.__

4. According to the passage, the *purpose* of administrative analysis in a public agency is to
   A. prevent injustice to the public employee
   B. promote the efficiency of the agency
   C. protect the interests of the public
   D. ensure the observance of procedural due process

   4.__

5. The passage implies that a considerable rise in the quality of work of public employees can be brought about by

    A.   encouraging positive employee attitudes toward work
    B.   controlling personnel officers who exceed their powers
    C.   creating warm personal associations among public employees in an agency
    D.   closing loopholes in personnel organization and procedures

5._____

6. Typist *X* can type 20 forms per hour and Typist *I* can type 30 forms per hour. If there are 30 forms to be typed and both typists are put to work on the job, *how soon* should they be expected to finish the work? _____ minutes.

    A.  32        B.  34        C.  36        D.  38

6._____

7. Assume that there were 18 working days in February and that the six clerks in your unit had the following number of absences:

                      Clerk F - 3 absences
                      Clerk G - 2 absences
                      Clerk H - 8 absences
                      Clerk I - 1 absence
                      Clerk J - 0 absences
                      Clerk K - 5 absences

The average percentage attendance for the six clerks in your unit in February was, *most nearly,*

    A.  80%        B.  82%        C.  84%        D.  86%

7._____

8. A certain employee is paid at the rate of $7.50 per hour, with time-and-a-half for over-time. Hours in excess of 40 hours a week count as overtime. During the past week the employee put in 48 working hours.
The employee's gross wages for the week are, *most nearly,*

    A.  $330        B.  $350        C.  $370        D.  $390

8._____

9. You are making a report on the number of inside and outside calls handled by a particular switchboard. Over a 15-day period, the total number of all inside and outside calls handled by the switchboard was 5,760. The average number of inside calls per day was 234. You cannot find one day's tally of outside calls, but the total number of outside calls for the other fourteen days was 2,065. From this information, how many *outside calls* must have been reported on the missing tally?

    A.  175        B.  185        C.  195        D.  205

9._____

10. A floor plan has been prepared for a new building, drawn to a scale of 3/4 inch = 1 foot. A certain area is drawn 1 and 1/2 feet long and 6 inches wide on the floor plan. What are the *actual* dimensions of this area in the new building? _____ feet long and _____ feet wide.

    A.  21; 8        B.  24; 8        C.  27; 9        D.  30; 9

10._____

Questions 11 - 15.

DIRECTIONS:  In answering Questions 11 through 15, assume that you are in charge of public information for an office which issues reports and answers questions from
other offices and from the public on changes in land use. The charts below
represent comparative land use in four neighborhoods. The area of each
neighborhood is expressed in city blocks. Assume that all city blocks are the
same size.

NEIGHBORHOOD A - 16 CITY BLOCKS

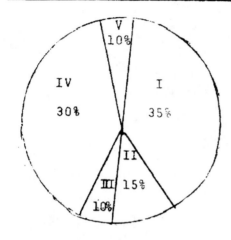

NEIGHBORHOOD B - 24 CITY BLOCKS

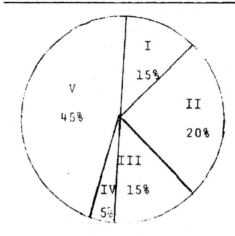

NEIGHBORHOOD C - 20 CITY BLOCKS

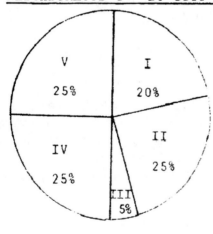

NEIGHBORHOOD D - 12 CITY BLOCKS

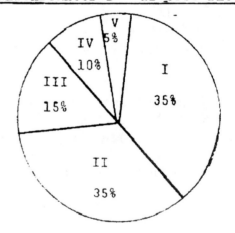

KEY:  I- one- and two-family houses    III. Office buildings
II- Apartment buildings    IV. Rental stores
V. Factories and warehouses

11.  In how many of these neighborhoods does residential use (categories I and II together)
account for at least 50% of the land use?

A.  One          B.  Two          C.  Three          D.  Four

12.  Which neighborhood has the largest land area occupied by apartment buildings? Neighborhood _____ .

A.  A          B.  B          C.  C          D.  D

13. In which neighborhood is the largest percentage of the land devoted to both office build-   13.____
    ings and retail stores? Neighborhood _____ .

    A.  A              B.  B              C.  C              D.  D

14. What is the difference, to the nearest city block, between the amount of land devoted to   14.____
    retail stores in Neighborhood B and the amount devoted to similar use in Neighborhood
    C? _____ block(s).

    A.  1              B.  2              C.  4              D.  6

15. Which one of the following types of buildings occupies the same amount of land area in   15.____
    Neighborhood B as the amount of land area occupied by retail stores in Neighborhood
    A?

    A.  Factories and warehouses
    B.  Office buildings
    C.  Retail stores
    D.  Apartment buildings

Questions 16 - 20.

DIRECTIONS:   Answer Questions 16 through 20 on the basis of the following passage.

*For a period of nearly fifteen years, beginning in the mid-1950's, higher education sus-
tained a phenomenal rate of growth. The factors principally responsible were continuing
improvement in the rate of college entrance by high school graduates, a 50-percent increase
in the size of the college-age (eighteen to twenty-one) group, and - until about 1967 - a rapid
expansion of university research activity supported by the federal government.*

*Today, as one looks ahead fifteen years to the year 2020, it is apparent that each of
these favorable stimuli will either be abated or turn into a negative factor. The rate of growth
of the college-age group has already diminished, and from 2010 to 2015 the size of the college-age group will shrink annually almost as fast as it grew from 1965 to 1970. From 2015 to
2020, this annual decrease will slow down so that by 2020 the age-group will be about the
same size as it was in 2019. This substantial net decrease in the size of the college-age
group over the next fifteen years will dramatically affect college enrollments since, currently,
83 percent of undergraduates are twenty-one and under, and another 11 percent are twenty-
one to twenty-four.*

16. Which one of the following factors is NOT mentioned in the above passage as contritut-   16.____
    ing to the high rate of growth of higher education?

    A.  A larger increase in the size of the eighteen to twenty-one age group
    B.  The equalization of educational opportunities among socio-economic groups
    C.  The federal budget impact on research and development spending in the higher
        education sector
    D.  The increasing rate at which high school graduates enter college

17. Based on the information in the above passage, the size of the college-age group in 2020 will be
    17.___

    A.  larger than it was in 2019
    B.  larger than it was in 2005
    C.  smaller than it was in 2015
    D.  about the same as it was in 2010

18. According to the above passage, the tremendous rate of growth of higher education started around
    18.___

    A.  1950        B.  1955        C.  1960        D.  1965

19. The percentage of undergraduates who are over age 24 is, *most nearly,*
    19.___

    A.  6%        B.  8%        C.  11%        D.  17%

20. Which one of the following conclusions can be substantiated by the information given in the above passage?
    20.___

    A.  The college-age group will be about the same size in 2010 as it was in 1965.
    B.  The annual decrease in the size of the college-age group from 2010 to 2015 will be about the same as the annual increase from 1965 to 1970.
    C.  The overall decrease in the size of the college-age group from 2010 to 2015 will be followed by an overall increase in its size from 2015 to 2020.
    D.  The size of the college-age group will decrease at a fairly constant rate from 1995 to 2010.

21. Because higher status is important to many employees, they will often make an effort to achieve it as an end in itself.
    21.___
    Of the following, the BEST course of action for the supervisor to take on the basis of the preceding statement is to

    A.  attach higher status to that behavior of subordinates which is directed toward reaching the goals of the organization
    B.  avoid showing sympathy toward subordinates' wishes for increased wages, improved working conditions, or other benefits
    C.  foster interpersonal competitiveness among subordinates so that personal friendliness is replaced by the desire to protect individual status
    D.  reprimand subordinates whenever their work is in some way unsatisfactory in order to adjust their status accordingly

22. Assume that a large office in a certain organization operates long hours and is thus on two shifts with a slight overlap. Those employees, including supervisors, who are most productive are given their choice of shifts. The earlier shift is considered preferable by most employees .
    22.__
    As a result of this method of assignment, which of the following is *most likely* to result?

    A.  Most non-supervisory employees will be assigned to the late shift; most supervisors will be assigned to the early shift.
    B.  Most supervisors will be assigned to the late shift; most non-supervisory employees will be assigned to the early shift.
    C.  The early shift will be more productive than the late shift.
    D.  The late shift will be more productive than the early shift.

23. Assume that a supervisor of a unit in which the employees are of avera.ge friendliness    23.____
tells a newly-hired employee on her first day that her co-workers are very friendly. The
other employees hear his remarks to the new employee.
Which of the following is the most *likely* result of this action of the supervisor? The

    A.   newly-hired employee will tend to feel less friendly than if the supervisor had said
        nothing
    B.   newly-hired employee will tend to believe that her co-workers are very friendly
    C.   other employees will tend to feel less friendly toward one another
    D.   other employees will tend to see the newly-hired employee as insincerely friendly

24. A recent study of employee absenteeism showed that, although unscheduled absence    24.____
for part of a week is relatively high for young employees, unscheduled absence for a full
week is low. However, although full-week unscheduled absence is least frequent for the
youngest employees, the frequency of such absence increases as the age of employees
increases.
Which of the following statements is the MOST logical explanation for the greater full-
week absenteeism among older employees?

    A.   *Older* employees are more likely to be males.
    B.   *Older* employees are more likely to have more relatively serious illnesses.
    C.   *Younger* employees are more likely to take longer vacations.
    D.   *Younger* employees are more likely to be newly-hired.

25. An employee can be motivated to fulfill his needs as he sees them. He is not motivated    25.____
by what others think he ought to have, but what he himself wants. Which of the following
statements follows MOST logically from the foregoing viewpoint?

    A.   A person's different traits may be separately classified, but they are all part of one
        system comprising a whole person.
    B.   Every job, however simple, entitles the person who does it to proper respect and
        recognition of his unique aspirations and abilities.
    C.   No matter what equipment and facilities an organization has, they cannot be put to
        use except by people who have been motivated.
    D.   To an observer, a person's need may be unrealistic but they are still controlling.

# KEY (CORRECT ANSWERS)

| | | | | |
|---|---|---|---|---|
| 1. | D | | 11. | B |
| 2. | C | | 12. | C |
| 3. | D | | 13. | A |
| 4. | B | | 14. | C |
| 5. | A | | 15. | D |
| 6. | C | | 16. | B |
| 7. | B | | 17. | C |
| 8. | D | | 18. | B |
| 9. | B | | 19. | A |
| 10. | B | | 20. | B |

| | |
|---|---|
| 21. | A |
| 22. | C |
| 23. | B |
| 24. | B |
| 25. | D |

———

# EXAMINATION SECTION

## TEST 1

DIRECTIONS: Each question or incomplete statement is followed by several suggested answers or completions. Select the one that BEST answers the question or completes the statement. *PRINT THE LETTER OF THE CORRECT ANSWER IN THE SPACE AT THE RIGHT.*

1. A certain system for handling office supplies requires that supplies be issued to the various agency offices only on a bi-weekly basis and that all supply requisitions be authorized by the unit supervisor.
   The BEST reason for establishing this supplies system is to
   A. standardize ordering descriptions and stock identification codes
   B. prevent the disordering of stock shelves and cabinets by unauthorized persons searching for supplies
   C. ensure that unit supervisors properly exercise their right to make determinations on supply orders
   D. encourage proper utilization of supplies to control the workload

   1.___

2. It is important that every office have a retention and disposal program for filing material. Suppose that you have been appointed administrative assistant in an office with a poorly organized records-retention program.
   In establishing a revised program for the transfer or disposal of records, the step which would logically be taken THIRD in the process is
   A. preparing a safe and inexpensive storage area and setting up an indexing system for records already in storage
   B. determining what papers to retain and for how long a period
   C. taking an inventory of what is filed, where it is filed, how much is filed, and how often it is used
   D. moving records from active to inactive files and destroying useless records

   2.___

3. In the effective design of office forms, the FIRST step to take is to
   A. decide what information should be included
   B. decide the purpose for which the form will be used
   C. identify the form by name and number
   D. identify the employees who will be using the form

   3.___

4. Some designers of office forms prefer to locate the instructions on how to fill out the form at the bottom of it. The MOST logical objection to placing such instructions at the bottom of the form is that
   A. instructions at the bottom require an excess of space
   B. all form instructions should be outlined with a separate paragraph

   4.___

C. the form may be partly filled out before the instructions are seen

D. the bottom of the form should be reserved only for authorization and signature

5. A formal business report may consist of many parts, including the following:
   I. Table of contents
  II. List of references
 III. Preface
  IV. Index
   V. List of tables
  VI. Conclusions or recommendations

    Of the following, in setting up a formal report, the PROPER order of the six parts listed is
    A. I, III, VI, V, II, IV    B. IV, III, II, V, VI, I
    C. III, I, V, VI, II, IV    D. II, V, III, I, IV, VI

5.___

6. Three of the basic functions of office management are considered to be planning, controlling, and organizing. Of the following, the one which might BEST be considered ORGANIZING activity is
    A. assigning personnel and materials to work units to achieve agreed-upon objectives
    B. determining future objectives and indicating conditions affecting the accomplishment of the goals
    C. evaluating accomplishments and applying necessary corrective measures to insure results
    D. motivating employees to perform their work in accordance with objectives

6.___

7. The following four statements relate to office layout.
    I. Position supervisors' desks at the front of their work group so that they can easily be recognized as persons in authority
   II. Arrange file cabinets and frequently used equipment near the employees who utilize them most often
  III. Locate the receptionist's desk near the entrance of the office so that visitor traffic will not distract other workers
  IV. Divide a large office area into many smaller offices by using stationary partitions so that all employees may have privacy and prestige
According to authorities in office management and administration, which of these statements are GENERALLY recommended guides to effective office layout?
    A. I, II, III    B. II, III, IV
    C. II, III    D. All of the above

7.___

8. For which of the following purposes would a flow chart have the GREATEST applicability?
    A. Training new employees in performance of routinized duties
    B. Determining adequacy of performance of employees
    C. Determining the accuracy of the organization chart
    D. Locating causes of delays in carrying out an operation

8.___

9. Office work management concerns tangible accomplishment or     9.___
production. It has to do with results; it does not deal
with the amount of energy expended by the individual who
produces the results.
According to this statement, the production in which of
the following kinds of jobs would be MOST difficult to
measure accurately?  A(n)
   A. file clerk             B. secretary
   C. computer operator     D. office administrator

10. The FIRST step in the statistical analysis of a great     10.___
mass of data secured from a survey is to
   A. scan the data to determine which is atypical of
       the survey
   B. determine the number of deviations from the average
   C. arrange the data into groups on the basis of likenesses
       and differences
   D. plot the data on a graph to determine trends

11. Suppose that, as an administrative assistant in charge of     11.___
an office, you are required to change the layout of your
office to accommodate expanding functions.
The LEAST important factor to be considered in planning
the revised layout is the
   A. relative productivity of individuals in the office
   B. communication and work flow needs
   C. need for screening confidential activities from
       unauthorized persons
   D. areas of noise concentration

12. Suppose you have instructed a new employee to follow a     12.___
standardized series of steps to accomplish a job. He is
to use a rubber stamp, then a red pencil on the first
paper, and a numbering machine on the second. Then, he
is to staple the two sheets of paper together and put them
to one side. You observe, however, that he sometimes uses
the red pencil first, sometimes the numbering machine first.
At other times, he does the stapling before using the
numbering machine.
For you as supervisor to suggest that the clerk use the
standardized method when doing this job would be
   A. *bad* because the clerk should be given a chance to use
       his independent judgment on the best way to do his job
   B. *good* because the clerk's sequence of actions results
       in a loss of efficiency
   C. *bad* because it is not wise to interrupt the work habit
       the clerk has already developed
   D. *good* because the clerk should not be permitted to make
       unauthorized changes in standard office routines

13. Suppose study of the current records management system     13.___
for students' transcripts reveals needless recopying of
transcript data throughout various offices within the
university. On this basis, a recommendation is made that
this unnecessary recopying of information be eliminated.

This decision to eliminate waste in material, time, and space is an application of the office management principle of

   A. work simplification      B. routing and scheduling
   C. job analysis           D. cost and budgetary control

14. It is generally LEAST practical for an office manager to prepare for known peak work periods by      14.___
   A. putting job procedures into writing so that they can be handled by more than one person
   B. arranging to make assignments of work on a short-interval scheduling basis
   C. cleaning up as much work as possible ahead of known peak periods
   D. rotating jobs and assignments among different employees to assure staff flexibility

15. The four statements below are about office manuals used for various purposes.      15.___
If you had the job of designing and controlling several kinds of office manuals to be used in your agency, which one of these statements would BEST apply as a general rule for you to follow?
   A. Office manual content should be classified into main topics with proper subdivisions arranged in strict alphabetical order.
   B. Manual additions and revisions should be distributed promptly to all holders of manuals for their approval, correction, and criticism.
   C. The language used in office manuals should be simple, and charts and diagrams should be interspersed within the narrative material for further clarity.
   D. Office manual content should be classified into main topics arranged in strict alphabetical order with subtopics in sequence according to importance.

16. Suppose that, as an administrative assistant, you have been assigned to plan the reorganization of an office which has not been operating efficiently because of the uncoordinated manner in which new functions have been assigned to it over the past year.      16.___
The FIRST thing you should do is
   A. call a meeting of the office staff and explain the purposes of the planned reorganization
   B. make a cost-value analysis of the present operations to determine what should be changed or eliminated
   C. prepare a diagram of the flow of work as you think it should be
   D. define carefully the current objectives to be achieved by this reorganization

17. Effective organization requires that specific actions be taken in proper sequence.      17.___
The following are four actions essential to effective organization:

    I. Group activities on the basis of human and
       material resources
   II. Coordinate functions and provide for good communications
  III. Formulate objectives, policies, and plans
   IV. Determine activities necessary to accomplish goals

The PROPER sequence of these four actions is:
   A. III, II, IV, I          B. IV, III, I, II
   C. III, IV, I, II          D. IV, I, III, II

18. For an administrative assistant to give each of his sub-        18.___
    ordinates exactly the same type of supervision is
        A. *advisable*, because he will gain a reputation for
           being fair and impartial
        B. *inadvisable*, because subordinates work more diligently
           when they think they are receiving preferential
           treatment
        C. *advisable*, because most human problems can be classi-
           fied into categories which make them easier to handle
        D. *inadvisable*, because people differ and there is no
           one supervisory procedure that applies in every case
           to dealing with individuals

19. Suppose that, as an administrative assistant, you find         19.___
    that some of your subordinates are coming to you with
    complaints you think are trivial.
    For you to hear them through is
        A. *poor practice*; subordinates should be trained to
           come to you only with major grievances
        B. *good practice*; major grievances sometimes are the
           underlying cause of minor complaints
        C. *poor practice*; you should delegate this kind of
           matter and spend your time on more important problems
        D. *good practice*; this will make you more popular with
           your subordinates

20. Suppose that a new departmental policy has just been           20.___
    established which you feel may be resented by your sub-
    ordinates, but which they must understand and follow.
    Which would it be most advisable for you as their super-
    visor to do FIRST?
        A. Make clear to your subordinates that you are not
           responsible for making this policy.
        B. Tell your subordinates that you agree with the
           policy whether you do or not.
        C. Explain specifically to your subordinates the
           reasons for the policy and how it is going to affect
           them.
        D. Distribute a memo outlining the new policy and
           require your subordinates to read it.

21. An office assistant under your supervision tells you that      21.___
    she is reluctant to speak to one of her subordinates about
    poor work habits because this subordinate is strong-willed,
    and she does not want to antagonize her.
    For you to refuse the office assistant's request that you
    speak to her subordinate about this matter is

A. *inadvisable*, since you are in a position of greater authority
B. *advisable*, since supervision of this subordinate is a basic responsibility of that office assistant
C. *inadvisable*, since the office assistant must work more closely with her subordinate than you do
D. *advisable*, since you should not risk antagonizing her subordinate yourself

22. The GREATEST advantage to a supervisor of using oral communications as compared to written is the
    A. opportunity provided for immediate feedback
    B. speed with which orders can be given and carried out
    C. reduction in amount of paper work
    D. establishment of an informal atmosphere

22.___

23. Of the following, the MOST important reason for an administrative assistant to have private, face-to-face discussions with subordinates about their performance is
    A. encourage a more competitive spirit among employees
    B. give special praise to employees who perform well
    C. discipline employees who perform poorly
    D. help employees improve their work

23.___

24. For a supervisor to keep records of reprimands to subordinates about violations of rules is
    A. *poor practice*; such records are evidence of the supervisor's inability to maintain discipline
    B. *good practice*; these records are valuable to support disciplinary actions recommended or taken
    C. *poor practice*; the best way to prevent recurrences is to apply penalties without delay
    D. *good practice*; such records are evidence that the supervisor is doing a good job

24.___

25. As an administrative assistant supervising a small office, you decide to hold a staff meeting to try to find an acceptable solution to a problem that is causing serious conflicts within the group.
    At this meeting, your role should be to present the problem and
    A. see that the group keeps the problem in focus and does not discuss irrelevant matters
    B. act as chairman of the meeting, but take no other part in the discussion
    C. see to it that each member of the group offers a suggestion for its solution
    D. state your views on the matter before any discussion gets under way

25.___

# KEY (CORRECT ANSWERS)

| | | | | |
|---|---|---|---|---|
| 1. D | 6. A | 11. A | 16. D | 21. B |
| 2. A | 7. C | 12. B | 17. C | 22. A |
| 3. B | 8. D | 13. A | 18. D | 23. D |
| 4. C | 9. D | 14. B | 19. B | 24. B |
| 5. C | 10. C | 15. C | 20. C | 25. A |

# TEST 2

DIRECTIONS: Each question or incomplete statement is followed by several suggested answers or completions. Select the one that BEST answers the question or completes the statement. *PRINT THE LETTER OF THE CORRECT ANSWER IN THE SPACE AT THE RIGHT.*

1. Suppose that one of your subordinates who supervises two young office assistants has been late for work a number of times and you have decided to talk to him about it.
   In your discussion, it would be MOST constructive for you to emphasize that
   A. personal problems cannot be used as an excuse for these latenesses
   B. the department suffers financially when he is late
   C. you will be forced to give him a less desirable assignment if his latenesses continue
   D. his latenesses set a bad example to those he supervises

   1.___

2. Suppose that, as a newly-appointed administrative assistant, you are in charge of a small but very busy office. Your four subordinates are often required to make quick decisions on a wide range of matters while answering telephone or in-person inquiries.
   You can MOST efficiently help your subordinates meet such situations by
   A. delegating authority to make such decisions to only one or two trusted subordinates
   B. training each subordinate in the proper response for each kind of inquiry that might be made
   C. making certain that subordinates understand clearly the basic policies that affect these decisions
   D. making each subordinate an expert in one area

   2.___

3. Of the following, the MOST recent development in methods of training supervisors that involves the human relations approach is
   A. conference training      B. the lecture method
   C. the case method          D. sensitivity training

   3.___

4. Which of the following is MOST likely to result in failure as a supervisor?
   A. Showing permissiveness in relations with subordinates
   B. Avoiding delegation of tasks to subordinates
   C. Setting high performance standards for subordinates
   D. Using discipline only when necessary

   4.___

5. The MOST important long-range benefit to an organization of proper delegation of work by supervisors is *generally* that
   A. subordinates will be developed to assume greater responsibilities

   5.___

B. subordinates will perform the work as their supervisors would
C. errors in delegated work will be eliminated
D. more efficient communication among organizational components will result

6. Which of the following duties would it be LEAST appropriate for an administrative assistant in charge of an office to delegate to an immediate subordinate?
   A. Checking of figures to be used in a report to the head of the department
   B. On-the-job training of newly appointed college office assistants
   C. Reorganization of assignments for higher level office staff
   D. Contacting other school offices for needed information

6.___

7. Decisions should be delegated to the lowest point in the organization at which they can be made effectively.
   The one of the following which is MOST likely to be a result of the application of this accepted management principle is that
   A. upward communications will be facilitated
   B. potential for more rapid decisions and implementation is increased
   C. coordination of decisions that are made will be simplified
   D. no important factors will be overlooked in making decisions

7.___

8. The lecture-demonstration method would be LEAST desirable in a training program set up for
   A. changing the attitudes of long-term employees
   B. informing subordinates about new procedures
   C. explaining how a new office machine works
   D. orientation of new employees

8.___

9. Which one of the following conditions would be LEAST likely to indicate a need for employee training?
   A. Large number of employee suggestions
   B. Large amount of overtime
   C. High number of chronic latenesses
   D. Low employee morale

9.___

10. An administrative assistant is planning to make a recommendation to change a procedure which would substantially affect the work of his subordinates.
    For this supervisor to consult with his subordinates about the recommendation before sending it through would be
    A. *undesirable*; subordinates may lose respect for a supervisor who evidences such indecisiveness
    B. *desirable*; since the change in procedure would affect their work, subordinates should decide whether the change should be made
    C. *undesirable*; since subordinates would not receive credit if the procedure were changed, their morale would be lowered
    D. *desirable*; the subordinates may have some worthwhile suggestions concerning the recommendation

10.___

11. The BEST way to measure improvement in a selected group    11.___
    of office assistants who have undergone a training course
    in the use of specific techniques is to
    A. have the trainees fill out questionnaires at the
       completion of the course as to what they have learned
       and giving their opinions as to the value of the course
    B. compare the performance of the trainees who completed
       the course with the performance of office assistants
       who did not take the course
    C. compare the performance of the trainees in these
       techniques before and after the training course
    D. compare the degree of success on the next promotion
       examination of trainees and non-trainees

12. When an administrative assistant finds it necessary to    12.___
    call in a subordinate for a disciplinary interview, his
    MAIN objective should be to
    A. use techniques which can penetrate any deception
       and get at the truth
    B. stress correction of, rather than punishment for,
       past errors
    C. maintain a reputation for being an understanding
       superior
    D. decide on disciplinary action that is consistent
       with penalties applied for similar infractions

13. Suppose that a newly promoted office assistant does satis-   13.___
    factory work during the first five months of her probationary
    period. However, her supervisor notices shortly after
    this time that her performance is falling below acceptable
    standards. The supervisor decides to keep records of this
    employee's performance, and if there is no significant
    improvement by the end of 11 months, to recommend that this
    employee not be given tenure in the higher title.
    This, as the sole course of action, is
    A. *justified*; employees who do not perform satisfactorily
       should not be promoted
    B. *unjustified*; the supervisor should attempt to determine
       the cause of the poor performance as soon as possible
    C. *justified*; the supervisor will have given the sub-
       ordinate the full probationary period to improve herself
    D. *unjustified*; the subordinate should be demoted to
       her previous title as soon as her work becomes
       unsatisfactory

14. Suppose that you are conducting a conference-style    14.___
    training course for a group of 12 office assistants. Miss
    Jones is the only conferee who has not become involved
    in the discussion.
    The BEST method of getting Miss Jones to participate is to
    A. ask her to comment on remarks made by the best-
       informed participant
    B. ask her to give a brief talk at the next session on
       a topic that interests her
    C. set up a role-play situation and assign her to take
       a part
    D. ask her a direct question which you know she can answer

15. Which of the following is NOT part of the "control" function of office management?
    A. Deciding on alternative courses of action
    B. Reporting periodically on productivity
    C. Evaluating performance against the standards
    D. Correcting deviations when required
15.___

16. Which of the following is NOT a principal aspect of the process of delegation?
    A. Developing improvements in methods used to carry out assignments
    B. Granting of permission to do what is necessary to carry out assignments
    C. Assignment of duties by a supervisor to an immediate subordinate
    D. Obligation on the part of a subordinate to carry out his assignment
16.___

17. Reluctance of a supervisor to delegate work effectively may be due to any or all of the following EXCEPT the supervisor's
    A. unwillingness to take calculated risks
    B. lack of confidence in subordinates
    C. inability to give proper directions as to what he wants done
    D. retention of ultimate responsibility for delegated work
17.___

18. A man cannot serve two masters.
    This statement emphasizes the importance in an organization of following the principle of
    A. specialization of work
    B. unity of command
    C. uniformity of assignment
    D. span of control
18.___

19. In general, the number of subordinates an administrative assistant can supervise effectively tends to vary
    A. *directly* with both similarity and complexity of their duties
    B. *directly* with similarity of their duties and *inversely* with complexity of their duties
    C. *inversely* with both similarity and complexity of their duties
    D. *inversely* with similarity of their duties and *directly* with complexity of their duties
19.___

20. When an administrative assistant practices "general" rather than "close" supervision, which one of the following is MOST likely to happen?
    A. His subordinates will not be as well-trained as employees who are supervised more closely.
    B. Standards are likely to be lowered because subordinates will be under fewer pressures and will not be motivated to work toward set goals.
20.___

C. He will give fewer specific orders and spend more
time on planning and coordinating than those
supervisors who practice close supervision.
D. This supervisor will spend more time checking and
correcting mistakes made by subordinates than would
one who supervises closely.

Questions 21-25.

DIRECTIONS:    Questions 21 to 25 are to be answered SOLELY on the
basis of the information contained in the following
paragraph.

*Since an organization chart is pictorial in nature, there is a
tendency for it to be drawn in an artistically balanced and appealing
fashion, regardless of the realities of actual organizational structure. In addition to being subject to this distortion, there is the
difficulty of communicating in any organization chart the relative
importance or the relative size of various component parts of an
organizational structure. Furthermore, because of the need for
simplicity of design, an organization chart can never indicate the
full extent of the interrelationships among the component parts of
an organization. These interrelationships are often just as vital
as the specifications which an organization chart endeavors to
indicate. Yet, if an organization chart were to be drawn with all
the wide variety of criss-crossing communication and cooperation
networks existent within a typical organization, the chart would
probably be much more confusing than informative. It is also
obvious that no organization chart as such can 'prove' or 'disprove'
that the organizational structure it represents is effective in
realizing the objectives of the organization. At best, an
organization chart can only illustrate some of the various factors
to be taken into consideration in understanding, devising, or
altering organizational arrangements.*

21. According to the above paragraph, an organization chart          21.____
can be expected to portray the
    A. structure of the organization along somewhat ideal
       lines
    B. relative size of the organizational units quite
       accurately
    C. channels of information distribution within the
       organization graphically
    D. extent of the obligation of each unit to meet the
       organizational objectives

22. According to the above paragraph, those aspects of              22.____
internal functioning which are NOT shown on an organization
chart
    A. can be considered to have little practical application
       in the operations of the organization
    B. might well be considered to be as important as the
       structural relationships which a chart does present
    C. could be the cause of considerable confusion in the
       operation of an organization which is quite large
    D. would be most likely to provide the information needed
       to determine the overall effectiveness of an organization

23. In the above paragraph, the one of the following conditions which is NOT implied as being a defect of an organization chart is that an organizat    chart may
    A. present a picture of the organizat   al structure which is different from the structure that actually exists
    B. fail to indicate the comparative size of various organizational units
    C. be limited in its ability to convey some of the meaningful aspects of organizational relationships
    D. become less useful over a period of time during which the organizational facts which it illustrated have changed

23.____

24. The one of the following which is the MOST suitable title for the above paragraph is
    A. The Design and Construction of an Organization Chart
    B. The Informal Aspects of an Organization Chart
    C. The Inherent Deficiencies of an Organization Chart
    D. The Utilization of a Typical Organization Chart

24.____

25. It can be INFERRED from the above paragraph that the function of an organization chart is to
    A. contribute to the comprehension of the organization form and arrangements
    B. establish the capabilities of the organization to operate effectively
    C. provide a balanced picture of the operations of the organization
    D. eliminate the need for complexity in the organization's structure

25.____

# KEY (CORRECT ANSWERS)

| | | | |
|---|---|---|---|
| 1. D | | 11. C | |
| 2. C | | 12. B | |
| 3. D | | 13. B | |
| 4. B | | 14. D | |
| 5. A | | 15. A | |
| 6. C | | 16. A | |
| 7. B | | 17. D | |
| 8. A | | 18. B | |
| 9. A | | 19. B | |
| 10. D | | 20. C | |

21. A
22. B
23. D
24. C
25. A

# TEST 3

DIRECTIONS: Each question or incomplete statement is followed by several suggested answers or completions. Select the one that BEST answers the question or completes the statement. *PRINT THE LETTER OF THE CORRECT ANSWER IN THE SPACE AT THE RIGHT.*

1. Of the following problems that might affect the conduct and outcome of an interview, the MOST troublesome and usually the MOST difficult for the interviewer to control is the
   A. tendency of the interviewee to anticipate the needs and preferences of the interviewer
   B. impulse to cut the interviewee off when he seems to have reached the end of an idea
   C. tendency of interviewee attitudes to bias the results
   D. tendency of the interviewer to do most of the talking

1.___

2. The administrative assistant MOST likely to be a good interviewer is one who
   A. is adept at manipulating people and circumstances toward his objectives
   B. is able to put himself in the position of the interviewee
   C. gets the more difficult questions out of the way at the beginning of the interview
   D. develops one style and technique that can be used in any type of interview

2.___

3. A good interviewer guards against the tendency to form an overall opinion about an interviewee on the basis of a single aspect of the interviewee's make-up.
   This statement refers to a well-known source of error in interviewing known as the
   A. assumption error      B. expectancy error
   C. extension effect      D. halo effect

3.___

4. In conducting an "exit interview" with an employee who is leaving voluntarily, the interviewer's MAIN objective should be to
   A. see that the employee leaves with a good opinion of the organization
   B. learn the true reasons for the employee's resignation
   C. find out if the employee would consider a transfer
   D. try to get the employee to remain on the job

4.___

5. During an interview, an interviewee unexpectedly discloses a relevant but embarrassing personal fact.
   It would be BEST for the interviewer to
   A. listen calmly, avoiding any gesture or facial expression that would suggest approval or disapproval of what is related
   B. change the subject, since further discussion in this area may reveal other embarrassing, but irrelevant, personal facts

5.___

    C. apologize to the interviewee for having led him to
       reveal such a fact and promise not to do so again
    D. bring the interview to a close as quickly as possible
       in order to avoid a discussion which may be distress-
       ful to the interviewee

6. Suppose that while you are interviewing an applicant for    6. ___
a position in your office, you notice a contradiction in
facts in two of his responses.
For you to call the contradictions to his attention would
be
    A. *inadvisable*, because it reduces the interviewee's level
       of participation
    B. *advisable*, because getting the facts is essential to a
       successful interview
    C. *inadvisable*, because the interviewer should use more
       subtle techniques to resolve any discrepancies
    D. *advisable*, because the interviewee should be impressed
       with the necessity for giving consistent answers

7. An interviewer should be aware that an undesirable result    7. ___
of including "leading questions" in an interview is to
    A. cause the interviewee to give "yes" or "no" answers
       with qualification or explanation
    B. encourage the interviewee to discuss irrelevant topics
    C. encourage the interviewee to give more meaningful
       information
    D. reduce the validity of the information obtained from
       the interviewee

8. The kind of interview which is PARTICULARLY helpful in    8. ___
getting an employee to tell about his complains and
grievances is one in which
    A. a pattern has been worked out involving a sequence
       of exact questions to be asked
    B. the interviewee is expected to support his statements
       with specific evidence
    C. the interviewee is not made to answer specific questions
       but is encouraged to talk freely
    D. the interviewer has specific items on which he wishes to
       get or give information

9. Suppose you are scheduled to interview a student aide under    9. ___
your supervision concerning a health problem. You know that
some of the questions you will be asking him will seem embarrassing to him, and that he may resist answering these
questions.
In general, to hold these questions for the last part of the
interview would be
    A. *desirable;* the intervening time period gives the inter-
       viewer an opportunity to plan how to ask these sensitive
       questions
    B. *undesirable;* the student aide will probably feel that he
       has been tricked when he suddenly must answer embarrass-
       ing questions

    C. *desirable*; the student aide will probably have
       increased confidence in the interviewer and be
       more willing to answer these questions
    D. *undesirable*; questions that are important should
       not be deferred until the end of the interview

10. The House passed an amendment to delete from the omnibus    10.\_\_\_
    higher education bill a section that would have prohibited
    coeducational colleges and universities from considering
    sex as a factor in their admissions policy.
    According to the above passage, consideration of sex as
    a factor in the admissions policy of coeducational colleges
    and universities would
    A. be permitted by the omnibus higher education bill if
       passed without further amendment
    B. be prohibited by the amendment to the omnibus higher
       education bill
    C. have been prohibited by the deletion of a section from
       the omnibus higher education bill
    D. have been permitted if the House had failed to pass
       the amendment

Questions 11-14.

DIRECTIONS:    Answer Questions 11 to 14 only according to the
               information given in the passage below.

*The proposition that administrative activity is essentially
the same in all organizations appears to underlie some of the
practices in the administration of private higher education. Although
the practice is unusual in public education, there are numerous
instances of industrial, governmental, or military administrators
being assigned to private institutions of higher education and, to
a lesser extent, of college and university presidents assuming
administrative positions in other types of organizations. To test
this theory that administrators are interchangeable, there is a
need for systematic observation and classification. The myth that
an educational administrator must first have experience in the
teaching profession is firmly rooted in a long tradition that has
historical prestige. The myth is bound up in the expectations of
the public and personnel surrounding the administrator. Since
administrative success depends significantly on how well an
administrator meets the expectations others have of him, the myth
may be more powerful than the special experience in helping the
administrator attain organizational and educational objectives.
Educational administrators who have risen through the teaching
profession have often expressed nostalgia for the life of a teacher
or scholar, but there is no evidence that this nostalgia contributes
to administrative success.*

11. Which of the following statements as completed is MOST    11.\_\_\_
    consistent with the above passage?
    The greatest number of administrators has moved from
    A. industry and the military to government and universities
    B. government and universities to industry and the military
    C. government, the armed forces, and industry to colleges
       and universities
    D. colleges and universities to government, the armed forces,
       and industry

12. Of the following, the MOST reasonable inference from the   12.___
above passage is that a specific area requiring further
research is the
   A. place of myth in the tradition and history of the
educational profession
   B. relative effectiveness of educational administrators
from inside and outside the teaching profession
   C. performance of administrators in the administration
of public colleges
   D. degree of reality behind the nostalgia for scholarly
pursuits often expressed by educational administrators

13. According to the above passage, the value to an education-   13.___
al administrator of experience in the teaching profession
   A. lies in the firsthand knowledge he has acquired of
immediate educational problems
   B. may lie in the belief of his colleagues, subordinates,
and the public that such experience is necessary
   C. has been supported by evidence that the experience
contributes to administrative success in educational
fields
   D. would be greater if the administrator were able to
free himself from nostalgia for his former duties

14. Of the following, the MOST appropriate title for the   14.___
above passage is
   A. Educational Administration, Its Problems
   B. The Experience Needed for Educational Administration
   C. Administration in Higher Education
   D. Evaluating Administrative Experience

Questions 15-20.

DIRECTIONS: Answer Questions 15 to 20 only according to the
information contained in the following paragraph.

*Methods of administration of office activities, much of which
consists of providing information and 'know-how' needed to coordinate
both activities within that particular office and other offices,
have been among the last to come under the spotlight of management
analysis. Progress has been rapid during the past decade, however,
and is now accelerating at such a pace that an 'information revolution'
in office management appears to be in the making. Although triggered
by technological breakthroughs in electronic computers and other
giant steps in mechanization, this information revolution must be
attributed to underlying forces, such as the increased complexity of
both governmental and private enterprise, and ever-keener competition
Size, diversification, specialization of function, and decentralizati
are among the forces which make coordination of activities both more
imperative and more difficult. Increased competition, both domestic
and international, leaves little margin for error in managerial
decisions. Several developments during recent years indicate an
evolving pattern. In 1960, the American Management Association
expanded the scope of its activities and changed the name of its
Office Management Division to Administrative Services Division. Also
in 1960, the magazine "Office Management" merged with the magazine
"American Business", and this new publication was named "Administrative Management".*

15. A REASONABLE inference that can be made from the informa-     15.____
tion in the above paragraph is that an important role of
the office manager today is to
    A. work toward specialization of functions performed
       by his subordinates
    B. inform and train subordinates regarding any new
       developments in computer technology and mechanization
    C. assist the professional management analysts with the
       management analysis work in the organization
    D. supply information that can be used to help coordinate
       and manage the other activities of the organization

16. An IMPORTANT reason for the 'information revolution' that     16.____
has been taking place in office management is the
    A. advance made in management analysis in the past decade
    B. technological breakthrough in electronic computers
       and mechanization
    C. more competitive and complicated nature of private
       business and government
    D. increased efficiency of office management techniques
       in the past ten years

17. According to the above paragraph, specialization of func-     17.____
tion in an organization is MOST likely to result in
    A. the elimination of errors in managerial decisions
    B. greater need to coordinate activities
    C. more competition with other organizations, both
       domestic and international
    D. a need for office managers with greater flexibility

18. The word *evolving*, as used in the third from last sentence  18.____
in the above paragraph, means *most nearly*
    A. developing by gradual changes
    B. passing on to others
    C. occurring periodically
    D. breaking up into separate, constituent parts

19. Of the following, the MOST reasonable implication of the      19.____
changes in names mentioned in the last part of the above
paragraph is that these groups are attempting to
    A. professionalize the field of office management and
       the title of Office Manager
    B. combine two publications into one because of the
       increased costs of labor and materials
    C. adjust to the fact that the field of office management
       is broadening
    D. appeal to the top managerial people rather than the
       office management people in business and government

20. According to the above paragraph, intense competition         20.____
among domestic and international enterprises makes it
MOST important for an organization's managerial staff to
    A. coordinate and administer office activities with
       other activities in the organization
    B. make as few errors in decision-making as possible

C. concentrate on decentralization and reduction of
   size of the individual divisions of the organization
D. restrict decision-making only to top management
   officials

---

# KEY (CORRECT ANSWERS)

|       |   |       |   |
|-------|---|-------|---|
| 1. | A | 11. | C |
| 2. | B | 12. | B |
| 3. | D | 13. | B |
| 4. | B | 14. | B |
| 5. | A | 15. | D |
|    |   |     |   |
| 6. | B | 16. | C |
| 7. | D | 17. | B |
| 8. | C | 18. | A |
| 9. | C | 19. | C |
| 10. | A | 20. | B |

---

# EXAMINATION SECTION

DIRECTIONS FOR THIS SECTION:
Each question or incomplete statement is followed by several suggested answers or completions. Select the one that BEST answers the question or completes the statement. *PRINT THE LETTER OF THE CORRECT ANSWER IN THE SPACE AT THE RIGHT.*

# TEST 1

1. A supervisor notices that one of his more competent subordinates has recently been showing less interest in his work. The work performed by this employee has also fallen off and he seems to want to do no more than the minimum acceptable amount of work. When his supervisor questions the subordinate about his decreased interest and his mediocre work performance, the subordinates replies: "Sure, I've lost interest in my work. I don't see any reason why I should do more than I have to. When I do a good job, nobody notices it. But, let me fall down on one minor job and the whole place knows about it! So why should I put myself out on this job?"
   If the subordinate's contentions are true, it would be CORRECT to *assume* that the
   A. subordinate has not received adequate training
   B. subordinate's workload should be decreased
   C. supervisor must share responsibility for this employee's reaction
   D. supervisor has not been properly enforcing work standards

2. How many subordinates should report directly to each supervisor? While there is agreement that there are limits to the number of subordinates that a manager can supervise well, this limit is determined by a number of important factors.
   Which of the following factors is *most likely* to increase the number of subordinates that can be EFFECTIVELY supervised by one supervisor in a particular unit?
   A. The unit has a great variety of activities.
   B. A staff assistant handles the supervisor's routine duties.
   C. The unit has a relatively inexperienced staff.
   D. The office layout is being rearranged to make room for more employees.

3. Mary Smith, an administrative assistant, heads the inspection records unit of Department Y. She is a dedicated supervisor who not only strives to maintain an efficient operation, but also tries to improve the competence of each individual member of her staff. She keeps these considerations in mind when assigning work to her staff. Her bureau chief asks her to compile some data based on information contained in her records. She feels that any member of her staff should be able to do this job.
   The one of the following members of her staff who would *probably* be given LEAST consideration for this assignment is:
   A. Jane Abel, a capable supervising clerk with considerable experience in the unit
   B. Kenneth Brown, a senior clerk recently transferred to

1. ...

2. ...

3. ...

1

the unit, who has had several opportunities to
demonstrate his capabilities

    C. Laura Chance, a clerk who spends full time on a
single routine assignment

    D. Michael Dutton, a clerk who works on several minor
jobs but still has the lightest work load

4. There are very few aspects of a supervisor's job that do    4. ...
not involve communication, either in writing or orally.
Which of the following statements regarding *oral* and
*written* orders is NOT correct?

    A. Oral orders usually permit more immediate feedback
than do written orders.

    B. Written orders, rather than oral orders, should
generally be given when the subordinate will be held
strictly accountable.

    C. Oral orders are usually preferable when the order
contains lengthy detailed instructions.

    D. Written orders, rather than oral orders, should
usually be given to a subordinate who is slow to
understand or is forgetful.

5. Assume that you are the head of a large clerical unit in    5. ...
Department R.  Your department's personnel office has appointed a clerk, Roberta Rowe, to fill a vacancy in your
unit.  Before bringing this appointee to your office, the
personnel officer has given Roberta the standard orientation on salary, fringe benefits, working conditions, attendance, and the department's personnel rules.  In addition, he
has supplied her with literature covering these areas.
Of the following, the action that you should take FIRST
after Roberta has been brought to your office is to

    A. give her an opportunity to read the literature furnished
by the personnel office so that she can ask you questions about it

    B. escort her to the desk she will use and assign her to
work with an experienced employee who will act as her
trainer

    C. explain the duties and responsibilities of her job and
its relationship with the jobs being performed by the
other employees of the unit

    D. summon the employee who is currently doing the work
that will be performed by Roberta and have him explain
and demonstrate how to perform the required tasks

6. Your superior informs you that the employee turnover rate    6. ...
in your office is well above the norm and must be reduced.
Which one of the following initial steps would be LEAST
appropriate in attempting to overcome this problem?

    A. Decide to be more lenient about performance standards
and about employee requests for time off, so that
your office will gain a reputation as an easy place
to work

    B. Discuss the problem with a few of your key people whose
judgment you trust to see if they can shed some light
on the underlying causes of the problem

    C. Review the records of employees who have left during
the past year to see if there is a pattern that will
help you understand the problem

      D. Carefully review your training procedures to see
         whether they can be improved

7. In issuing instructions to a subordinate on a job assign-    7. ...
ment, the supervisor should ordinarily explain why the
assignment is being made.
*Omission* of such an explanation is BEST justified when the
    A. subordinate is restricted in the amount of discretion
       he can exercise in carrying out the assignment
    B. assignment is one that will be unpopular with the
       subordinate
    C. subordinate understands the reason as a result of
       previous similar assignments
    D. assignment is given to an employee who is in need of
       further training

8. When a supervisor allows sufficient time for training and    8. ...
makes an appropriate effort in the training of his subordinates, his CHIEF goal is to
    A. increase the dependence of one subordinate upon
       another in their everyday work activities
    B. spend more time with his subordinates in order to
       become more involved in their work
    C. increase the capability and independence of his
       subordinates in carrying out their work
    D. increase his frequency of contact with his subordi-
       nates in order to better evaluate their performance

9. In preparing an evaluation of a subordinate's performance,   9. ...
which one of the following items is *usually* IRRELEVANT?
    A. Remarks about tardiness or absenteeism
    B. Mention of any unusual contributions or accomplishments
    C. A summary of the employee's previous job experience
    D. An assessment of the employee's attitude toward the job

10. The ability to delegate responsibility while maintaining   10. ...
adequate controls is one key to a supervisor's success.
Which one of the following methods of control would MINI-
MIZE the amount of responsibility assumed by the subordinate?
    A. Asking for a monthly status report in writing
    B. Asking to receive copies of important correspondence so
       that you can be aware of potential problems
    C. Scheduling periodic project status conferences with
       your subordinate
    D. Requiring that your subordinate confer with you before
       making decisions on a project

11. You wish to assign an important project to a subordinate   11. ...
who you think has good potential.
Which one of the following approaches would be MOST effective in successfully completing the project while developing the subordinate's abilities?
    A. Describe the project to the subordinate in general
       terms and emphasize that it must be completed as
       quickly as possible
    B. Outline the project in detail to the subordinate and
       emphasize that its successful completion could lead
       to career advancement
    C. Develop a detailed project outline and timetable,
       discuss the details and timing with him, and assign
       the subordinate to carry out the plan on his own

D. Discuss the project objectives and suggested approaches with the subordinate, and ask the subordinate to develop a detailed project outline and timetable for your approval

12. Research studies reveal that an important difference between high-production and low-production supervisors lies not in their interest in eliminating mistakes, but in their manner of handling mistakes.
High-production supervisors are *most likely* to look upon mistakes as PRIMARILY a(n)　　12. ...
    A. opportunity to provide training
    B. by-product of subordinate negligence
    C. opportunity to fix blame in a situation
    D. result of their own incompetence

13. Supervisors should try to establish what has been called "positive discipline," an atmosphere in which subordinates willingly abide by rules which they consider fair.
When a supervisor notices a subordinate violating an important rule, his FIRST course of action should be to　　13. ...
    A. stop the subordinate and tell him what he is doing wrong
    B. wait a day or two before approaching the employee involved
    C. call a meeting of all subordinates to discuss the rule
    D. forget the matter in the hope that it will not happen again

14. The working climate is the feeling, degree of freedom, the tone and the mood of the working environment.
Which of the following contributes MOST to determining the working climate in a unit or group?  The　　14. ...
    A. rules set for rest periods
    B. example set by the supervisor
    C. rules set for morning check in
    D. wages paid to the employees

15. John Polk is a bright, ingenious clerk with a lot of initiative.  He has made many good suggestions to his supervisor in the training division of Department T, where he is employed.  However, last week one of his bright ideas literally "blew up."  In setting up some electronic equipment in the training classroom, he crossed some wires, resulting in a damaged tape recorder and a classroom so filled with smoke that the training class had to be held in another room.  When Mr. Brown, his supervisor, learned of this occurrence, he immediately summoned John to his private office.  There Mr. Brown spent five minutes bawling John out, calling him an over-zealous, overgrown kid, and sent him back to his job without letting John speak once.
Of the following, the action of Mr. Brown that MOST deserves *approval* is that he　　15. ...
    A. took disciplinary action immediately without regard for past performance
    B. kept the disciplinary interview to a brief period
    C. concentrated his criticism on the root cause of the occurrence
    D. held the disciplinary interview in his private office

16. Typically, when the technique of "supervision by results" is practiced, higher management sets down, either implicitly or　　16. ...

4

explicitly,certain **performance** standards or goals that the sub-
ordinate is expected to meet.  So long as these standards
are met, management interferes very little.
The *most likely* result of the use of this technique is that
it will
  A. lead to ambiguity in terms of goals
  B. be successful only to the extent that close direct
     supervision is practiced
  C. make it possible to evaluate both employee and super-
     visory effectiveness
  D. allow for complete automomy on the subordinate's part

17. Assume that you are the supervisor of a large clerical        17. ...
    unit performing routine clerical operations.  One of your
    clerks consistenly produces much less work than other
    members of your staff performing similar tasks.
    Of the following, the action you should take FIRST is to
      A. ask the clerk if he wants to be transferred to another
         unit
      B. reprimand the clerk for his poor performance and warn
         him that further disciplinary action will be taken if
         his work does not improve
      C. quietly ask the clerk's co-workers whether they know
         why his performance is poor
      D. discuss this matter with the clerk to work out plans
         for improving his performance

18. When making written evaluations and reviews of the per-       18. ...
    formance of subordinates, it is *usually* advisable to
      A. avoid informing the employee of the evaluation if it
         is critical because it may create hard feelings
      B. avoid informing the employee of the evaluation whether
         critical or favorable because it is tension-producing
      C. to permit the employee to see the evaluation but not
         to discuss it with him because the supervisor cannot
         be certain where the discussion might lead
      D. to discuss the evaluation openly with the employee
         because it helps the employee understand what is
         expected of him

19. There are a number of well-known and respected human re-      19. ...
    lations principles that successful supervisors have been
    using for years in building good relationships with their
    employees.
    Which of the following does NOT illustrate such a principle?
      A. Give clear and complete instructions
      B. Let each person know how he is getting along
      C. Keep an open-door policy
      D. Make all relationships personal ones

20. Assume that it is your responsibility to maintain certain     20. ...
    personnel records that are continually being updated.  You
    have three senior clerks assigned specifically to this task.
    Recently you have noticed that the volume of work has in-
    creased substantially, and the processing of personnel re-
    cords by the clerks is backlogged.  Your supervisor is now
    receiving complaints due to the processing delay.
    Of the following, the *best* course of action for you to take
    FIRST is to

5

A. have a meeting with the clerks, advise them of the
problem, and ask that they do their work faster; then
confirm your meeting in writing for the record
B. request that an additional position be authorized for
your unit
C. review the procedures being used for processing the
work, and try to determine if you can improve the flow
of work
D. get the system moving faster by spending some of your
own time processing the backlog

21. Assume that you are in charge of a payroll unit consisting    21. ...
of four clerks.  It is Friday, November 14.  You have just
arrived in the office after a conference.  Your staff is
preparing a payroll that must be forwarded the following
Monday.
Which of the following new items on your desk should you
attend to FIRST?  A
A. telephone message regarding very important information
needed for the statistical summary of salaries paid
for the month of November
B. memorandum regarding a new procedure that should be
followed in preparing the payroll
C. telephone message from an employee who is threatening
to endorse his pay check "Under Protest" because he
is dissatisfied with the amount
D. memorandum from your supervisor reminding you to submit the probationary period report on a new employee

22. You are in charge of a unit that orders and issues sup-    22. ...
plies.  On a particular day you are faced with the following four situations.  Which one should you take care of
FIRST?
A. One of your employees who is in the process of taking
the quarterly inventory of supplies has telephoned
and asked that you return his call as soon as possible.
B. A representative of a company that is noted for producing excellent office supplies will soon arrive with
samples for you to distribute to the various offices
in your agency.
C. A large order of supplies which was delivered this
morning has been checked and counted and a deliveryman
is waiting for you to sign the receipt.
D. A clerk from the purchase division asks you to search
for a bill you failed to send to them which is urgently
needed in order for them to complete a report due this
morning.

23. Assume that it is necessary for you to give an unpleasant    23. ...
assignment to one of your subordinates.  You expect this
employee to raise some objections to this assignment.
The *most appropriate* of the following actions for you to
take FIRST is to issue the assignment
A. orally, with the further statement that you will not
listen to any complaints
B. in writing, to forestall any complaints by the employee
C. orally, permitting the employee to express his feelings
D. in writing, with a note that any comments should be
submitted in writing

6

24. Your office has recently acquired its own electrostatic
    copier. During the first two months of use, copying costs
    have greatly exceeded the budgeted amount, and you have
    been asked to take steps to reduce this cost.
    Which one of the following steps would be LEAST effective
    in solving this problem?
    A. Making sure that employees use carbons, rather than
       the copier, for file copies of ordinary correspondence
    B. Turning off the copier for two hours each day
    C. Analyzing the need for copies of routine reports, and
       eliminating useless copies
    D. Requiring that a different copying process, such as
       memeograph, be used when large numbers of copies are
       needed

25. A Centrex telephone system allows both incoming and outgo-
    ing calls to be completed directly without going through a
    switchboard operator. An outside caller can reach a par-
    ticular employee by direct dialing.
    For which one of the following types of offices would this
    system be MOST desirable? A(n)
    A. office dealing chiefly with complaints from tenants
    B. office whose primary function is to maintain account-
       ing records
    C. office that receives and processes applications for
       certain kinds of permits
    D. purchasing office where each employee maintains con-
       tact with a number of regular suppliers

24. ...

25. ...

# TEST 2

1. Cycling is an arrangement where papers are processed
   throughout a period according to an orderly plan rather
   than as a group all at one time. This technique has been
   used for a long time by public utilities in their cycle
   billing.
   Of the following practices, the one that BEST illustrates
   this technique is that in which
   A. paychecks for per annum employees are issued bi-weekly
      and those for per diem employees are issued weekly
   B. field inspectors report in person to their offices one
      day a week, on Fridays, when they do all their paper-
      work and also pick up their paychecks
   C. the dates for issuing relief checks to clients vary
      depending on the last digit of the clients' social
      security numbers
   D. the last day for filing and paying income taxes is
      the same for Federal, State, and City income taxes

2. The employees in your division have recently been given
   an excellent up-to-date office manual, but you find that
   a good number of employees are not following the procedures
   outlined in it.
   Which one of the following would be *most likely* to ensure
   that employees begin using the manual EFFECTIVELY?
   A. Require each employee to keep a copy of the manual
      in plain sight on his desk

1. ...

2. ...

7

      B. Issue warnings periodically to those employees who
         deviate most from procedures prescribed in the manual
      C. Tell an employee to check his manual when he does not
         follow the proper procedures
      D. Suggest to the employees that the manual be studied
         thoroughly

3. The one of the following factors which should be considered 3. ...
   FIRST in the design of office forms is the
      A. information to be included in the form
      B. sequence of the information
      C. purpose of the form
      D. persons who will be using the form

4. Window envelopes are being used to an increasing extent by 4. ...
   government and private industry.
   The *one* of the following that is NOT an advantage of window
   envelopes is that they
      A. cut down on addressing costs
      B. eliminate the need to attach envelopes to letters being
         sent forward for signature by a superior
      C. are less costly to buy than regular envelopes
      D. reduce the risk of having letters placed in wrong
         envelopes

5. Your bureau's typing unit is getting bogged down with work. 5. ...
   Your bureau head wants you to look into this problem.  You
   find that much time is spent by the typists in inserting
   and then removing carbons used in preparing form notices
   in quadruplicate.  The carbon copies are kept by the units
   to which they are routed for a maximum of two years.  You
   suggest, as a time-saver, that these notices be printed as
   4-part carbon interleaved sets.
   In selecting the paper to be used for these 4-part carbon
   interleaved forms, you would find it MOST desirable to use
      A. 16-lb., 100% rag content paper
      B. 16-lb., 100% sulphite paper
      C. 20-lb., 25% rag content paper  D. 20-lb., ledger paper

6. Your bureau head asks you to prepare the office layouts for 6. ...
   several of his units being moved to a higher floor in your
   office building.
   Of the following possibilities, the *one* that you should
   AVOID in preparing the layouts is to
      A. place the desks of the first-line supervisors near
         those of the staffs they supervise
      B. place the desks of employees whose work is most close-
         ly related near one another
      C. arrange the desks so that employees do not face one
         another
      D. locate desks with many outside visitors farthest from
         the office entrance

7. Which one of the following conditions would be LEAST impor- 7. ...
   tant in considering a change of the layout in a particular
   office?
      A. Installation of a new office machine
      B. Assignment of five additional employees to your office
      C. Poor flow of work
      D. Employees' personal preferences of desk location

8. Your bureau head asks you to design an application form that will be filled out either in handwriting or by type-writer. The information supplied on this form will be key-punched for subsequent processing on a computer. In design-ing this form, you intend to make it as easy as possible for the keypunch operator to transcribe the information that is to be keypunched.
The *one* of the following considerations that will contribute LEAST to carrying out this intention is the
   A. color of the ink to be used in printing the form
   B. similarity in sequence of items on the form and the key punch card
   C. size of the type to be used in printing the form
   D. substance and weight of the paper used for the form

9. Which of the following duplicating processes should be used to make 10,000 copies of a letter-sized form?
   A. Photo-offset process     B. Xerox process
   C. **Mimeograph process**     D. Spirit duplicating process

10. Suppose Mr. Blount, an administrative assistant, is dic-tating a letter to a stenographer. His dictation begins with the name of the addressee and continues to the body of the letter. However, Mr. Blount does not dictate the address of the recipient of the letter. He expects the stenographer to locate it.
The use of this practice by Mr. Blount is
   A. *acceptable,* especially if he gives the stenographer the letter to which he is responding
   B. *acceptable,* especially if the letter is lengthy and detailed
   C. *unacceptable,* because it is not part of a steno-rapher's duties to search for information
   D. *unacceptable,* because he should not rely on the ac-curacy of the stenographer

11. Assume that there are no rules, directives, or instruc-tions concerning the filing of materials in your office or the retention of such files. A system is now being followed of placing in "inactive" files any materials that are more than one year old.
Of the following, the MOST appropriate thing to do with material that has been in an "inactive" file in your of-fice for over one year is to
   A. inspect the contents of the files to decide how to dispose of them
   B. transfer the material to a nearby location, where it can be obtained if necessary
   C. keep the material intact for a minimum of another three years
   D. destroy the material which has not been needed for at least a year

12. Suppose you have just returned to your desk after engag-ing in an all-morning conference. Joe Brent, a clerk, informs you that Clara McCloud, an administrator in another agency, telephoned during the morning and that, although she requested to speak with you, he was able to give her the desired information.

Of the following, the MOST appropriate action for you to take in regard to Mr. Brent's action is to
- A. thank him for assisting Ms. McCloud in your absence
- B. explain to him the proper telephone practice to use in the future
- C. reprimand him for not properly channeling Ms. McCloud's call
- D. issue a memo to all clerical employees regarding proper telephone practices

13. When interviewing subordinates with problems, supervisors    13. ...
frequently find that asking direct questions of the employee results only in evasive responses.  The supervisor may, therefore, resort to the "non-directive" interview technique.  In this technique the supervisor avoids pointed questions; he leads the employee to continue talking freely uninfluenced by the supervisor's preconceived notions. This technique often enables the employee to bring his problem into sharp focus and to reach a solution to his problem. Suppose that you are a supervisor interviewing a subordinate about his recent poor attendance record.  On calling his attention to his excessive lateness record, he replies: "I just don't seem to be able to get up in the morning.  Frankly, I've lost interest in this job.  I don't care about it.  When I get up in the morning, I have to skip breakfast and I'm still late.  I don't care about this job." If you are using the "non-directive" technique in this interview, the *most appropriate* of the following responses for you to make is:
- A. "You don't care about this job?"
- B. "Don't you think you are letting your department down?"
- C. "Are you having trouble at home?"
- D. "Don't you realize your actions are childish?"

Questions 14-18.
DIRECTIONS:    Questions 14 through 18 are to be answered SOLELY on the basis of the following passage.

General supervision, in contrast to close supervision, involves a high degree of delegation of authority and requires some indirect means to insure that employee behavior conforms to management needs. Not everyone works well under general supervision, however.  General supervision works best where subordinates desire responsibility. General supervision also works well where individuals in work groups have strong feelings about the quality of the finished work products. Strong identification with management goals is another trait of persons who work well under general supervision.  There are substantial differences in the amount of responsibility people are willing to accept on the job.  One person may flourish under supervision that another might find extremely restrictive.

Psychological research provides evidence that the nature of a person's personality affects his attitude toward supervision.  There are some employees with a low need for achievement and high fear of failure who shy away from challenges and responsibilities.  Many seek self-expression off the job and ask only to be allowed to daydream on it. There are others who have become so accustomed to the authoritarian approach in their culture, family, and previous work experience that they regard general supervision as no supervision at all.  They abuse the privileges it bestows on them and refuse to accept the responsibilities it demands.

10

Different groups develop different attitudes toward work. Most college graduates, for example, expect a great deal of responsibility and freedom. People with limited education, on the other hand, often have trouble accepting the concept that people should make decisions for themselves, particularly decisions concerning work. Therefore, the extent to which general supervision will be effective varies greatly with the subordinates involved.

14. According to the above passage, which one of the following 14. ...
    is a NECESSARY part of management policy regarding general
    supervision?
    A. Most employees should formulate their own work goals.
    B. Deserving employees should be rewarded periodically.
    C. Some controls on employee work patterns should be
       established.
    D. Responsibility among employees should generally be
       equalized.

15. It can be inferred from the above passage that an employee 15. ...
    who avoids responsibilities and challenges is *most likely*
    to
    A. gain independence under general supervision
    B. work better under close supervision than under
       general supervision
    C. abuse the liberal guidelines of general supervision
    D. become more restricted and cautious under general
       supervision

16. Based on the above passage, employees who succeed under     16. ...
    general supervision are *most likely* to
    A. have a strong identification with people and their
       problems
    B. accept work obligations without fear
    C. seek self-expression off the job
    D. value the intellectual aspects of life

17. Of the following, the BEST title for the passage is:        17. ...
    A. Benefits and Disadvantages of General Supervision
    B. Production Levels of Employees under General Supervision
    C. Employee Attitudes Toward Work and the Work Environment
    D. Employee Background and Personality as a Factor in
       Utilizing General Supervision

18. It can be inferred from the above passage that the one of   18. ...
    the following employees who is *most likely* to work BEST
    under general supervision is one who
    A. is a part-time graduate student
    B. was raised by very strict parents
    C. has little self-confidence
    D. has been closely supervised in past jobs

19. An employee in a work group made the following comment to   19. ...
    a co-worker: "It's great to be a lowly employee instead
    of an administrative assistant because you can work with-
    out thinking. The administrative assistant is getting paid
    to plan, schedule, and think. Let him see to it that you
    have a productive day."
    Which one of the following statements about this statement
    BEST reflects an understanding of good personnel management
    techniques and the role of the supervising administrative
    assistant? The employee is

11

    A. *wrong* in attitude and in his perception of the role of the administrative assistant

    B. *correct* in attitude but is *wrong* in his perception of the role of the administrative assistant

    C. *correct* in attitude and in his perception of the role of the administrative assistant

    D. *wrong* in attitude but is *right* in his perception of the role of the administrative assistant

20. An administrative assistant has been criticized for the    20. ...
low productivity in the group which he supervises.
Which of the following BEST reflects an understanding of
supervisory responsibilities in the area of productivity?
An administrative assistant should be held responsible for
his own

    A. individual productivity and the productivity of the group he supervises, because he is in a position where he maintains or increases production through others

    B. personal productivity only, because the supervisor is not likely to have any effect on the productivity of subordinates

    C. individual productivity but only for a drop in the productivity of the group he supervises, since subordinates will receive credit for increased productivity individually

    D. personal productivity only, because this is how he would be evaluated if he were not a supervisor

21. A supervisor has held a meeting in his office with an em-   21. ...
ployee about the employee's grievance. The grievance concerned the sharp way in which the supervisor reprimanded
the employee for an error the employee made in the performance of a task assigned to him. The problem was not resolved.
Which one of the following statements about this meeting
BEST reflects an understanding of good supervisory techniques?

    A. It is awkward for a supervisor to handle a grievance involving himself. The supervisor should not have held the meeting.

    B. It would have been better if the supervisor had held the meeting at the employee's workplace, even though there would have been frequent distractions, because the employee would have been more relaxed.

    C. The resolution of a problem is not the only sign of a successful meeting. The achievement of communication was worthwhile.

    D. The supervisor should have been forceful. There is nothing wrong with raising your voice to an employee every once in a while.

22. John Hart, the owner of a single family house, complains   22. ...
that he submitted an application for reduction of assessment that obviously was not acted upon before his final
assessment notice was sent to him. The timely receipt of
the application has been verified in a departmental log
book.
As the supervisor of the clerical unit through which this
application was processed and where this delay occurred,
you should be LEAST concerned with

    A. what happened          B. who is responsible
    C. why it happened        D. what can be learned from it
23. The one of the following that applies MOST appropriately    23. ...
    to the role of the first-line supervisor is that *usually*
    he is
    A. called upon to help determine agency policy
    B. involved in long-range agency planning
    C. responsible for determining some aspects of basic
       organization structure
    D. a participant in developing procedures and methods
24. Sally Jones, an administrative assistant, gives clear and    24. ...
    precise instructions to Robert Warren, a senior clerk.  In
    these instructions, Ms. Jones clearly delegates authority
    to Mr. Warren  to undertake a well-defined task.
    In this situation Ms. Jones should expect Mr. Warren to
    A. come to her to check out details as he progresses
       with the task
    B. come to her only with exceptional problems
    C. ask her permission if he wishes to use his delegated
       authority
    D. use his authority to re-define the task and its re-
       lated activities
25. Planning involves establishing department goals and    25. ...
    programs and determining ways of reaching them.
    The MAIN advantage of such planning is that
    A. there will be no need for adjustments once a plan
       is put into operation
    B. it insures that everyone is working on schedule
    C. it provides the framework for an effective operation
    D. unexpected work problems are easily overcome

# TEST 3

1. As a result of reorganization, the jobs in a large cleri-    1. ...
   cal unit were broken down into highly specialized tasks.
   Each specialized task was then assigned to a particular
   employee to perform.
   This action will *probably* lead to an INCREASE in
   A. flexibility          B. job satisfaction
   C. need for coordination    D. employee initiative
2. Your office carries on a large volume of correspondence    2. ...
   concerned with the purchase of supplies and equipment for
   city offices.  You use form letters to deal with many com-
   mon situations.
   In which one of the following situations would use of a
   form letter be LEAST appropriate?
   A. Informing suppliers of a change in city regulations
      concerning purchase contracts
   B. Telling a new supplier the standard procedures to be
      followed in billing
   C. Acknowledging receipt of a complaint and saying that
      the complaint will be investigated
   D. Answering a city councilman's request for additional
      information on a particular regulation affecting sup-
      pliers

3. Assume that you head a large clerical unit.  Because of      3. ...
   the great demands being made on your time, you have desig-
   nated Tom Smith, a supervising clerk, to be your assistant
   and to assume some of your duties.
   Of the following duties performed by you, the *most appro-*
   *priate* one to assign to Tom Smith is to
   - A. conduct the on-the-job training of new employees
   - B. prepare the performance appraisal reports on your
     staff members
   - C. represent your unit in dealings with the heads of
     other units
   - D. handle matters that require exception to general policy
4. In establishing rules for his subordinates, a superior      4. ...
   should be PRIMARILY concerned with
   - A. creating sufficient flexibility to allow for exceptions
   - B. making employees aware of the reasons for the rules and
     the penalties for infractions
   - C. establishing the strength of his own position in rela-
     tion to his subordinates
   - D. having his subordinates know that such rules will be
     imposed in a personal manner
5. The practice of conducting staff training sessions on a      5. ...
   periodic basis is *generally* considered
   - A. *poor;* it takes employees away from their work assign-
     ments
   - B. *poor;* all staff training should be done on an individ-
     ual basis
   - C. *good;* it permits the regular introduction of new
     methods and techniques
   - D. *good;* it ensures a high employee productivity rate
6. Suppose you have just announced at a staff meeting with      6. ...
   your subordinates that a radical reorganization of work
   will take place next week.  Your subordinates at the
   meeting appear to be excited, tense, and worried.
   Of the following, the BEST action for you to take at that
   time is to
   - A. schedule private conferences with each subordinate to
     obtain his reaction to the meeting
   - B. close the meeting and tell your subordinates to return
     immediately to their work assignments
   - C. give your subordinates some time to ask questions and
     discuss your announcement
   - D. insist that your subordinates do not discuss your an-
     nouncement among themselves or with other members of
     the agency
7. Assume that you supervise the duplicating and reproduction   7. ...
   unit of Department B.  One of your responsibilities is to
   prepare a daily schedule showing when and on which of your
   unit's four duplicating machines jobs are to be run off.
   Of the following, the factor that should be given LEAST con-
   sideration in preparing the schedule is the
   - A. priority of each of the jobs to be run off
   - B. production speed of the different machines that will be
     used
   - C. staff available to operate the machines
   - D. date on which the job order was received

8. Suppose that you were recently placed in charge of the     8. ...
   duplicating and stock unit of Department Y.  From your
   observation of the operations of your unit during your
   first week as its head, you get the impression that there
   are inefficiencies in its operations causing low productivity.
   To obtain an increase in its productivity, the FIRST of the
   following actions you should take is to
   - A. seek the advice of your immediate superior on how he
     would tackle this problem
   - B. develop plans to correct any unsatisfactory conditions
     arising from other than manpower deficiencies
   - C. identify the problems causing low productivity
   - D. discuss your productivity problem with other unit heads
     to find out how they handled similar problems

9. Assume that you were recently placed in charge of a large     9. ...
   clerical unit.  At a meeting, the head of another unit
   tells you, "My practice is to give a worker more than he
   can finish.  In that way you can be sure that you are getting
   the most out of him."
   For you to adopt this practice would be
   - A. *advisable*, since your actions would be consistent with
     those practiced in your agency
   - B. *inadvisable*, since such a practice is apt to create
     frustration and lower staff morale
   - C. *advisable*, since a high goal stimulates people to
     strive to attain it
   - D. *inadvisable*, since management may, in turn, set too
     high a productivity goal for the unit

10. Suppose that you are the supervisor of a unit in which     10. ...
    there is an increasing amount of friction among several
    of your staff members.  One of the reasons for this fric-
    tion is that the work of some of these staff members cannot
    be completed by them until other staff members complete re-
    lated work.
    Of the following, the MOST appropriate action for you to
    take is to
    - A. summon these employees to a meeting to discuss the
      responsibilities each has and to devise better
      methods of coordination
    - B. have a private talk with each employee involved and
      make each understand that there must be more coopera-
      tion among the employees
    - C. arrange for interviews with each of the employees
      involved to determine what his problems are
    - D. shift the assignments of these employees so that each
      will be doing a job different from his current one

11. An office supervisor has a number of responsibilities with 11. ...
    regard to his subordinates.
    Which one of the following functions should NOT be regarded
    as a *basic* responsibility of the office supervisor?
    - A. Telling employees how to solve personal problems that
      may be interfering with their work
    - B. Training new employees to do the work assigned to them
    - C. Evaluating employees' performance periodically and
      discussing the evaluation with each employee

15

   D. Bringing employee grievances to the attention of
      higher-level administrators and seeking satisfactory
      resolutions

12. One of your most productive subordinates frequently        12. ...
    demonstrates a poor attitude toward his job.  He seems
    unsure of himself, and he annoys his co-workers because
    he is continually belittling himself and the work that
    he is doing.
    In trying to help him overcome this problem, which of the
    following approaches is LEAST likely to be effective?
    A. Compliment him on his work and assign him some addi-
       tional responsibilities, telling him that he is being
       given these responsibilities because of his demonstrated
       ability
    B. Discuss with him the problem of his attitude, and warn
       him that you will have to report it on his next perform-
       ance evaluation
    C. Assign him a particularly important and difficult proj-
       ect, stressing your confidence in his ability to com-
       plete it successfully
    D. Discuss with him the problem of his attitude, and ask
       him for suggestions as to how you can help him over-
       come it

13. You come to realize that a personality conflict between    13. ...
    you and one of your subordinates is adversely affecting
    his performance.
    Which one of the following would be the most appropriate
    FIRST step to take?
    A. Report the problem to your superior and request as-
       sistance.  His experience may be helpful in resolving
       this problem
    B. Discuss the situation with several of the subordinate's
       co-workers to see if they can suggest any remedy
    C. Suggest to the subordinate that he get professional
       counseling or therapy
    D. Discuss the situation candidly with the subordinate,
       with the objective of resolving the problem between
       yourselves

# KEY (CORRECT ANSWERS)

| TEST 1 | | | | TEST 2 | | | | TEST 3 | | | |
|---|---|---|---|---|---|---|---|---|---|---|---|
| 1. | C | 11. | D | 1. | C | 11. | A | 1. | C | 7. | D |
| 2. | B | 12. | A | 2. | C | 12. | A | 2. | D | 8. | C |
| 3. | A | 13. | A | 3. | C | 13. | A | 3. | A | 9. | B |
| 4. | C | 14. | B | 4. | C | 14. | C | 4. | B | 10. | A |
| 5. | C | 15. | D | 5. | B | 15. | B | 5. | C | 11. | A |
| 6. | A | 16. | C | 6. | D | 16. | B | 6. | C | 12. | B |
| 7. | C | 17. | D | 7. | D | 17. | D | | | 13. | D |
| 8. | C | 18. | D | 8. | D | 18. | A | | | | |
| 9. | C | 19. | D | 9. | A | 19. | D | | | | |
| 10. | D | 20. | C | 10. | A | 20. | A | | | | |
| | 21. | B | | | 21. | C | | | | | |
| | 22. | C | | | 22. | B | | | | | |
| | 23. | C | | | 23. | D | | | | | |
| | 24. | B | | | 24. | B | | | | | |
| | 25. | D | | | 25. | C | | | | | |

# READING COMPREHENSION
## UNDERSTANDING AND INTERPRETING WRITTEN MATERIAL
# EXAMINATION SECTION
# TEST 1

DIRECTIONS:   Each question or incomplete statement is followed by several suggested answers or completions. Select the one that BEST answers the question or completes the statement. *PRINT THE LETTER OF THE CORRECT ANSWER IN THE SPACE AT THE RIGHT.*

Questions 1-2.

DIRECTIONS:   Questions 1 and 2 are to be answered SOLELY on the basis of the following passage.

The employees in a unit or division of a government agency may be referred to as a work group. Within a government agency which has existed for some time, the work groups will have evolved traditions of their own. The persons in these work groups acquire these traditions as part of the process of work adjustment within their groups. Usually, a work group in a large organization will contain *oldtimers*, *newcomers*, and *in-betweeners*. Like the supervisor of a group, who is not necessarily an oldtimer or the oldest member, oldtimers usually have great influence. They can recall events unknown to others and are a storehouse of information and advice about current problems in the light of past experience. They pass along the traditions of the group to the others who, in turn, become oldtimers themselves. Thus, the traditions of the group which have been honored and revered by long acceptance are continued.

1. According to the above passage, the traditions of a work group within a government agency are developed

    A. at the time the group is established
    B. over a considerable period of time
    C. in order to give recognition to oldtimers
    D. for the group before it is established

1.\_\_\_\_\_

2. According to the above passage, the oldtimers within a work group

    A. are the means by which long accepted practices and customs are perpetuated
    B. would best be able to settle current problems that arise
    C. are honored because of the changes they have made in the traditions
    D. have demonstrated that they have learned to do their work well

2.\_\_\_\_\_

Questions 3-4.

DIRECTIONS:   Questions 3 and 4 are to be answered SOLELY on the basis of the following passage.

In public agencies, the success of a person assigned to perform first-line supervisory duties depends in large part upon the personal relations between him and his subordinate employees. The goal of supervising effort is something more than to obtain compliance with procedures established by some central office. The major objective is work accomplishment. In order for this goal to be attained, employees must want to attain it and must exercise initiative in their work. Only if employees are generally satisfied with the type of supervision which exists in an organization will they put forth their best efforts.

3. According to the above passage, in order for employees to try to do their work as well as they can, it is essential that

   A. they participate in determining their working conditions and rates of pay
   B. their supervisors support the employees' viewpoints in meetings with higher management
   C. they are content with the supervisory practices which are being used
   D. their supervisors make the changes in working procedures that the employees request

4. It can be inferred from the above passage that the goals of a unit in a public agency will not be reached unless the employees in the unit

   A. wish to reach them and are given the opportunity to make individual contributions to the work
   B. understand the relationship between the goals of the unit and goals of the agency
   C. have satisfactory personal relationships with employees of other units in the agency
   D. carefully follow the directions issued by higher authorities

Questions 5-9.

DIRECTIONS: Questions 5 through 9 are to be answered SOLELY on the basis of the following passage.

If an employee thinks he can save money, time, or material for the city or has an idea about how to do something better than it is being done, he shouldn't keep it to himself. He should send his ideas to the Employees' Suggestion Program, using the special form which is kept on hand in all departments. An employee may send in as many ideas as he wishes. To make sure that each idea is judged fairly, the name of the suggester is not made known until an award is made. The awards are certificates of merit or cash prizes ranging from $10 to $500.

5. According to the above passage, an employee who knows how to do a job in a better way should

   A. be sure it saves enough time to be worthwhile
   B. get paid the money he saves for the city
   C. keep it to himself to avoid being accused of causing a speed-up
   D. send his idea to the Employees' Suggestion Program

6. In order to send his idea to the Employees' Suggestion Program, an employee should 6.____

   A. ask the Department of Personnel for a special form
   B. get the special form in his own department
   C. mail the idea using Special Delivery
   D. send it on plain, white letter-size paper

7. An employee may send to the Employees' Suggestion Program 7.____

   A. as many ideas as he can think of
   B. no more than one idea each week
   C. no more than ten ideas in a month
   D. only one idea on each part of the job

8. The reason the name of an employee who makes a suggestion is not made known at first is to 8.____

   A. give the employee a larger award
   B. help the judges give more awards
   C. insure fairness in judging
   D. only one idea on each part of the job

9. An employee whose suggestion receives an award may be given a 9.____

   A. bonus once a year
   C. cash prize of up to $500
   B. certificate for $10
   D. salary increase of $500

Questions 10-12.

DIRECTIONS: Questions 10 through 12 are to be answered SOLELY on the basis of the following passage.

According to the rules of the Department of Personnel, the work of every permanent city employee is reviewed and rated by his supervisor at least once a year. The civil service rating system gives the employee and his supervisor a chance to talk about the progress made during the past year as well as about those parts of the job in which the employee needs to do better. In order to receive a pay increase each year, the employee must have a satisfactory service rating. Service ratings also count toward an employee's final mark on a promotion examination.

10. According to the above passage, a permanent city employee is rated AT LEAST once 10.____

    A. before his work is reviewed
    B. every six months
    C. yearly by his supervisor
    D. yearly by the Department of Personnel

11. According to the above passage, under the rating system the supervisor and the employee can discuss how 11.____

    A. much more work needs to be done next year
    B. the employee did his work last year

C.   the work can be made easier next year
D.   the work of the Department can be increased

12.   According to the above passage, a permanent city employee will NOT receive a yearly     12
pay increase

A.   if he received a pay increase the year before
B.   if he used his service rating for his mark on a promotion examination
C.   if his service rating is unsatisfactory
D.   unless he got some kind of a service rating

Questions 13-16.

DIRECTIONS:   Questions 13 through 16 are to be answered SOLELY on the basis of the
following passage.

It is an accepted fact that the rank and file employee can frequently advance worthwhile
suggestions toward increasing efficiency. For this reason, an Employees' Suggestion System
has been developed and put into operation. Suitable means have been provided at each
departmental location for the confidential submission of suggestions. Numerous suggestions
have been received thus far and, after study, about five percent of the ideas submitted are
being translated into action. It is planned to set up, eventually, monetary awards for all worthwhile suggestions.

13.   According to the above passage, a MAJOR reason why an Employees' Suggestion Sys-     13
tem was established is that

A.   an organized program of improvement is better than a haphazard one
B.   employees can often give good suggestions to increase efficiency
C.   once a fact is accepted, it is better to act on it than to do nothing
D.   the suggestions of rank and file employees were being neglected

14.   According to the above passage, under the Employees' Suggestion System,     14

A.   a file of worthwhile suggestions will eventually be set up at each departmental
location
B.   it is possible for employees to turn in suggestions without fellow employees knowing of it
C.   means have been provided for the regular and frequent collection of suggestions
submitted
D.   provision has been made for the judging of worthwhile suggestions by an Employees' Suggestion Committee

15.   According to the above passage, it is reasonable to assume that     1

A.   all suggestions must be turned in at a central office
B.   employees who make worthwhile suggestions will be promoted
C.   not all the prizes offered will be monetary ones
D.   prizes of money will be given for the best suggestions

16. According to the above passage, of the many suggestions made,    16.____

    A. all are first tested
    B. a small part are put into use
    C. most are very worthwhile
    D. samples are studied

Questions 17-20.

DIRECTIONS:   Questions 17 through 20 are to be answered SOLELY on the basis of the following passage.

    Employees may be granted leaves of absence without pay at the discretion of the Personnel Officer. Such a leave without pay shall begin on the first working day on which the employee does not report for duty and shall continue to the first day on which the employee returns to duty. The Personnel Division may vary the dates of the leave for the record so as to conform with payroll periods, but in no case shall an employee be off the payroll for a different number of calendar days than would have been the case if the actual dates mentioned above had been used. An employee who has vacation or overtime to his credit, which is available for normal use, may take time off immediately prior to beginning a leave of absence without pay, chargeable against all or part of such vacation or overtime.

17. According to the above passage, the Personnel Officer must    17.____

    A. decide if a leave of absence without pay should be granted
    B. require that a leave end on the last working day of a payroll period
    C. see to it that a leave of absence begins on the first working day of a pay period
    D. vary the dates of a leave of absence to conform with a payroll period

18. According to the above passage, the exact dates of a leave of absence without pay may    18.____
be varied provided that the

    A. calendar days an employee is off the payroll equal the actual leave granted
    B. leave conforms to an even number of payroll periods
    C. leave when granted made provision for variance to simplify payroll records
    D. Personnel Officer approves the variation

19. According to the above passage, a leave of absence without pay must extend from the    19.____

    A. first day of a calendar period to the first day the employee resumes work
    B. first day of a payroll period to the last calendar day of the leave
    C. first working day missed to the first day on which the employee resumes work
    D. last day on which an employee works through the first day he returns to work

20. According to the above passage, an employee may take extra time off just before the    20.____
start of a leave of absence without pay if

    A. he charges this extra time against his leave
    B. he has a favorable balance of vacation or overtime which has been frozen
    C. the vacation or overtime that he would normally use for a leave without pay has not been charged in this way before
    D. there is time to his credit which he may use

Question 21.

DIRECTIONS:   Question 21 is to be answered SOLELY on the basis of the following passage.

In considering those things which are motivators and incentives to work, it might be just as erroneous not to give sufficient weight to money as an incentive as it is to give too much weight. It is not a problem of establishing a rank-order of importance, but one of knowing that motivation is a blend or mixture rather than a pure element. It is simple to say that cultural factors count more than financial considerations, but this leads only to the conclusion that our society is financial-oriented.

21.   Based on the above passage, in our society, cultural and social motivations to work are      21.__

    A.   things which cannot be avoided
    B.   melded to financial incentives
    C.   of less consideration than high pay
    D.   not balanced equally with economic or financial considerations

Question 22.

DIRECTIONS:   Question 22 is to be answered SOLELY on the basis of the following passage.

A general principle of training and learning with respect to people is that they learn more readily if they receive *feedback*. Essential to maintaining proper motivational levels is knowledge of results which indicate level of progress. Feedback also assists the learning process by identifying mistakes. If this kind of information were not given to the learner, then improper or inappropriate job performance may be instilled.

22.   Based on the above passage, which of the following is MOST accurate?      22.__

    A.   Learning will not take place without feedback.
    B.   In the absence of feedback, improper or inappropriate job performance will be learned.
    C.   To properly motivate a learner, the learner must have his progress made known to him.
    D.   Trainees should be told exactly what to do if they are to learn properly.

Question 23.

DIRECTIONS:   Question 23 is to be answered SOLELY on the basis of the following passage.

In a democracy, the obligation of public officials is twofold. They must not only do an efficient and satisfactory job of administration, but also they must persuade the public that it is an efficient and satisfactory job. It is a burden which, if properly assumed, will make democracy work and perpetuate reform government.

23.   The above passage means that      23.__

    A.   public officials should try to please everybody
    B.   public opinion is instrumental in determining the policy of public officials

C. satisfactory performance of the job of administration will eliminate opposition to its work
D. frank and open procedure in a public agency will aid in maintaining progressive government

Question 24.

DIRECTIONS: Question 24 is to be answered SOLELY on the basis of the following passage.

Upon retirement for service, a member shall receive a retirement allowance which shall consist of an annuity which shall be the actuarial equivalent of his accumulated deductions at the time of his retirement and a pension, in addition to his annuity, which shall be equal to one service-fraction of his final compensation, multiplied by the number of years of service since he last became a member credited to him, and a pension which is the actuarial equivalent of the reserve-for-increased-take-home-pay to which he may then be entitled, if any.

24. According to the above passage, a retirement allowance shall consist of a(n)          24._____

    A. annuity, plus a pension, plus an actuarial equivalent
    B. annuity, plus a pension, plus reserve-for-increased-take-home-pay, if any
    C. annuity, plus reserve-for-increased-take-home-pay, if any, plus final compensation
    D. pension, plus reserve-for-increased-take-home-pay, if any, plus accumulated deductions

Question 25.

DIRECTIONS: Question 25 is to be answered SOLELY on the basis of the following passage.

Membership in the retirement system shall cease upon the occurrence of any one of the following conditions: when the time out of service of any member who has total service of less than 25 years, shall aggregate more than 5 years; when the time out of service of any member who has total service of 25 years or more, shall aggregate more than 10 years; when any member shall have withdrawn more than 50% of his accumulated deductions; or when any member shall have withdrawn the cash benefit provided by Section B3-35.0 of the Administrative Code.

25. According to the information in the above passage, membership in the retirement system          25._____
shall cease when an employee

    A. with 17 years of service has been on a leave of absence for 3 years
    B. withdraws 50% of his accumulated deductions
    C. with 28 years of service has been out of service for 10 years
    D. withdraws his cash benefits

—————

# KEY (CORRECT ANSWERS)

| | | | | |
|---|---|---|---|---|
| 1. | B | | 11. | B |
| 2. | A | | 12. | C |
| 3. | C | | 13. | B |
| 4. | A | | 14. | B |
| 5. | D | | 15. | D |
| | | | | |
| 6. | B | | 16. | B |
| 7. | A | | 17. | A |
| 8. | C | | 18. | A |
| 9. | B | | 19. | C |
| 10. | C | | 20. | D |

| | |
|---|---|
| 21. | B |
| 22. | C |
| 23. | D |
| 24. | B |
| 25. | D |

———

# TEST 2

DIRECTIONS:  Each question or incomplete statement is followed by several suggested answers or completions. Select the one that BEST answers the question or completes the statement. *PRINT THE LETTER OF THE CORRECT ANSWER IN THE SPACE AT THE RIGHT.*

Questions 1-6.

DIRECTIONS:  Questions 1 through 6 are to be answered SOLELY on the basis of the following passage.

Since almost every office has some contact with data-processed records, a stenographer should have some understanding of the basic operations of data processing. Data processing systems now handle about one-third of all office paperwork. On punched cards, magnetic tape, or on other mediums, data are recorded before being fed into the computer for processing. A machine such as the keypunch is used to convert the data written on the source document into the coded symbols on punched cards or tapes. After data has been converted, it must be verified to guarantee absolute accuracy of conversion. In this manner, data becomes a permanent record which can be read by electronic computers that compare, store, compute, and otherwise process data at high speeds.

One key person in a computer installation is a programmer, the man or woman who puts business and scientific problems into special symbolic languages that can be read by the computer. Jobs done by the computer range all the way from payroll operations to chemical process control, but most computer applications are directed toward management data. About half of the programmers employed by business come to their positions with college degrees; the remaining half are promoted to their positions from within the organization on the basis of demonstrated ability without regard to education.

1.  Of the following, the BEST title for the above passage is                                          1.____

    A.  THE STENOGRAPHER AS DATA PROCESSOR
    B.  THE RELATION OF KEYPUNCHING TO STENOGRAPHY
    C.  UNDERSTANDING DATA PROCESSING
    D.  PERMANENT OFFICE RECORDS

2.  According to the above passage, a stenographer should understand the basic operations      2.____
    of data processing because

    A.  almost every office today has contact with data processed by computer
    B.  any office worker may be asked to verify the accuracy of data
    C.  most offices are involved in the production of permanent records
    D.  data may be converted into computer language by typing on a keypunch

3.  According to the above passage, the data which the computer understands is MOST           3.____
    often expressed as

    A.  a scientific programming language
    B.  records or symbols punched on tape, cards, or other mediums
    C.  records on cards
    D.  records on tape

4. According to the above passage, computers are used MOST often to handle
4.\_

   A. management data
   B. problems of higher education
   C. the control of chemical processes
   D. payroll operations

5. Computer programming is taught in many colleges and business schools.
The above passage implies that programmers in industry
5.\_

   A. must have professional training
   B. need professional training to advance
   C. must have at least a college education to do adequate programming tasks
   D. do not need college education to do programming work

6. According to the above passage, data to be processed by computer should be
6.\_

   A. recent           B. basic
   C. complete       D. verified

Questions 7-10.

DIRECTIONS: Questions 7 through 10 are to be answered SOLELY on the basis of the following passage.

There is nothing that will take the place of good sense on the part of the stenographer. You may be perfect in transcribing exactly what the dictator says and your speed may be adequate, but without an understanding of the dictator's intent as well as his words, you are likely to be a mediocre secretary.

A serious error that is made when taking dictation is putting down something that does not make sense. Most people who dictate material would rather be asked to repeat and explain than to receive transcribed material which has errors due to inattention or doubt. Many dictators request that their grammar be corrected by their secretaries, but unless specifically asked to do so, secretaries should not do it without first checking with the dictator. Secretaries should be aware that, in some cases, dictators may use incorrect grammar or slang expressions to create a particular effect.

Some people dictate commas, periods, and paragraphs, while others expect the stenographer to know when, where, and how to punctuate. A well-trained secretary should be able to indicate the proper punctuation by listening to the pauses and tones of the dictator's voice.

A stenographer who has taken dictation from the same person for a period of time should be able to understand him under most conditions, By increasing her tact, alertness, and efficiency, a secretary can become more competent.

7. According to the above passage, which of the following statements concerning the dictation of punctuation is CORRECT?
7

   A. Dictator may use incorrect punctuation to create a desired style
   B. Dictator should indicate all punctuation
   C. Stenographer should know how to punctuate based on the pauses and tones of the dictator
   D. Stenographer should not type any punctuation if it has not been dictated to her

8. According to the above passage, how should secretaries handle grammatical errors in a    8.\_\_\_\_
dictation? Secretaries should

    A. *not correct* grammatical errors unless the dictator is aware that this is being done
    B. *correct* grammatical errors by having the dictator repeat the line with proper pauses
    C. *correct* grammatical errors if they have checked the correctness in a grammar book
    D. *correct* grammatical errors based on their own good sense

9. If a stenographer is confused about the method of spacing and indenting of a report    9.\_\_\_\_
which has just been dictated to her, she GENERALLY should

    A. do the best she can
    B. ask the dictator to explain what she should do
    C. try to improve her ability to understand dictated material
    D. accept the fact that her stenographic ability is not adequate

10. In the last line of the first paragraph, the word *mediocre* means MOST NEARLY    10.\_\_\_\_

    A. superior                  B. respected
    C. disregarded           D. second-rate

Questions 11-12.

DIRECTIONS:   Questions 11 and 12 are to be answered SOLELY on the basis of the following passage.

    The number of legible carbon copies required to be produced determines the weight of the carbon paper to be used. When only one copy is made, heavy carbon paper is satisfactory. Most typists, however, use medium-weight carbon paper and find it serviceable for up to three or four copies. If five or more copies are to be made, it is wise to use light carbon paper. On the other hand, the finish of carbon paper to be used depends largely on the stroke of the typist and, in lesser degree, on the number of copies to be made and on whether the typewriter has pica or elite type. A soft-finish carbon paper should be used if the typist's touch is light or if a noiseless machine is used. It is desirable for the average typist to use medium-finish carbon paper for ordinary work, when only a few carbon copies are required. Elite type requires a harder carbon finish than pica type for the same number of copies.

11. According to the above passage, the lighter the carbon paper used,    11.\_\_\_\_

    A. the softer the finish of the carbon paper will be
    B. the greater the number of legible carbon copies that can be made
    C. the greater the number of times the carbon paper can be used
    D. the lighter the typist's touch should be

12. According to the above passage, the MOST important factor which determines whether    12.\_\_\_\_
the finish of carbon paper to be used in typing should be hard, medium, or soft is

    A. the touch of the typist
    B. the number of carbon copies required
    C. whether the type in the typewriter is pica or elite
    D. whether a machine with pica type will produce the same number of carbon copies as a machine with elite type

Questions 13-16.

DIRECTIONS:   Questions 13 through 16 are to be answered SOLELY on the basis of the following passage.

Modern office methods, geared to ever higher speeds and aimed at ever greater efficiency, are largely the result of the typewriter. The typewriter is a substitute for handwriting
and, in the hands of a skilled typist, not only turns out letters and other documents at least
three times faster than a penman can do the work, but turns out the greater volume more uni-
formly and legibly. With the use of carbon paper and onionskin paper, identical copies can be
made at the same time.

The typewriter, besides its effect on the conduct of business and government, has had a
very important effect on the position of women. The typewriter has done much to bring
women into business and government, and today there are vastly more women than men typists. Many women have used the keys of the typewriter to climb the ladder to responsible
managerial positions.

The typewriter, as its name implies, employs type to make an ink impression on paper.
For many years, the manual typewriter was the standard machine used. Today, the electric
typewriter is dominant, and completely automatic electronic typewriters are coming into wider
use.

The mechanism of the office manual typewriter includes a set of keys arranged system-
atically in rows; a semicircular frame of type, connected to the keys by levers; the carriage, or
paper carrier; a rubber roller, called a platen, against which the type strikes; and an inked rib-
bon which make the impression of the type character when the key strikes it.

13.   The above passage mentions a number of good features of the combination of a skilled        13.__
typist and a typewriter. Of the following, the feature which is NOT mentioned in the passage is

    A.   speed                              B.   reliability
    C.   uniformity                         D.   legibility

14.   According to the above passage, a skilled typist can                                          14.__

    A.   turn out at least five carbon copies of typed matter
    B.   type at least three times faster than a penman can write
    C.   type more than 80 words a minute
    D.   readily move into a managerial position

15.   According to the above passage, which of the following is NOT part of the mechanism of       15.__
a manual typewriter?

    A.   Carbon paper                       B.   Platen
    C.   Paper carrier                      D.   Inked ribbon

16.   According to the above passage, the typewriter has helped                                     16.__

    A.   men more than women in business
    B.   women in career advancement into management
    C.   men and women equally, but women have taken better advantage of it
    D.   more women than men, because men generally dislike routine typing work

Questions 17-21.

DIRECTIONS: Questions 17 through 21 are to be answered SOLELY on the basis of the following passage.

The recipient gains an impression of a typewritten letter before he begins to read the
message. Factors which provide for a good first impression include margins and spacing that
are visually pleasing, formal parts of the letter which are correctly placed according to the
style of the letter, copy which is free of obvious erasures and over-strikes, and transcript that
is even and clear. The problem for the typist is that of how to produce that first, positive
impression of her work.

There are several general rules which a typist can follow when she wishes to prepare a
properly spaced letter on a sheet of letterhead. Ordinarily, the width of a letter should not be
less than four inches nor more than six inches. The side margins should also have a desirable
relation to the bottom margin and the space between the letterhead and the body of the letter.
Usually the most appealing arrangement is when the side margins are even and the bottom
margin is slightly wider than the side margins. In some offices, however, standard line length
is used for all business letters, and the secretary then varies the spacing between the date
line and the inside address according to the length of the letter.

17. The BEST title for the above passage would be                                              17._____

    A. WRITING OFFICE LETTERS
    B. MAKING GOOD FIRST IMPRESSIONS
    C. JUDGING WELL-TYPED LETTERS
    D. GOOD PLACING AND SPACING FOR OFFICE LETTERS

18. According to the above passage, which of the following might be considered the way in      18._____
    which people very quickly judge the quality of work which has been typed? By

    A. measuring the margins to see if they are correct
    B. looking at the spacing and cleanliness of the typescript
    C. scanning the body of the letter for meaning
    D. reading the date line and address for errors

19. What, according to the above passage, would be definitely UNDESIRABLE as the aver-        19._____
    age line length of a typed letter?

    A. 4"                                    B. 6"
    C. 5"                                    D. 7"

20. According to the above passage, when the line length is kept standard, the secretary       20._____

    A. does not have to vary the spacing at all since this also is standard
    B. adjusts the spacing between the date line and inside address for different lengths
       of letters
    C. uses the longest line as a guideline for spacing between the date line and inside
       address
    D. varies-the number of spaces between the lines

21. According to the above passage, side margins are MOST pleasing when they        21._

    A. are even and somewhat smaller than the bottom margin
    B. are slightly wider than the bottom margin
    C. vary with the length of the letter
    D. are figured independently from the letterhead and the body of the letter

Questions 22-25.

DIRECTIONS:   Questions 22 through 25 are to be answered SOLELY on the basis of the following passage.

   Typed pages can reflect the simplicity of modern art in a machine age. Lightness and evenness can be achieved by proper layout and balance of typed lines and white space. Instead of solid, cramped masses of uneven, crowded typing, there should be a pleasing balance up and down as well as horizontal.

   To have real balance, your page must have a center. The eyes see the center of the sheet slightly above the real center. This is the way both you and the reader see it. Try imagining a line down the center of the page that divides the paper in equal halves. On either side of your paper, white space and blocks of typing need to be similar in size and shape. Although left and right margins should be equal, top and bottom margins need not be as exact. It looks better to hold a bottom border wider than a top margin, so that your typing rests upon a cushion of white space. To add interest to the appearance of the page, try making one paragraph between one-half and two-thirds the size of an adjacent paragraph.

   Thus, by taking full advantage of your typewriter, the pages that you type will not only be accurate but will also be attractive.

22. It can be inferred from the above passage that the basic importance of proper balancing  22._
on a typed page is that proper balancing

    A. makes a typed page a work of modern art
    B. provides exercise in proper positioning of a typewriter
    C. increases the amount of typed copy on the paper
    D. draws greater attention and interest to the page

23. A reader will tend to see the center of a typed page  23._

    A. somewhat higher than the true center
    B. somewhat lower than the true center
    C. on either side of the true center
    D. about two-thirds of an inch above the true center

24. Which of the following suggestions is NOT given by the above passage?  24._

    A. Bottom margins may be wider than top borders.
    B. Keep all paragraphs approximately the same size.
    C. Divide your page with an imaginary line down the middle.
    D. Side margins should be equalized.

25.  Of the following, the BEST title for the above passage is          25._____
     A.  INCREASING THE ACCURACY OF THE TYPED PAGE
     B.  DETERMINATION OF MARGINS FOR TYPED COPY
     C.  LAYOUT AND BALANCE OF THE TYPED PAGE
     D.  HOW TO TAKE FULL ADVANTAGE OF THE TYPEWRITER

———————

# KEY (CORRECT ANSWERS)

| | | | |
|---|---|---|---|
| 1. | C | 11. | B |
| 2. | A | 12. | A |
| 3. | B | 13. | C |
| 4. | A | 14. | B |
| 5. | D | 15. | A |
| 6. | D | 16. | B |
| 7. | C | 17. | D |
| 8. | A | 18. | B |
| 9. | B | 19. | D |
| 10. | D | 20. | B |

21.  A
22.  D
23.  A
24.  B
25.  C

———————

# TEST 3

Questions 1-5.

DIRECTIONS: Questions 1 through 5 are to be answered SOLELY on the basis of the following passage.

A written report is a communication of information from one person to another. It is an account of some matter especially investigated, however routine that matter may be. The ultimate basis of any good written report is facts, which become known through observation and verification. Good written reports may seem to be no more than general ideas and opinions. However, in such cases, the facts leading to these opinions were gathered, verified, and reported earlier, and the opinions are dependent upon these facts. Good style, proper form, and emphasis cannot make a good written report out of unreliable information and bad judgment; but on the other hand, solid investigation and brilliant thinking are not likely to become very useful until they are effectively communicated to others. If a person's work calls for written reports, then his work is often no better than his written reports.

1. Based on the information in the above passage, it can be concluded that opinions expressed in a report should be

   A. based on facts which are gathered and reported
   B. emphasized repeatedly when they result from a special investigation
   C. kept to a minimum
   D. separated from the body of the report

2. In the above passage, the one of the following which is mentioned as a way of establishing facts is

   A. authority                    B. reporting
   C. communication                D. verification

3. According to the above passage, the characteristic shared by ALL written reports is that they are

   A. accounts of routine matters  B. transmissions of information
   C. reliable and logical         D. written in proper form

4. Which of the following conclusions can logically be drawn from the information given in the above passage?

   A. Brilliant thinking can make up for unreliable information in a report.
   B. One method of judging an individual's work is the quality of the written reports he is required to submit.
   C. Proper form and emphasis can make a good report out of unreliable information.
   D. Good written reports that seem to be no more than general ideas should be rewritten.

5. Which of the following suggested titles would be MOST appropriate for the above passage?

    A. GATHERING AND ORGANIZING FACTS
    B. TECHNIQUES OF OBSERVATION
    C. NATURE AND PURPOSE OF REPORTS
    D. REPORTS AND OPINIONS: DIFFERENCES AND SIMILARITIES

5.___

Questions 6-8.

DIRECTIONS: Questions 6 through 8 are to be answered SOLELY on the basis of the following passage.

The most important unit of the mimeograph machine is a perforated metal drum over which is stretched a cloth ink pad. A reservoir inside the drum contains the ink which flows through the perforations and saturates the ink pad. To operate the machine, the operator first removes from the machine the protective sheet, which keeps the ink from drying while the machine is not in use. He then hooks the stencil face down on the drum, draws the stencil smoothly over the drum, and fastens the stencil at the bottom. The speed with which the drum turns determines the blackness of the copies printed. Slow turning gives heavy, black copies; fast turning gives light, clear-cut reproductions. If reproductions are run on other than porous paper, slip-sheeting is necessary to prevent smearing. Often, the printed copy fails to drop readily as it comes from the machine. This may be due to static electricity. To remedy this difficulty, the operator fastens a strip of tinsel from side to side near the impression roller so that the printed copy just touches the soft stems of the tinsel as it is ejected from the machine, thus grounding the static electricity to the frame of the machine.

6. According to the above passage,

    A. turning the drum fast produces light copies
    B. stencils should be placed face up on the drum
    C. ink pads should be changed daily
    D. slip-sheeting is necessary when porous paper is being used

6.___

7. According to the above passage, when a mimeograph machine is not in use,

    A. the ink should be drained from the drum
    B. the ink pad should be removed
    C. the machine should be covered with a protective sheet
    D. the counter should be set at zero

7.___

8. According to the above passage, static electricity is grounded to the frame of the mimeograph machine by means of

    A. a slip-sheeting device
    B. a strip of tinsel
    C. an impression roller
    D. hooks located at the top of the drum

8.___

Questions 9-10.

DIRECTIONS:   Questions 9 and 10 are to be answered SOLELY on the basis of the following
passage.

The proofreading of material typed from copy is performed more accurately and more
speedily when two persons perform this work as a team. The person who did not do the typing should read aloud the original copy while the person who did the typing should check the
reading against the typed copy. The reader should speak very slowly and repeat the figures,
using a different grouping of numbers when repeating the figures. For example, in reading
1967, the reader may say *one-nine-six-seven* on first reading the figure and *nineteen-sixty-
seven* on repeating the figure. The reader should read all punctuation marks, taking nothing
for granted. Since mistakes can occur anywhere, everything typed should be proofread. To
avoid confusion, the proofreading team should use the standard proofreading marks, which
are given in most dictionaries.

9.   According to the above passage, the

    A.   person who holds the typed copy is called the reader
    B.   two members of a proofreading team should take turns in reading the typed copy
        aloud
    C.   typed copy should be checked by the person who did the typing
    D.   person who did not do the typing should read aloud from the typed copy

9.

10.   According to the above passage,

    A.   it is unnecessary to read the period at the end of a sentence
    B.   typographical errors should be noted on the original copy
    C.   each person should develop his own set of proofreading marks
    D.   figures should be read twice

10

Questions 11-16.

DIRECTIONS:   Questions 11 through 16 are to be answered SOLELY on the basis of the
above passage.

Basic to every office is the need for proper lighting. Inadequate lighting is a familiar cause
of fatigue and serves to create a somewhat dismal atmosphere in the office. One requirement
of proper lighting is that it be of an appropriate intensity. Intensity is measured in foot candles.
According to the Illuminating Engineering Society of New York, for casual seeing tasks such
as in reception rooms, inactive file rooms, and other service areas, it is recommended that
the amount of light be 30 foot-candles. For ordinary seeing tasks such as reading, work in
active file rooms, and in mailrooms, the recommended lighting is 100 foot-candles. For very
difficult seeing tasks such as accounting, transcribing, and business machine use, the recommended lighting is 150 foot-candles.

Lighting intensity is only one requirement. Shadows and glare are to be avoided. For
example, the larger the proportion of a ceiling filled with lighting units, the more glare-free and
comfortable the lighting will be. Natural lighting from windows is not too dependable because
on dark wintry days, windows yield little usable light, and on sunny summer afternoons, the
glare from windows may be very distracting. Desks should not face the windows. Finally, the
main lighting source ought to be overhead and to the left of the user,

11. According to the above passage, insufficient light in the office may cause      11._____

    A. glare                    B. tiredness
    C. shadows             D. distraction

12. Based on the above passage, which of the following must be considered when planning      12._____
lighting arrangements? The

    A. amount of natural light present
    B. amount of work to be done
    C. level of difficulty of work to be done
    D. type of activity to be carried out

13. It can be inferred from the above passage that a well-coordinated lighting scheme is      13._____
LIKELY to result in

    A. greater employee productivity
    B. elimination of light reflection
    C. lower lighting cost
    D. more use of natural light

14. Of the following, the BEST title for the above passage is      14._____

    A. CHARACTERISTICS OF LIGHT
    B. LIGHT MEASUREMENT DEVICES
    C. FACTORS TO CONSIDER WHEN PLANNING LIGHTING SYSTEMS
    D. COMFORT VS. COST WHEN DEVISING LIGHTING ARRANGEMENTS

15. According to the above passage, a foot-candle is a measurement of the      15._____

    A. number of bulbs used
    B. strength of the light
    C. contrast between glare and shadow
    D. proportion of the ceiling filled with lighting units

16. According to the above passage, the number of foot-candles of light that would be      16._____
needed to copy figures onto a payroll is _____ foot-candles.

    A. less than 30           B. 100
    C. 30                D. 150

Questions 17-23.

DIRECTIONS: Questions 17 through 23 are to be answered SOLELY on the basis of the following passage, which is the Fee Schedule of a hypothetical college.

## FEE SCHEDULE

A. A candidate for any baccalaureate degree is not required to pay tuition fees for undergraduate courses until he exceeds 128 credits, Candidates exceeding 128 credits in undergraduate courses are charged at the rate of $100 a credit for each credit of undergraduate course work in excess of 128. Candidates for a baccalaureate degree who are taking graduate courses must pay the same fee as any other student taking graduate courses

B. Non-degree students and college graduates are charged tuition fees for courses, whether undergraduate or graduate, at the rate of $180 a credit. For such students, there is an additional charge of $150 for each class hour per week in excess of the number of course credits. For example, if a three-credit course meets five hours a week, there is an additional charge for the extra two hours. Graduate courses are shown with a (G) before the course number.

C. All students are required to pay the laboratory fees indicated after the number of credits given for that course.

D. All students must pay a $250 general fee each semester.

E. Candidates for a baccalaureate degree are charged a $150 medical insurance fee for each semester. All other students are charged a $100 medical insurance fee each semester.

17. Miss Burton is not a candidate for a degree. She registers for the following courses in the spring semester: Economics 12, 4 hours a week, 3 credits; History (G) 23, 4 hours a week, 3 credits; English 1, 2 hours a week, 2 credits. The TOTAL amount in fees that Miss Burton must pay is      17.

    A. less than $2000                      B. at least $2000 but less than $2100
    C. at least $2100 but less than $2200    D. $2200 or over

18. Miss Gray is not a candidate for a degree. She registers for the following courses in the fall semester: History 3, 3 hours a week, 3 credits; English 5, 3 hours a week, 2 credits; Physics 5, 6 hours a week, 3 credits, laboratory fee $ 60; Mathematics 7, 4 hours a week, 3 credits. The TOTAL amount in fees that Miss Gray must pay is      18.

    A. less than $3150                      B. at least $3150 but less than $3250
    C. at least $3250 but less than $3350    D. $3350 or over

19. Mr. Wall is a candidate for the Bachelor of Arts degree and has completed 126 credits. He registers for the following courses in the spring semester, his final semester at college: French 4, 3 hours a week, 3 credits; Physics (G) 15, 6 hours a week, 3 credits, laboratory fee $80; History (G) 33, 4 hours a week, 3 credits. The TOTAL amount in fees that this candidate must pay is      19.

    A. less than $2100                      B. at least $2100 but less than $2300
    C. at least $2300 but less than $2500    D. $2500

20. Mr. Tindall, a candidate for the B.A. degree, has completed 122 credits of undergraduate courses. He registers for the following courses in his final semester: English 31, 3 hours a week, 3 credits; Philosophy 12, 4 hours a week, 4 credits; Anthropology 15, 3 hours a week, 3 credits; Economics (G) 68, 3 hours a week, 3 credits. The TOTAL amount in fees that Mr. Tindall must pay in his final semester is      20.

    A. less than $1200                      B. at least $1200 but less than $1400
    C. at least $1400 but less than $1600    D. $1600

21. Mr. Cantrell, who was graduated from the college a year ago, registers for graduate courses in the fall semester. Each course for which he registers carries the same number of credits as the number of hours a week it meets.
If he pays a total of $1530; including a $100 laboratory fee, the number of credits for which he is registered is

   A. 4        B. 5        C. 6        D. 7

21.____

22. Miss Jayson, who is not a candidate for a degree, has, registered for several courses including a lecture course in History. She withdraws from the course in History for which she had paid the required course fee of $690. The number of hours that this course is scheduled to meet is

   A. 4        B. 5        C. 2        D. 3

22.____

23. Mr. Van Arsdale, a graduate of a college is Iowa, registers for the following courses in one semester: Chemistry 35, 5 hours a week, 3 credits; Biology 13, 4 hours a week, 3 credits, laboratory fee $150; Mathematics (G) 179, 3 hours a week, 3 credits.
The TOTAL amount in fees that Mr. Van Arsdale must pay is

   A. less than $2400
   B. at least $2400 but less than $2500
   C. at least $2500 but less than $2600
   D. at least $2600 or over

23.____

Questions 24-25.

DIRECTIONS: Questions 24 and 25 are to be answered SOLELY on the basis of the following passage.

A duplex envelope is an envelope composed of two sections securely fastened together so that they become one mailing piece. This type of envelope makes it possible for a first class letter to be delivered simultaneously with third or fourth class matter and yet not require payment of the much higher first class postage rate on the entire mailing. First class postage is paid only on the letter which goes in the small compartment, third or fourth class postage being paid on the contents of the larger compartment. The larger compartment generally has an ungummed flap or clasp for sealing. The first class or smaller compartment has a gummed flap for sealing. Postal regulations require that the exact amount of postage applicable to each compartment be separately attached to it.

24. On the basis of the above passage, it is MOST accurate to state that

   A. the smaller compartment is placed inside the larger compartment before mailing
   B. the two compartments may be detached and mailed separately
   C. two classes of mailing matter may be mailed as a unit at two different postage rates
   D. the more expensive postage rate is paid on the matter in the larger compartment

24.____

25. When a duplex envelope is used, the                                    25.___

    A. first class compartment may be sealed with a clasp
    B. correct amount of postage must be placed on each compartment
    C. compartment containing third or fourth class mail requires a gummed flap for sealing
    D. full amount of postage for both compartments may be placed on the larger compartment

___

# KEY (CORRECT ANSWERS)

| | | | |
|---|---|---|---|
| 1. A | | 11. C | |
| 2. D | | 12. D | |
| 3. B | | 13. A | |
| 4. B | | 14. C | |
| 5. C | | 15. B | |
| 6. A | | 16. D | |
| 7. C | | 17. B | |
| 8. B | | 18. A | |
| 9. C | | 19. B | |
| 10. D | | 20. B | |

21. C
22. A
23. C
24. C
25. B

___

# PREPARING WRITTEN MATERIAL

# PARAGRAPH REARRANGEMENT
## COMMENTARY

The sentences which follow are in scrambled order. You are to rearrange them in proper order and indicate the letter choice containing the correct answer at the space at the right.

Each group of sentences in this section is actually a paragraph presented in scrambled order. Each sentence in the group has a place in that paragraph; no sentence is to be left out. You are to read each group of sentences and decide upon the best order in which to put the sentences so as to form as well-organized paragraph.

The questions in this section measure the ability to solve a problem when all the facts relevant to its solution are not given.

More specifically, certain positions of responsibility and authority require the employee to discover connections between events sometimes, apparently, unrelated. In order to do this, the employee will find it necessary to correctly infer that unspecified events have probably occurred or are likely to occur. This ability becomes especially important when action must be taken on incomplete information.

Accordingly, these questions require competitors to choose among several suggested alternatives, each of which presents a different sequential arrangement of the events. Competitors must choose the MOST logical of the suggested sequences.

In order to do so, they may be required to draw on general knowledge to infer missing concepts or events that are essential to sequencing the given events. Competitors should be careful to infer only what is essential to the sequence. The plausibility of the wrong alternatives will always require the inclusion of unlikely events or of additional chains of events which are NOT essential to sequencing the given events.

It's very important to remember that you are looking for the best of the four possible choices, and that the best choice of all may not even be one of the answers you're given to choose from.

There is no one right way to these problems. Many people have found it helpful to first write out the order of the sentences, as they would have arranged them, on their scrap paper before looking at the possible answers. If their optimum answer is there, this can save them some time. If it isn't, this method can still give insight into solving the problem. Others find it most helpful to just go through each of the possible choices, contrasting each as they go along. You should use whatever method feels comfortable, and works, for you.

While most of these types of questions are not that difficult, we've added a higher percentage of the difficult type, just to give you more practice. Usually there are only one or two questions on this section that contain such subtle distinctions that you're unable to answer confidently, and you then may find yourself stuck deciding between two possible choices, neither of which you're sure about.

———

# PREPARING WRITTEN MATERIAL
## EXAMINATION SECTION

DIRECTIONS: The following groups of sentences need to be arranged so that the entire passage is correctly organized from start to finish. Select the letter preceding the sequence that represents the best sentence order. *PRINT THE LETTER OF THE CORRECT ANSWER IN THE SPACE AT THE RIGHT.*

## Question 1

1._____

1. A large Naval station on Alameda Island, near Oakland, held many warships in port, and the War Department was worried that if the bridge were to be blown up by the enemy, passage to and from the bay would be hopelessly blocked.

2. Though many skeptics were opposed to the idea of building such an enormous bridge, the most vocal opposition came from a surprising source: the United States War Department.

3. The War Department's concerns led to a showdown at San Francisco City Hall between Strauss and the Secretary of War, who demanded to know what would happen if a military enemy blew up the bridge.

4. In 1933, by submitting a construction cost estimate of $17 million, an engineer named Joseph Strauss won the contract to build the Golden Gate Bridge of San Francisco, which would then become one of the world's largest bridges.

5. Strauss quickly ended the debate by explaining that the Golden Gate Bridge was to be a suspension bridge, whose roadway would hang in the air from cables strung between two huge towers, and would immediately sink into three hundred feet of water if it were destroyed.

The best order is
A.  2 3 1 4 5
B.  1 2 3 5 4
C.  4 2 1 3 5
D.  4 1 3 5 2

**Question 2**

1. Plastic surgeons have already begun to use virtual reality to map out the complex nerve and tissue structures of a particular patient's face, in order to prepare for delicate surgery.

2. A virtual reality program responds to these movements by adjusting the images that a person sees on a screen or through goggles, thereby creating an "interactive" world in which a person can see and touch three-dimensional graphic objects.

3. No more than a computer program that is designed to build and display graphic images, the virtual reality program takes graphic programs a step further by sensing a person's head and body movements.

4. The computer technology known as virtual reality, now in its very first stages of development, is already revolutionizing some aspects of contemporary life.

5. Virtual reality computers are also being used by the space program, most recently to simulate conditions for the astronauts who were launched on a repair mission to the Hubble telescope.

The best order is
   A. 4 2 1 5 3
   B. 3 1 5 2 4
   C. 4 3 2 1 5
   D. 3 1 2 4 5

**Question 3**

1. Before you plant anything, the soil in your plant bed should be carefully raked level, a small section at a time, and any clods or rocks that can't be broken up should be removed.

2. Your plant should be placed in a hole that will position it at the same level it was at the nursery, and a small indentation should be pressed into the soil around the plant in order to hold water near it roots.

3. Before placing the plant in the soil, lightly separate any roots that may have been matted together in the container, cutting away any thick masses that can't be separated, so that the remaining roots will be able to grow outward.

4. After the bed is ready, remove your plant from its container by turning it upside down and tapping or pushing on the bottom – never remove it by pulling on the plant.

5. When you bring home a small plant in an individual container from the nursery, there are several things to remember while preparing to plant it in your own garden.

The best order is
   A. 5 4 3 2 1
   B. 5 1 4 3 2
   C. 1 4 2 3 5
   D. 1 4 5 2 3

**Question 4**                                                            4._____

1. The motte and its tower were usually built first, so that sentries could use it as a lookout to warn the castle workers of any danger that might approach the castle.

2. Though the moat and palisade offered the bailey a good deal of protection, it was linked to the motte by a set of stairs that led to a retractable drawbridge at the motte's gate, to enable people to evacuate and retreat onto the motte in case of an attack.

3. The *motte* of these early castles was a fortified hill, sometimes as high as one hundred feet, on which stood a palisade and tower.

4. The *bailey* was a clear, level spot below the motte, also enclosed by a palisade, which in turn was surrounded by a large trench or moat.

5. The earliest castles built in Europe were not the magnificent stone giants that still tower over much of the European landscape, but simpler wooden constructions called motte-and-bailey castles.

The best order is
   A.  5 3 1 4 2
   B.  5 4 1 2 3
   C.  1 4 3 2 5
   D.  1 3 2 4 5

**Question 5**                                                            5._____

1. If an infant is left alone or abandoned for a short while, its immediate response is to cry loudly, accompanying its screams with aggressive flailing of its legs and limbs.

2. If a child has been abandoned for a longer period of time, it becomes completely still and quiet, as if realizing that now its only chance for survival is to shut its mouth and remain motionless.

3. Along with their intense fear of the dark, the crying behavior of human infants offers insights into how prehistoric newborn children might have evolved instincts that would prevent them from becoming victims of predators.

4. This behavior often surprises people who enter a hospital's maternity ward for the first time and encounter total silence from a roomful of infants.

5. This violent screaming response is quite different from an infant's cries of discomfort or hunger, and seems to serve as either the child's first line of defense against an unwanted intruder, or a desperate attempt to communicate its position to the mother.

The best order is
   A.  3 2 4 1 5
   B.  3 1 5 2 4
   C.  1 5 4 2 3
   D.  2 4 1 5 3

3

**Question 6**

1. When two cats meet who are strangers, their first actions and gestures determine who the "dominant" cat will be, at least for the time being.

2. Unlike dogs, cats are typically a solitary animal species who avoid social interaction, but they do display specific social responses to each other upon meeting.

3. This is unlikely, however; before such a point of open hostility is reached, one of the cats will usually take the "submissive" position of crouching down while looking away from the other cat.

4. If a cat desires dominance or sees the other cat as a threat to its territory, it will stare directly at the intruder with a lowered tail.

5. If the other cat responds with a similar gesture, or with the strong defensive posture of an arched back, laid-back ears and raised tail, a fight or chase is likely if neither cat gives in.

    The best order is
    A.  4  2  1  5  3
    B.  1  2  4  5  3
    C.  1  4  5  3  2
    D.  2  1  4  5  3


**Question 7**

1. A star or planet's gravitational force can best be explained in this way: anything passing through this "dent" in space will veer toward the star or planet as if it were rolling into a hole.

2. Objects that are massive or heavy, such as stars or planets, "sink" into this surface, creating a sort of dent or concavity in the surrounding space.

3. Black holes, the most massive objects known to exist in space, create dents so large and deep that the space surrounding them actually folds in on itself, preventing anything that falls in – even light – from ever escaping again.

4. The sort of dent a star or planet makes depends on how massive it is; planets generally have weak gravitational pulls, but stars, which are larger and heavier, make a bigger "dent" that will attract more matter.

5. In outer space, the force of gravity works as if the surrounding space is a soft, flat surface.

    The best order is
    A.  3  5  2  1  4
    B.  3  4  1  5  2
    C.  5  2  1  4  3
    D.  1  5  2  4  3

4

**Question 8**

1. Eventually, the society of Kyoto gave the world one of its first and greatest novels when Japan's most prominent writer, Lady Murasaki Shikibu, wrote her chronicle of Kyoto's society, *The Tale of Genji*, which preceded the first European novels by more than 500 years.

2. The society of Kyoto was dedicated to the pleasures of art; the courtiers experimented with new and colorful methods of sculpture, painting, writing, decorative gardening, and even making clothes.

3. Japanese culture began under the powerful authority of Chinese Buddhism, which influenced every aspect of Japanese life from religion to politics and art.

4. This new, vibrant culture was so sophisticated that all the people in Kyoto's imperial court considered themselves poets, and the line between life and art hardly existed – lovers corresponded entirely through written verses, and even government officials communicated by writing poems to each other.

5. In the eighth century, when the emperor established the town of Kyoto as the capital of the Japanese empire, Japanese society began to develop its own distinctive style.

The best order is  ·
A.  5  2  4  1  3
B.  2  1  5  4  3
C.  5  3  4  1  2
D.  3  5  2  4  1

**Question 9**

1. Instead of wheels, the HSST uses two sets of magnets, one which sits on the track, and another that is carried by the train; these magnets generate an identical magnetic field which forces the two sets apart.

2. In the last few decades, railway travel has become less popular throughout the world, because it is much slower than travel by airplane, and not much less expensive.

3. The HSST's designers say that the train can take passengers from one town to another as quickly as a jet plane – while consuming less than half the energy.

4. This repellent effect is strong enough to lift the entire train above the trackway, and the train, literally traveling on air, rockets along at speeds of up to 300 miles per hour.

5. The revolutionary technology of magnetic levitation, currently being tested by Japan's experimental HSST (High Speed Surface Transport), may yet bring passenger trains back from the dead.

The best order is
A.  2  5  1  4  3
B.  2  1  4  3  5
C.  5  2  3  1  4
D.  5  1  3  4  2

**Question 10**

1. When European countries first began to colonize the African continent, their impression of the African people was of a vast group of loosely organized tribal societies, without any great centralized source of power or wealth.

2. The legend of Timbuktu persisted until the nineteenth century, when a French adventurer visited Timbuktu and found that raids by neighboring tribesmen had made the city a shadow of its former self.

3. In the fifteenth century, when the stories of travelers who had traveled Africa's Sudan region began circulating around Europe, this impression began to change.

4. In 1470, an Italian merchant named Benedetto Dei traveled to Timbuktu and confirmed these rumors, describing a thriving metropolis where rich and poor people worshipped together in the city's many ornate mosques – there was even a university in Timbuktu, much like its European counterparts, where African scholars pursued their studies in the arts and sciences.

5. The travelers' legends told of an enormous city in the western Sudan, Timbuktu, where the streets were crowded with goods brought by faraway caravans, and where there was a stone palace as large as any in Europe.

The best order is
A. 3 5 1 4 2
B. 1 2 4 3 5
C. 1 3 5 4 2
D. 2 1 3 4 5

**Question 11**

1. Also, our reference points in sighting the moon may make us believe that its size is changing; when the moon is rising through the trees, it seems huge, because our brains unconsciously compare the size of the moon with the size of the trees in the foreground.

2. To most people, the sky itself appears more distant at the horizon than directly overhead, and if the moon's size – which remains constant – is projected from the horizon, the apparent distance of the horizon makes the moon look bigger.

3. Up higher in the sky, the moon is set against tiny stars in the background, which will make the moon seem smaller.

4. People often wonder why the moon becomes bigger when it approaches the horizon, but most scientists agree that this is a complicated optical illusion, produced by at least three factors.

5. The moon illusion may also be partially explained by a phenomenon that has nothing to do with errors in our perception – light that enters the earth's atmosphere is sometimes refracted, and so the atmosphere may act as a kind of magnifying glass for the moon's image.

The best order is
A. 4 3 5 2 1
B. 4 2 1 3 5
C. 5 2 1 3 4
D. 2 1 3 4 5

**Question 12**

1. When the Native Americans were introduced to the horses used by white explorers, they were amazed at their new alternative – here was an animal that was strong and swift, would patiently carry a person or other loads on its back, and, they later discovered, was right at home on the plains.

2. Before the arrival of European explorers to North America, the natives of the American plains used large dogs to carry their travois-long lodgepoles loaded with clothing, gear, and food.

3. These horses, it is now known, were not really strangers to North America; the very first horses originated here, on this continent, tens of thousands of years ago, and migrated into Asia across the Bering Land Bridge, a strip of land that used to link our continent with the Eastern world.

4. At first, the natives knew so little about horses that at least one tribe tried to feed their new animals pieces of dried meat and animal fat, and were surprised when the horses turned their heads away and began to eat the grass of the prairie.

5. The American horse eventually became extinct, but its Asian cousins were reintroduced to the New World when the European explorers brought them to live among the Native Americans.

   The best order is
   A.  2  1  4  3  5
   B.  2  4  1  3  5
   C.  1  2  4  3  5
   D.  1  3  5  2  4

**Question 13**

1. The dress worn by the dancer is believed to have been adorned in the past by shells which would strike each other as the dancer performed, creating a lovely sound.

2. Today's jingle-dress is decorated with the tin lids of snuff cans, which are rolled into cones and sewn onto the dress.

3. During the jingle-dress dance, the dancer must blend complicated footwork with a series of gentle hops that cause the cones to jingle in rhythm to a drumbeat.

4. When contemporary Native American tribes meet for a pow-wow, one of the most popular ceremonies to take place is the women's jingle-dress dance.

5. Besides being more readily available than shells, the lids are thought by many dancers to create a softer, more subtle sound.

   The best order is
   A.  2  4  5  1  3
   B.  4  2  1  3  5
   C.  2  1  3  5  4
   D.  4  1  2  5  3

**Question 14**

1. If a homeowner lives where seasonal climates are extreme, deciduous shade trees – which will drop their leaves in the winter and allow sunlight to pass through the windows – should be planted near the southern exposure in order to keep the house cool during the summer.

2. This trajectory is shorter and lower in the sky than at any other time of year during the winter, when a house most requires heating; the northern- facing parts of a house do not receive any direct sunlight at all.

3. In designing an energy-efficient house, especially in colder climates, it is important to remember that most of the house's windows should face south.

4. Though the sun always rises in the east and sets in the west, the sun of the northern hemisphere is permanently situated in the southern portion of the sky.

5. The explanation for why so many architects and builders want this "southern exposure" is related to the path of the sun in the sky.

The best order is
   A.  3  1  5  4  2
   B.  3  5  4  2  1
   C.  1  3  4  2  5
   D.  1  2  5  4  3

**Question 15**

1. His journeying lasted twenty-four years and took him over an estimated 75,000 miles, a distance that would not be surpassed by anyone other than Magellan – who sailed around the world – for another six hundred years.

2. Perhaps the most far-flung of these lesser-known travelers was Ibn Batuta, an African Moslem who left his birthplace of Tangier in the summer of 1325.

3. Ibn Batuta traveled all over Africa and Asia, from Niger to Peking, and to the islands of Maldive and Indonesia.

4. However, a few explorers of the Eastern world logged enough miles and adventures to make Marco Polo's voyage look like an evening stroll.

5. In America, the most well-known of the Old World's explorers are usually Europeans such as Marco Polo, the Italian who brought many elements of Chinese culture to the Western world.

The best order is
   A.  5  4  2  3  1
   B.  5  4  3  2  1
   C.  3  2  1  4  5
   D.  2  3  1  4  5

**Question 16**

1. In the rain forests of South America, a rare species of frog practices a reproductive method that is entirely different from this standard process.

2. She will eventually carry each of the tadpoles up into the canopy and drop each into its own little pool, where it will be easy to locate and safe from most predators.

3. After fertilization, the female of the species, who lives almost entirely on the forest floor, lays between 2 and 16 eggs among the leaf litter at the base of a tree, and stands watch over these eggs until they hatch.

4. Most frogs are pond-dwellers who are able to deposit hundreds of eggs in the water and then leave them alone, knowing that enough eggs have been laid to insure the survival of some of their offspring.

5. Once the tadpoles emerge, the female backs in among them, and a tadpole will wriggle onto her back to be carried high into the forest canopy, where the female will deposit it in a little pool of water cupped in the leaf of a plant.

The best order is
A.  1 4 3 2 5
B.  1 3 5 2 4
C.  4 3 2 5 1
D.  4 1 3 5 2

**Question 17**

1. Eratosthenes had heard from travelers that at exactly noon on June 21, in the ancient city of Aswan, Egypt, the sun cast no shadow in a well, which meant that the sun must be directly overhead.

2. He knew the sun always cast a shadow in Alexandria, and so he figured that if he could measure the length of an Alexandria shadow at the time when there was no shadow in Aswan, he could calculate the angle of the sun, and therefore the circumference of the earth.

3. The evidence for a round earth was not new in 1492; in fact, Eratosthenes, an Alexandrian geographer who lived nearly sixteen centuries before Columbus's voyage (275-195 B.C.), actually developed a method for calculating the circumference of the earth that is still in use today.

4. Eratosthenes's method was correct, but his result – 28,700 miles – was about 15 percent too high, probably because of the inaccurate ancient methods of keeping time, and because Aswan was not due south of Alexandria, as Eratosthenes had believed.

5. When Christopher Columbus sailed across the Atlantic Ocean for the first time in 1492, there were still some people in the world who ignored scientific evidence and believed that the earth was flat, rather than round.

The best order is
A.  1 2 5 3 4
B.  5 3 4 1 2
C.  5 3 1 2 4
D.  3 5 1 2 4

**Question 18**

1. The first name for the child is considered a trial naming, often impersonal and neutral, such as the Ngoni name *Chabwera*, meaning "it has arrived."

2. This sort of name is not due to any parental indifference to the child, but is a kind of silent recognition of Africa's sometimes high infant death rate; most parents ease the pain of losing a child with the belief that it is not really a person until it has been given a final name.

3. In many tribal African societies, families often give two different names to their children, at different periods in time.

4. After the trial naming period has subsided and it is clear that the child will survive, the parents choose a final name for the child, an act that symbolically completes the act of birth.

5. In fact, some African first-given names are explicitly uncomplimentary, translating as "I am dead" or "I am ugly," in order to avoid the jealousy of ancestral spirits who might wish to take a child that is especially healthy or attractive.

The best order is
A. 3 1 2 5 4
B. 3 4 2 1 5
C. 4 3 1 2 5
D. 4 5 3 1 2

**Question 19**

1. Though uncertain of the definite reasons for this behavior, scientists believe the birds digest the clay in order to counteract toxins contained in the seeds of certain fruits that are eaten by macaws.

2. For example, all macaws flock to riverbanks at certain times of the year to eat the clay that is found in river mud.

3. The macaws of South America are not only among the largest and most beautifully colored of the world's flying birds, but they are also one of the smartest.

4. It is believed that macaws are forced to resort to these toxic fruits during the dry season, when foods are more scarce.

5. The macaw's intelligence has led to intense study by scientists, who have discovered some macaw behaviors that have not yet been explained.

The best order is
A. 3 4 1 2 5
B. 3 5 2 1 4
C. 5 2 1 4 3
D. 4 1 2 3 5

**Question 20**

1. Although Maggie Kuhn has since passed away, the Gray Panthers are still waging a campaign to reinstate the historical view of the elderly as people whose experience allows them to make their greatest contribution in their later years.

2. In 1972, an elderly woman named Maggie Kuhn responded to this sort of treatment by forming a group called the Gray Panthers, an organization of both old and young adults with the common goal of creating change.

3. This attitude is reflected strongly in the way elderly people are treated by our society; many are forced into early retirement, or are placed in rest homes in which they are isolated from their communities.

4. Unlike most other cultures around the world, Americans tend to look upon old age with a sense of dread and sadness.

5. Kuhn believed that when the elderly are forced to withdraw into lives that lack purpose, society loses one of its greatest resources: people who have a lifetime of experience and wisdom to offer their communities.

The best order is
   A. 4 3 2 5 1
   B. 4 2 1 3 5
   C. 2 4 3 5 1
   D. 2 1 4 3 5

**Question 21**

1. The current theory among most anthropologists is that humans evolved from apes who lived in trees near the grasslands of Africa.

2. Still, some anthropologists insist that such an invention was necessary for the survival of early humans, and point to the Kung Bushmen of central Africa as a society in which the sling is still used in this way.

3. Two of these inventions – fire, and weapons such as spears and clubs – were obvious defenses against predators, and there is archaeological evidence to support the theory of their use.

4. Once people had evolved enough to leave the safety of trees and walk upright, they needed the protection of several inventions in order to survive.

5. But another invention, a leather or fiber sling that allowed mothers to carry children while leaving their hands free to gather roots or berries, would certainly have decomposed and left behind no trace of itself.

The best order is
   A. 1 2 3 5 4
   B. 4 1 2 3 5
   C. 1 4 3 5 2
   D. 4 3 5 2 1

**Question 22**

22._____

1.  The person holding the bird should keep it in hot water up to its neck, and the person cleaning should work a mild solution of dishwashing liquid into the bird's plumage, paying close attention to the head and neck.

2.  When rinsing the bird, after all the oil has been removed, the running water should be directed against the lay of its feathers, until water begins to bead off the surface of the feathers – a sign that all the detergent has been rinsed out.

3.  If you have rescued a sea bird from an oil spill and want to restore it to clean and normal living, you need a large sink, a constant supply of running hot water (a little over 100° F), and regular dishwashing liquid.

4.  This cleaning with detergent solution should be repeated as many times as it takes to remove all traces of oil from the bird's feathers, sometimes over a period of several days.

5.  But before you begin to clean the bird, you must first find a partner, because cleaning an oiled bird is a two-person job.

    The best order is
    A.  3 1 2 4 5
    B.  3 5 1 4 2
    C.  3 1 4 5 2
    D.  3 4 5 1 2

**Question 23**

23._____

1.  The most difficult time of year for the Tsaatang is the spring calving, when the reindeer leave their wintering ground and rush to their accustomed calving place, without stopping by night or by day.

2.  Reindeer travel in herds, and though some animals are tamed by the Tsaatang for riding or milking, the herds are allowed to roam free.

3.  This journey is hard for the Tsaatang, who carry all their possessions with them, but once it's over it proves worthwhile; the Tsaatang can immediately begin to gather milk from reindeer cows who have given birth.

4.  The Tsaatang, a small tribe who live in the far northwest corner of Mongolia, practice a lifestyle that is completely dependent on the reindeer, their main resource for food, clothing, and transport.

5.  The people must follow their yearly migrations, living in portable shelters that resemble Native American tepees.

    The best order is
    A.  1 3 2 5 4
    B.  1 4 2 5 3
    C.  4 1 3 5 2
    D.  4 2 5 1 3

12

**Question 24**

1. The Romans later improved this system by installing these heated pipe networks throughout walls and ceilings, supplying heat to even the uppermost floors of a building – a system that, to this day, hasn't been much improved.

2. Air-conditioning, the method by which humans control indoor temperatures, was practiced much earlier than most people think.

3. The earliest heating devices other than open fires were used in 350 B.C. by the ancient Greeks, who directed air that had been heated by underground fires into baked clay pipes that ran under the floor.

4. Ironically, the first successful cooling system, patented in England in 1831, used fire as its main energy source – fires were lit in the attic of a building, creating an updraft of air that drew cool air into the building through ducts that had underground openings near the river Thames.

5. Cooling buildings was more of a challenge, and wasn't attempted until 1500: a water-based system, designed by Leonardo da Vinci, does not appear to have been successful, since it was never used again.

The best order is
A. 3 5 4 1 2
B. 3 1 2 5 4
C. 2 3 1 5 4
D. 4 2 3 1 5

**Question 25**

1. Cold, dry air from Canada passes over the Rocky Mountains and sweeps down onto the plains, where it collides with warm, moist air from the waters of the Gulf of Mexico, and when the two air masses meet, the resulting disturbance sometimes forms a violent funnel cloud that strikes the earth and destroys virtually everything in its path.

2. Hurricanes, storms which are generally not this violent and last much longer, are usually given names by meteorologists, but this tradition cannot be applied to tornados, which have a life span measured in minutes and disappear in the same way as they are born – unnamed.

3. A tornado funnel forms rotating columns of air whose speed reaches three hundred miles and hour – a speed that can only be estimated, because no wind-measuring devices in the direct path of a storm have ever survived.

4. The natural phenomena known as tornados occur primarily over the midwestern grasslands of the United States.

5. It is here, meteorologists tell us, that conditions for the formation of tornados are sometimes perfect during the spring months.

The best order is
A. 2 4 5 1 3
B. 2 3 1 5 4
C. 4 5 1 3 2
D. 4 3 1 5 2

# KEY (CORRECT ANSWERS)

| | | |
|---|---|---|
| 1. C | 11. B | 21. C |
| 2. C | 12. A | 22. B |
| 3. B | 13. D | 23. D |
| 4. A | 14. B | 24. C |
| 5. B | 15. A | 25. C |
| | | |
| 6. D | 16. D | |
| 7. C | 17. C | |
| 8. D | 18. A | |
| 9. A | 19. B | |
| 10. C | 20. A | |

# PREPARING WRITTEN MATERIAL

## EXAMINATION SECTION
## TEST 1

DIRECTIONS:  Each of the sentences in the Tests that follow may be classified under one of the following four categories:

    A.  *Faulty* because of incorrect grammar or word usage
    B.  *Faulty* because of incorrect punctuation
    C.  *Faulty* because of incorrect capitalization or incorrect spelling
    D.  *Correct*

Examine each sentence carefully to determine under which of the above four options it is best classified. Then, in the space to the right, print the capital letter preceding the option which is the best of the four suggested above.

(Note that each faulty sentence contains but one type of error. Consider a sentence to be correct if it contains none of the types of errors mentioned, even though there may be other correct ways of expressing the same thought.)

1. He sent the notice to the clerk who you hired yesterday.      1._____

2. It must be admitted, however that you were not informed of this change.      2._____

3. Only the employees who have served in this grade for at least two years are eligible for promotion.      3._____

4. The work was divided equally between she and Mary.      4._____

5. He thought that you were not available at that time.      5._____

6. When the messenger returns; please give him this package.      6._____

7. The new secretary prepared, typed, addressed, and delivered, the notices.      7._____

8. Walking into the room, his desk can be seen at the rear.      8._____

9. Although John has worked here longer than She, he produces a smaller amount of work.      9._____

10. She said she could of typed this report yesterday.      10._____

11. Neither one of these procedures are adequate for the efficient performance of this task.      11._____

12. The typewriter is the tool of the typist; the cashe register, the tool of the cashier.      12._____

13. "The assignment must be completed as soon as possible" said the supervisor.      13._____

14. As you know, office handbooks are issued to all new Employees.      14._____

15. Writing a speech is sometimes easier than to deliver it before an audience.      15._____

16. Mr. Brown our accountant, will audit the accounts next week.      16._____

17.   Give the assignment to whomever is able to do it most efficiently.          17.____

18.   The supervisor expected either your or I to file these reports.              18.____

―――――

# KEY (CORRECT ANSWERS)

| | | | |
|---|---|---|---|
| 1. | A | 10. | A |
| 2. | B | 11. | A |
| 3. | D | 12. | C |
| 4. | A | 13. | B |
| 5. | D | 14. | C |
| 6. | B | 15. | A |
| 7. | B | 16. | B |
| 8. | A | 17. | A |
| 9. | C | 18. | A |

―――――

# TEST 2

1.   The fire apparently started in the storeroom, which is usually locked.          1._____

2.   On approaching the victim two bruises were noticed by this officer.          2._____

3.   The officer, who was there examined the report with great care.          3._____

4.   Each employee in the office had a seperate desk.          4._____

5.   All employees including members of the clerical staff, were invited to the lecture.          5._____

6.   The suggested Procedure is similar to the one now in use.          6._____

7.   No one was more pleased with the new procedure than the chauffeur.          7._____

8.   He tried to persaude her to change the procedure.          8._____

9.   The total of the expenses charged to petty cash were high.          9._____

10.   An understanding between him and I was finally reached.          10._____

———————

# KEY (CORRECT ANSWERS)

| | | | | |
|---|---|---|---|---|
| 1. | D | | 6. | C |
| 2. | A | | 7. | D |
| 3. | B | | 8. | C |
| 4. | C | | 9. | A |
| 5. | B | | 10. | A |

———

# TEST 3

DIRECTIONS:   Each of the sentences in the Tests that follow may be classified under one of
the following four categories:
A.  *Faulty* because of incorrect grammar or word usage
B.  *Faulty* because of incorrect punctuation
C.  *Faulty* because of incorrect capitalization or incorrect spelling
D.  *Correct*

Examine each sentence carefully to determine under which of the above four options it is
best classified. Then, in the space to the right, print the capital letter preceding the option
which is the best of the four suggested above.

(Note that each faulty sentence contains but one type of error. Consider a sentence to be
correct if it contains none of the types of errors mentioned, even though there may be other
correct ways of expressing the same thought.)

1.  They told both he and *I* that the prisoner had escaped.                                                    1.____

2.  Any superior officer, who, disregards the just complaints of his subordinates, is remiss in           2.____
    the performance of his duty.

3.  Only those members of the national organization who resided in the Middle West                       3.____
    attended the conference in Chicago.

4.  We told him to give the investigation assignment to whoever was available.                             4.____

5.  Please do not disappoint and embarass us by not appearing in court.                                    5.____

6.  Although the officer's speech proved to be entertaining, the topic was not relevent to the          6.____
    main theme of the conference.

7.  In February all new officers attended a training course in which they were learned in their         7.____
    principal duties and the fundamental operating procedures of the department.

8.  I personally seen inmate Jones threaten inmates Smith and Green with bodily harm if                 8.____
    they refused to participate in the plot.

9.  To the layman, who on a chance visit to the prison observes everything functioning                  9.____
    smoothly, the maintenance of prison discipline may seem to be a relatively easily realiz-
    able objective.

10. The prisoners in cell block fourty were forbidden to sit on the cell cots during the recre-         10.____
    ation hour.

# KEY (CORRECT ANSWERS)

| | | | |
|---|---|---|---|
| 1. | A | 6. | C |
| 2. | B | 7. | A |
| 3. | C | 8. | A |
| 4. | D | 9. | D |
| 5. | C | 10. | C |

———

# TEST 4

DIRECTIONS: Each of the sentences in the Tests that follow may be classified under one of the following four categories:
- A. *Faulty* because of incorrect grammar or word usage
- B. *Faulty* because of incorrect punctuation
- C. *Faulty* because of incorrect capitalization or incorrect spelling
- D. *Correct*

Examine each sentence carefully to determine under which of the above four options it is best classified. Then, in the space to the right, print the capital letter preceding the option which is the best of the four suggested above.

(Note that each faulty sentence contains but one type of error. Consider a sentence to be correct if it contains none of the types of errors mentioned, even though there may be other correct ways of expressing the same thought.)

1. I cannot encourage you any.          1._____

2. You always look well in those sort of clothes.          2._____

3. Shall we go to the park?          3._____

4. The man whome he introduced was Mr. Carey.          4._____

5. She saw the letter laying here this morning.          5._____

6. It should rain before the Afternoon is over.          6._____

7. They have already went home.          7._____

8. That Jackson will be elected is evident.          8._____

9. He does not hardly approve of us.          9._____

10. It was he, who won the prize.          10._____

# KEY (CORRECT ANSWERS)

| | | | |
|---|---|---|---|
| 1. | A | 6. | C |
| 2. | A | 7. | A |
| 3. | D | 8. | D |
| 4. | C | 9. | A |
| 5. | A | 10. | B |

———

# TEST 5

DIRECTIONS: Each of the sentences in the Tests that follow may be classified under one of the following four categories:

DIRECTIONS: Each of the sentences in the Tests that follow may be classified under one of the following four categories:
    A. *Faulty* because of incorrect grammar or word usage
    B. *Faulty* because of incorrect punctuation
    C. *Faulty* because of incorrect capitalization or incorrect spelling
    D. *Correct*

Examine each sentence carefully to determine under which of the above four options it is best classified. Then, in the space to the right, print the capital letter preceding the option which is the best of the four suggested above.

Note that each faulty sentence contains but one type of error. Consider a sentence to be correct if it contains none of the types of errors mentioned, even though there may be other correct ways of expressing the same thought.)

1. Shall we go to the park.                                               1._____

2. They are, alike, in this particular.                            2._____

3. They gave the poor man sume food when he knocked on the door.    3._____

4. I regret the loss caused by the error.                         4._____

5. The students' will have a new teacher.                      5._____

6. They sweared to bring out all the facts.                     6._____

7. He decided to open a branch store on 33rd street.           7._____

8. His speed is equal and more than that of a racehorse.         8._____

9. He felt very warm on that Summer day.                     9._____

10. He was assisted by his friend, who lives in the next house.     10._____

———

# KEY (CORRECT ANSWERS)

| | | | |
|---|---|---|---|
| 1. | B | 6. | A |
| 2. | B | 7. | C |
| 3. | C | 8. | A |
| 4. | D | 9. | C |
| 5. | B | 10. | D |

———

# TEST 6

DIRECTIONS: Each of the sentences in the Tests that follow may be classified under one of the following four categories:

DIRECTIONS: Each of the sentences in the Tests that follow may be classified under one of the following four categories:
    A. *Faulty* because of incorrect grammar or word usage
    B. *Faulty* because of incorrect punctuation
    C. *Faulty* because of incorrect capitalization or incorrect spelling
    D. *Correct*

Examine each sentence carefully to determine under which of the above four options it is best classified. Then, in the space to the right, print the capital letter preceding the option which is the best of the four suggested above.

Note that each faulty sentence contains but one type of error. Consider a sentence to be correct if it contains none of the types of errors mentioned, even though there may be other correct ways of expressing the same thought.)

1.  The climate of New York is colder than California.      1._____

2.  I shall wait for you on the corner.      2._____

3.  Did we see the boy who, we think, is the leader.      3._____

4.  Being a modest person, John seldom talks about his invention .      4._____

5.  The gang is called the smith street boys.      5._____

6.  He seen the man break into the store.      6._____

7.  We expected to lay still there for quite a while.      7._____

8.  He is considered to be the Leader of his organization.      8._____

9.  Although I recieved an invitation, I won't go.      9._____

10. The letter must be here some place.      10._____

———

# KEY (CORRECT ANSWERS)

| | | | |
|---|---|---|---|
| 1. | A | 6. | A |
| 2. | D | 7. | A |
| 3. | B | 8. | C |
| 4. | D | 9. | C |
| 5. | C | 10. | A |

———

# TEST 7

DIRECTIONS: Each of the sentences in the Tests that follow may be classified under one of the following four categories:

DIRECTIONS: Each of the sentences in the Tests that follow may be classified under one of the following four categories:
      A. *Faulty* because of incorrect grammar or word usage
      B. *Faulty* because of incorrect punctuation
      C. *Faulty* because of incorrect capitalization or incorrect spelling
      D. *Correct*

Examine each sentence carefully to determine under which of the above four options it is best classified. Then, in the space to the right, print the capital letter preceding the option which is the best of the four suggested above.

Note that each faulty sentence contains but one type of error. Consider a sentence to be correct if it contains none of the types of errors mentioned, even though there may be other correct ways of expressing the same thought.)

1. I though it to be he.         1._____

2. We expect to remain here for a long time.         2._____

3. The committee was agreed.         3._____

4. Two-thirds of the building are finished.         4._____

5. The water was froze.         5._____

6. Everyone of the salesmen must supply their own car.         6._____

7. Who is the author of Gone With the Wind?         7._____

8. He marched on and declaring that he would never surrender.         8._____

9. Who shall I say called?         9._____

10. Everyone has left but they.         10._____

# KEY (CORRECT ANSWERS)

| | | | |
|---|---|---|---|
| 1. | A | 6. | A |
| 2. | D | 7. | B |
| 3. | D | 8. | A |
| 4. | A | 9. | D |
| 5. | A | 10. | D |

———

# TEST 8

DIRECTIONS: Each of the sentences in the Tests that follow may be classified under one of the following four categories:

DIRECTIONS: Each of the sentences in the Tests that follow may be classified under one of the following four categories:
      A. *Faulty* because of incorrect grammar or word usage
      B. *Faulty* because of incorrect punctuation
      C. *Faulty* because of incorrect capitalization or incorrect spelling
      D. *Correct*

Examine each sentence carefully to determine under which of the above four options it is best classified. Then, in the space to the right, print the capital letter preceding the option which is the best of the four suggested above.

Note that each faulty sentence contains but one type of error. Consider a sentence to be correct if it contains none of the types of errors mentioned, even though there may be other correct ways of expressing the same thought.)

1. Who did we give the order to?       1.____

2. Send your order in immediately.       2.____

3. I believe I paid the Bill.       3.____

4. I have not met but one person.       4.____

5. Why aren't Tom, and Fred, going to the dance?       5.____

6. What reason is there for him not going?       6.____

7. The seige of Malta was a tremendous event.       7.____

8. I was there yesterday I assure you.       8.____

9. Your ukelele is better than mine.       9.____

10. No one was there only Mary.       10.____

# KEY (CORRECT ANSWERS)

|     |   |     |   |
|-----|---|-----|---|
| 1.  | A | 6.  | A |
| 2.  | D | 7.  | C |
| 3.  | C | 8.  | B |
| 4.  | A | 9.  | C |
| 5.  | B | 10. | A |

———

# TEST 9

DIRECTIONS:   In each of the following groups of sentences, one of the four sentences is faulty in grammar, punctuation, or capitalization. Select the incorrect sentence in each case.

1.   A.   If you had stood at home and done your homework, you would not have failed in arithmetic.
     B.   Her affected manner annoyed every member of the audience.
     C.   How will the new law affect our income taxes?
     D.   The plants were not affected by the long, cold winter, but they succumbed to the drought of summer.

1.____

2.   A.   He is one of the most able men who have been in the Senate.
     B.   It is he who is to blame for the lamentable mistake.
     C.   Haven't you a helpful suggestion to make at this time?
     D.   The money was robbed from the blind man's cup.

2.____

3.   A.   The amount of children in this school is steadily increasing.
     B.   After taking an apple from the table, she went out to play.
     C.   He borrowed a dollar from me.
     D.   I had hoped my brother would arrive before me.

3.____

4.   A.   Whom do you think I hear from every week?
     B.   Who do you think is the right man for the job?
     C.   Who do you think I found in the room?
     D.   He is the man whom we considered a good candidate for the presidency.

4.____

5.   A.   Quietly the puppy laid down before the fireplace.
     B.   You have made your bed; now lie in it.
     C.   I was badly sunburned because I had lain too long in the sun.
     D.   I laid the doll on the bed and left the room.

5.____

———————

# KEY (CORRECT ANSWERS)

1. A
2. D
3. A
4. C
5. A

———

# PHILOSOPHY, PRINCIPLES, PRACTICES AND TECHNICS
## OF
## SUPERVISION, ADMINISTRATION, MANAGEMENT AND ORGANIZATION

## TABLE OF CONTENTS

# TABLE OF CONTENTS (CONTINUED)

# PHILOSOPHY, PRINCIPLES, PRACTICES, AND TECHNICS
## OF
## SUPERVISION, ADMINISTRATION, MANAGEMENT AND ORGANIZATION

## I. MEANING OF SUPERVISION

The extension of the democratic philosophy has been accompanied by an extension in the scope of supervision. Modern leaders and supervisors no longer think of supervision in the narrow sense of being confined chiefly to visiting employees, supplying materials, or rating the staff. They regard supervision as being intimately related to all the concerned agencies of society, they speak of the supervisor's function in terms of "growth", rather than the "improvement," of employees.

This modern concept of supervision may be defined as follows:

Supervision is leadership and the development of leadership within groups which are cooperatively engaged in inspection, research, training, guidance and evaluation.

## II. THE OLD AND THE NEW SUPERVISION

*TRADITIONAL*
1. Inspection
2. Focused on the employee
3. Visitation
4. Random and haphazard
5. Imposed and authoritarian
6. One person usually

*MODERN*
1. Study and analysis
2. Focused on aims, materials, methods, supervisors, employees, environment
3. Demonstrations, intervisitation, workshops, directed reading, bulletins, etc.
4. Definitely organized and planned (scientific)
5. Cooperative and democratic
6. Many persons involved (creative)

## III THE EIGHT (8) BASIC PRINCIPLES OF THE NEW SUPERVISION

1. *PRINCIPLE OF RESPONSIBILITY*
Authority to act and responsibility for acting must be joined.
   a. If you give responsibility, give authority.
   b. Define employee duties clearly.
   c. Protect employees from criticism by others.
   d. Recognize the rights as well as obligations of employees.
   e. Achieve the aims of a democratic society insofar as it is possible within the area of your work.
   f. Establish a situation favorable to training and learning.
   g. Accept ultimate responsibility for everything done in your section, unit, office, division, department.
   h. Good administration and good supervision are inseparable.

## 2. *PRINCIPLE OF AUTHORITY*
The success of the supervisor is measured by the extent to which the power of authority is not used.

    a. Exercise simplicity and informality in supervision.
    b. Use the simplest machinery of supervision.
    c. If it is good for the organization as a whole, it is probably justified.
    d. Seldom be arbitrary or authoritative.
    e. Do not base your work on the power of position or of personality.
    f. Permit and encourage the free expression of opinions.

## 3. *PRINCIPLE OF SELF-GROWTH*
The success of the supervisor is measured by the extent to which, and the speed with which, he is no longer needed.

    a. Base criticism on principles, not on specifics.
    b. Point out higher activities to employees.
    c. Train for self-thinking by employees, to meet new situations.
    d. Stimulate initiative, self-reliance and individual responsibility.
    e. Concentrate on stimulating the growth of employees rather than on removing defects.

## 4. *PRINCIPLE OF INDIVIDUAL WORTH*
Respect for the individual is a paramount consideration in supervision.

    a. Be human and sympathetic in dealing with employees.
    b. Don't nag about things to be done.
    c. Recognize the individual differences among employees and seek opportunities to permit best expression of each personality.

## 5. *PRINCIPLE OF CREATIVE LEADERSHIP*
The best supervision is that which is not apparent to the employee.

    a. Stimulate, don't drive employees to creative action.
    b. Emphasize doing good things.
    c. Encourage employees to do what they do best.
    d. Do not be too greatly concerned with details of subject or method.
    e. Do not be concerned exclusively with immediate problems and activities.
    f. Reveal higher activities and make them both desired and maximally possible.
    g. Determine procedures in the light of each situation but see that these are derived from a sound basic philosophy.
    h. Aid, inspire and lead so as to liberate the creative spirit latent in all good employees.

## 6. *PRINCIPLE OF SUCCESS AND FAILURE*
There are no unsuccessful employees, only unsuccessful supervisors who have failed to give proper leadership.

    a. Adapt suggestions to the capacities, attitudes, and prejudices of employees.
    b. Be gradual, be progressive, be persistent.
    c. Help the employee find the general principle; have the employee apply his own problem to the general principle.
    d. Give adequate appreciation for good work and honest effort.
    e. Anticipate employee difficulties and help to prevent them.
    f. Encourage employees to do the desirable things they will do anyway.
    g. Judge your supervision by the results it secures.

7. *PRINCIPLE OF SCIENCE*

Successful supervision is scientific, objective, and experimental. It is based on facts, not on prejudices.

a. Be cumulative in results.
b. Never divorce your suggestions from the goals of training.
c. Don't be impatient of results.
d. Keep all matters on a professional, not a personal level.
e. Do not be concerned exclusively with immediate problems and activities.
f. Use objective means of determining achievement and rating where possible.

8. *PRINCIPLE OF COOPERATION*

Supervision is a cooperative enterprise between supervisor and employee.

a. Begin with conditions as they are.
b. Ask opinions of all involved when formulating policies.
c. Organization is as good as its weakest link.
d. Let employees help to determine policies and department programs.
e. Be approachable and accessible - physically and mentally.
f. Develop pleasant social relationships.

## IV. WHAT IS ADMINISTRATION?

Administration is concerned with providing the environment, the material facilities, and the operational procedures that will promote the maximum growth and development of supervisors and employees. (Organization is an aspect, and a concomitant, of administration.)

There is no sharp line of demarcation between supervision and administration; these functions are intimately interrelated and, often, overlapping. They are complementary activities.

1. *PRACTICES COMMONLY CLASSED AS "SUPERVISORY"*
a. Conducting employees conferences
b. Visiting sections, units, offices, divisions, departments
c. Arranging for demonstrations
d. Examining plans
e. Suggesting professional reading
f. Interpreting bulletins
g. Recommending in-service training courses
h. Encouraging experimentation
i. Appraising employee morale
j. Providing for intervisitation

2. *PRACTICES COMMONLY CLASSIFIED AS "ADMINISTRATIVE"*
a. Management of the office
b. Arrangement of schedules for extra duties
c. Assignment of rooms or areas
d. Distribution of supplies
e. Keeping records and reports
f. Care of audio-visual materials
g. Keeping inventory records
h. Checking record cards and books
i. Programming special activities
j. Checking on the attendance and punctuality of employees

3. *PRACTICES COMMONLY CLASSIFIED AS BOTH "SUPERVISORY" AND "ADMINISTRATIVE"*
   a. Program construction
   b. Testing or evaluating outcomes
   c. Personnel accounting
   d. Ordering instructional materials

## V. RESPONSIBILITIES OF THE SUPERVISOR

A person employed in a supervisory capacity must constantly be able to improve his own efficiency and ability. He represents the employer to the employees and only continuous self-examination can make him a capable supervisor.

Leadership and training are the supervisor's responsibility. An efficient working unit is one in which the employees work with the supervisor. It is his job to bring out the best in his employees. He must always be relaxed, courteous and calm in his association with his employees. Their feelings are important, and a harsh attitude does not develop the most efficient employees.

## VI. COMPETENCIES OF THE SUPERVISOR

1. Complete knowledge of the duties and responsibilities of his position.
2. To be able to organize a job, plan ahead and carry through.
3. To have self-confidence and initiative.
4. To be able to handle the unexpected situation and make quick decisions.
5. To be able to properly train subordinates in the positions they are best suited for.
6. To be able to keep good human relations among his subordinates.
7. To be able to keep good human relations between his subordinates and himself and to earn their respect and trust.

## VII. THE PROFESSIONAL SUPERVISOR-EMPLOYEE RELATIONSHIP

There are two kinds of efficiency: one kind is only apparent and is produced in organizations through the exercise of mere discipline; this is but a simulation of the second, or true, efficiency which springs from spontaneous cooperation. If you are a manager, no matter how great or small your responsibility, it is your job, in the final analysis, to create and develop this involuntary cooperation among the people whom you supervise. For, no matter how powerful a combination of money, machines, and materials a company may have, this is a dead and sterile thing without a team of willing, thinking and articulate people to guide it.

The following 21 points are presented as indicative of the exemplary basic relationship that should exist between supervisor and employee:

1. Each person wants to be liked and respected by his fellow employee and wants to be treated with consideration and respect by his superior.
2. The most competent employee will make an error. However, in a unit where good relations exist between the supervisor and his employees, tenseness and fear do not exist. Thus, errors are not hidden or covered up and the efficiency of a unit is not impaired.
3. Subordinates resent rules, regulations, or orders that are unreasonable or unexplained.
4. Subordinates are quick to resent unfairness, harshness, injustices and favoritism.
5. An employee will accept responsibility if he knows that he will be complimented for a job well done, and not too harshly chastised for failure; that his supervisor will check the cause of the failure, and, if it was the supervisor's fault, he will assume the blame therefore. If it was the employee's fault, his supervisor will explain the correct method or means of handling the responsibility.

6. An employee wants to receive credit for a suggestion he has made, that is used. If a suggestion cannot be used, the employee is entitled to an explanation. The supervisor should not say "no" and close the subject.

7. Fear and worry slow up a worker's ability. Poor working environment can impair his physical and mental health. A good supervisor avoids forceful methods, threats and arguments to get a job done.

8. A forceful supervisor is able to train his employees individually and as a team, and is able to motivate them in the proper channels.

9. A mature supervisor is able to properly evaluate his subordinates and to keep them happy and satisfied.

10. A sensitive supervisor will never patronize his subordinates.

11. A worthy supervisor will respect his employees' confidences.

12. Definite and clear-cut responsibilities should be assigned to each executive.

13. Responsibility should always be coupled with corresponding authority.

14. No change should be made in the scope or responsibilities of a position without a definite understanding to that effect on the part of all persons concerned.

15. No executive or employee, occupying a single position in the organization, should be subject to definite orders from more than one source.

16. Orders should never be given to subordinates over the head of a responsible executive. Rather than do this, the officer in question should be supplanted.

17. Criticisms of subordinates should, whoever possible, be made privately, and in no case should a subordinate be criticized in the presence of executives or employees of equal or lower rank.

18. No dispute or difference between executives or employees as to authority or responsibilities should be considered too trivial for prompt and careful adjudication.

19. Promotions, wage changes, and disciplinary action should always be approved by the executive immediately superior to the one directly responsible.

20. No executive or employee should ever be required, or expected, to be at the same time an assistant to, and critic of, another.

21. Any executive whose work is subject to regular inspection should, whever practicable, be given the assistance and facilities necessary to enable him to maintain an independent check of the quality of his work.

## VIII. MINI-TEXT IN SUPERVISION, ADMINISTRATION, MANAGEMENT, AND ORGANIZATION

### A. BRIEF HIGHLIGHTS

Listed concisely and sequentially are major headings and important data in the field for quick recall and review.

### 1. *LEVELS OF MANAGEMENT*

Any organization of some size has several levels of management. In terms of a ladder the levels are:

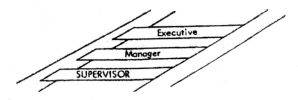

The first level is very important because it is the beginning point of management leadership.

## 2. WHAT THE SUPERVISOR MUST LEARN
A supervisor must learn to:
    (1) Deal with people and their differences
    (2) Get the job done through people
    (3) Recognize the problems when they exist
    (4) Overcome obstacles to good performance
    (5) Evaluate the performance of people
    (6) Check his own performance in terms of accomplishment

## 3. A DEFINITION OF SUPERVISOR
The term supervisor means any individual having authority, in the interests of the employer, to hire, transfer, suspend, lay-off, recall, promote, discharge, assign, reward, or discipline other employees or responsibility to direct them, or to adjust their grievances, or effectively to recommend such action, if, in connection with the foregoing, exercise of such authority is not of a merely routine or clerical nature but requires the use of independent judgment.

## 4. ELEMENTS OF THE TEAM CONCEPT
What is involved in teamwork? The component parts are:
    (1) Members    (3) Goals    (5) Cooperation
    (2) A leader    (4) Plans    (6) Spirit

## 5. PRINCIPLES OF ORGANIZATION
    (1) A team member must know what his job is.
    (2) Be sure that the nature and scope of a job are understood.
    (3) Authority and responsibility should be carefully spelled out.
    (4) A supervisor should be permitted to make the maximum number of decisions affecting his employees.
    (5) Employees should report to only one supervisor.
    (6) A supervisor should direct only as many employees as he can handle effectively.
    (7) An organization plan should be flexible.
    (8) Inspection and performance of work should be separate.
    (9) Organizational problems should receive immediate attention.
    (10) Assign work in line with ability and experience.

## 6. THE FOUR IMPORTANT PARTS OF EVERY JOB
    (1) Inherent in every job is the *accountability* for results.
    (2) A second set of factors in every job is *responsibilities*.
    (3) Along with duties and responsibilities one must have the *authority* to act within certain limits without obtaining permission to proceed.
    (4) No job exists in a vacuum. The supervisor is surrounded by key *relationships*.

## 7. PRINCIPLES OF DELEGATION
Where work is delegated for the first time, the supervisor should think in terms of these questions:
    (1) Who is best qualified to do this?
    (2) Can an employee improve his abilities by doing this?
    (3) How long should an employee spend on this?
    (4) Are there any special problems for which he will need guidance?
    (5) How broad a delegation can I make?

## 8. PRINCIPLES OF EFFECTIVE COMMUNICATIONS
     (1) Determine the media
     (2) To whom directed?
     (3) Identification and source authority
     (4) Is communication understood?

## 9. PRINCIPLES OF WORK IMPROVEMENT
     (1) Most people usually do only the work which is assigned to them
     (2) Workers are likely to fit assigned work into the time available to perform it
     (3) A good workload usually stimulates output
     (4) People usually do their best work when they know that results will be reviewed or inspected
     (5) Employees usually feel that someone else is responsible for conditions of work, workplace layout, job methods, type of tools/equipment, and other such factors
     (6) Employees are usually defensive about their job security
     (7) Employees have natural resistance to change
     (8) Employees can support or destroy a supervisor
     (9) A supervisor usually earns the respect of his people through his personal example of diligence and efficiency

## 10. AREAS OF JOB IMPROVEMENT
The areas of job improvement are quite numerous, but the most common ones which a supervisor can identify and utilize are:

  (1) Departmental layout      (5) Work methods
  (2) Flow of work      (6) Materials handling
  (3) Workplace layout      (7) Utilization
  (4) Utilization of manpower      (8) Motion economy

## 11. SEVEN KEY POINTS IN MAKING IMPROVEMENTS
     (1) Select the job to be improved
     (2) Study how it is being done now
     (3) Question the present method
     (4) Determine actions to be taken
     (5) Chart proposed method
     (6) Get approval and apply
     (7) Solicit worker participation

## 12. CORRECTIVE TECHNIQUES OF JOB IMPROVEMENT

| Specific Problems | General Improvement | Corrective Techniques |
| --- | --- | --- |
| (1) Size of workload | (1) Departmental layout | (1) Study with scale model |
| (2) Inability to meet schedules | (2) Flow of work | (2) Flow chart study |
| (3) Strain and fatigue | (3) Work plan layout | (3) Motion analysis |
| (4) Improper use of men and skills | (4) Utilization of manpower | (4) Comparison of units produced to standard allowance |
| (5) Waste, poor quality, unsafe conditions | (5) Work methods | (5) Methods analysis |
| (6) Bottleneck conditions that hinder output | (6) Materials handling | (6) Flow chart & equipment study |
| (7) Poor utilization of equipment and machine | (7) Utilization of equipment | (7) Down time vs. running time |
| (8) Efficiency and productivity of labor | (8) Motion economy | (8) Motion analysis |

## 13. A *PLANNING CHECKLIST*
(1) Objectives
(2) Controls
(3) Delegations
(4) Communications
(5) Resources

(6) Resources
(7) Manpower
(8) Equipment
(9) Supplies and materials
(10) Utilization of time

(11) Safety
(12) Money
(13) Work
(14) Timing of improvements

## 14. *FIVE CHARACTERISTICS OF GOOD DIRECTIONS*
In order to get results, directions must be:
(1) Possible of accomplishment
(2) Agreeable with worker interests
(3) Related to mission
(4) Planned and complete
(5) Unmistakably clear

## 15. *TYPES OF DIRECTIONS*
(1) Demands or direct orders
(2) Requests
(3) Suggestion or implication
(4) Volunteering

## 16. *CONTROLS*
A typical listing of the overall areas in which the supervisor should establish controls might be:
(1) Manpower
(2) Materials
(3) Quality of work
(4) Quantity of work
(5) Time
(6) Space
(7) Money
(8) Methods

## 17. *ORIENTING THE NEW EMPLOYEE*
(1) Prepare for him
(2) Welcome the new employee
(3) Orientation for the job
(4) Follow-up

## 18. *CHECKLIST FOR ORIENTING NEW EMPLOYEES*

Yes  No

(1) Do your appreciate the feelings of new employees when they first report for work?
(2) Are you aware of the fact that the new employee must make a big adjustment to his job?
(3) Have you given him good reasons for liking the job and the organization?
(4) Have you prepared for his first day on the job?
(5) Did you welcome him cordially and make him feel needed?
(6) Did you establish rapport with him so that he feels free to talk and discuss matters with you?
(7) Did you explain his job to him and his relationship to you?
(8) Does he know that his work will be evaluated periodically on a basis that is fair and objective?
(9) Did you introduce him to his fellow workers in such a way that they are likely to accept him?
(10) Does he know what employee benefits he will receive?
(11) Does he understand the importance of being on the job and what to do if he must leave his duty station?
(12) Has he been impressed with the importance of accident prevention and safe practice?
(13) Does he generally know his way around the department?
(14) Is he under the guidance of a sponsor who will teach the right ways of doing things?
(15) Do you plan to follow-up so that he will continue to adjust successfully to his job?

19. *PRINCIPLES OF LEARNING*
      (1) Motivation    (2) Demonstration or explanation    (3) Practice

20. *CAUSES OF POOR PERFORMANCE*
      (1) Improper training for job
      (2) Wrong tools
      (3) Inadequate directions
      (4) Lack of supervisory follow-up
      (5) Poor communications
      (6) Lack of standards of performance
      (7) Wrong work habits
      (8) Low morale
      (9) Other

21. *FOUR MAJOR STEPS IN ON-THE-JOB INSTRUCTION*
      (1) Prepare the worker
      (2) Present the operation
      (3) Tryout performance
      (4) Follow-up

22. *EMPLOYEES WANT FIVE THINGS*
      (1) Security  (2) Opportunity  (3) Recognition  (4) Inclusion  (5) Expression

23. *SOME DON'TS IN REGARD TO PRAISE*
      (1) Don't praise a person for something he hasn't done
      (2) Don't praise a person unless you can be sincere
      (3) Don't be sparing in praise just because your superior withholds it from you
      (4) Don't let too much time elapse between good performance and recognition of it

24. *HOW TO GAIN YOUR WORKERS' CONFIDENCE*
Methods of developing confidence include such things as:
      (1) Knowing the interests, habits, hobbies of employees
      (2) Admitting your own inadequacies
      (3) Sharing and telling of confidence in others
      (4) Supporting people when they are in trouble
      (5) Delegating matters that can be well handled
      (6) Being frank and straightforward about problems and working conditions
      (7) Encouraging others to bring their problems to you
      (8) Taking action on problems which impede worker progress

25. *SOURCES OF EMPLOYEE PROBLEMS*
On-the-job causes might be such things as:
      (1) A feeling that favoritism is exercised in assignments
      (2) Assignment of overtime
      (3) An undue amount of supervision
      (4) Changing methods or systems
      (5) Stealing of ideas or trade secrets
      (6) Lack of interest in job
      (7) Threat of reduction in force
      (8) Ignorance or lack of communications
      (9) Poor equipment
    (10) Lack of knowing how supervisor feels toward employee
    (11) Shift assignments

Off-the-job problems might have to do with:
      (1) Health    (2) Finances    (3) Housing    (4) Family

## 26. THE SUPERVISOR'S KEY TO DISCIPLINE

There are several key points about discipline which the supervisor should keep in mind:

(1) Job discipline is one of the disciplines of life and is directed by the supervisor.

(2) It is more important to correct an employee fault than to fix blame for it.

(3) Employee performance is affected by problems both on the job and off.

(4) Sudden or abrupt changes in behavior can be indications of important employee problems.

(5) Problems should be dealt with as soon as possible after they are identified.

(6) The attitude of the supervisor may have more to do with solving problems than the techniques of problem solving.

(7) Correction of employee behavior should be resorted to only after the supervisor is sure that training or counseling will not be helpful.

(8) Be sure to document your disciplinary actions.

(9) Make sure that you are disciplining on the basis of facts rather than personal feelings.

(10) Take each disciplinary step in order, being careful not to make snap judgments, or decisions based on impatience.

## 27. FIVE IMPORTANT PROCESSES OF MANAGEMENT

(1) Planning  (2) Organizing  (3) Scheduling
(4) Controlling  (5) Motivating

## 28. WHEN THE SUPERVISOR FAILS TO PLAN

(1) Supervisor creates impression of not knowing his job

(2) May lead to excessive overtime

(3) Job runs itself -- supervisor lacks control

(4) Deadlines and appointments missed

(5) Parts of the work go undone

(6) Work interrupted by emergencies

(7) Sets a bad example

(8) Uneven workload creates peaks and valleys

(9) Too much time on minor details at expense of more important tasks

## 29. FOURTEEN GENERAL PRINCIPLES OF MANAGEMENT

(1) Division of work
(2) Authority and responsibility
(3) Discipline
(4) Unity of command
(5) Unity of direction
(6) Subordination of individual interest to general interest
(7) Remuneration of personnel
(8) Centralization
(9) Scalar chain
(10) Order
(11) Equity
(12) Stability of tenure of personnel
(13) Initiative
(14) Esprit de corps

## 30. CHANGE

Bringing about change is perhaps attempted more often, and yet less well understood, than anything else the supervisor does. How do people generally react to change? (People tend to resist change that is imposed upon them by other individuals or circumstances.

Change is characteristic of every situation. It is a part of every real endeavor where the efforts of people are concerned.

A. Why do people resist change?
People may resist change because of:
(1) Fear of the unknown
(2) Implied criticism
(3) Unpleasant experiences in the past
(4) Fear of loss of status
(5) Threat to the ego
(6) Fear of loss of economic stability

B. How can we best overcome the resistance to change?
In initiating change, take these steps:
(1) Get ready to sell
(2) Identify sources of help
(3) Anticipate objections
(4) Sell benefits
(5) Listen in depth
(6) Follow up

## B. BRIEF TOPICAL SUMMARIES

## I. WHO/WHAT IS THE SUPERVISOR?
1. The supervisor is often called the "highest level employee and the lowest level manager."
2. A supervisor is a member of both management and the work group. He acts as a bridge between the two.
3. Most problems in supervision are in the area of human relations, or people problems.
4. Employees expect: Respect, opportunity to learn and to advance, and a sense of belonging, and so forth.
5. Supervisors are responsible for directing people and organizing work. Planning is of paramount importance.
6. A position description is a set of duties and responsibilities inherent to a given position.
7. It is important to keep the position description up-to-date and to provide each employee with his own copy.

## II. THE SOCIOLOGY OF WORK
1. People are alike in many ways; however, each individual is unique.
2. The supervisor is challenged in getting to know employee differences. Acquiring skills in evaluating individuals is an asset.
3. Maintaining meaningful working relationships in the organization is of great importance.
4. The supervisor has an obligation to help individuals to develop to their fullest potential.
5. Job rotation on a planned basis helps to build versatility and to maintain interest and enthusiasm in work groups.
6. Cross training (job rotation) provides backup skills.
7. The supervisor can help reduce tension by maintaining a sense of humor, providing guidance to employees, and by making reasonable and timely decisions. Employees respond favorably to working under reasonably predictable circumstances.
8. Change is characteristic of all managerial behavior. The supervisor must adjust to changes in procedures, new methods, technological changes, and to a number of new and sometimes challenging situations.
9. To overcome the natural tendency for people to resist change, the supervisor should become more skillful in initiating change.

## III. PRINCIPLES AND PRACTICES OF SUPERVISION

1. Employees should be required to answer to only one superior.
2. A supervisor can effectively direct only a limited number of employees, depending upon the complexity, variety, and proximity of the jobs involved.
3. The organizational chart presents the organization in graphic form. It reflects lines of authority and responsibility as well as interrelationships of units within the organization.
4. Distribution of work can be improved through an analysis using the "Work Distribution Chart."
5. The "Work Distribution Chart" reflects the division of work within a unit in understandable form.
6. When related tasks are given to an employee, he has a better chance of increasing his skills through training.
7. The individual who is given the responsibility for tasks must also be given the appropriate authority to insure adequate results.
8. The supervisor should delegate repetitive, routine work. Preparation of recurring reports, maintaining leave and attendance records are some examples.
9. Good discipline is essential to good task performance. Discipline is reflected in the actions of employees on the job in the absence of supervision.
10. Disciplinary action may have to be taken when the positive aspects of discipline have failed. Reprimand, warning, and suspension are examples of disciplinary action.
11. If a situation calls for a reprimand, be sure it is deserved and remember it is to be done in private.

## IV. DYNAMIC LEADERSHIP

1. A style is a personal method or manner of exerting influence.
2. Authoritarian leaders often see themselves as the source of power and authority.
3. The democratic leader often perceives the group as the source of authority and power.
4. Supervisors tend to do better when using the pattern of leadership that is most natural for them.
5. Social scientists suggest that the effective supervisor use the leadership style that best fits the problem or circumstances involved.
6. All four styles -- telling, selling, consulting, joining -- have their place. Using one does not preclude using the other at another time.
7. The theory X point of view assumes that the average person dislikes work, will avoid it whenever possible, and must be coerced to achieve organizational objectives.
8. The theory Y point of view assumes that the average person considers work to be as natural as play, and, when the individual is committed, he requires little supervision or direction to accomplish desired objectives.
9. The leader's basic assumptions concerning human behavior and human nature affect his actions, decisions, and other managerial practices.
10. Dissatisfaction among employees is often present, but difficult to isolate. The supervisor should seek to weaken dissatisfaction by keeping promises, being sincere and considerate, keeping employees informed, and so forth.
11. Constructive suggestions should be encouraged during the natural progress of the work.

## V. PROCESSES FOR SOLVING PROBLEMS

1. People find their daily tasks more meaningful and satisfying when they can improve them.
2. The causes of problems, or the key factors, are often hidden in the background. Ability to solve problems often involves the ability to isolate them from their backgrounds. There is some substance to the cliché that some persons "can't see the forest for the trees."
3. New procedures are often developed from old ones. Problems should be broken down into manageable parts. New ideas can be adapted from old ones.

4. People think differently in problem-solving situations. Using a logical, patterned approach is often useful. One approach found to be useful includes these steps:

|                          |                      |
|--------------------------|----------------------|
| (a) Define the problem   | (d) Weigh and decide |
| (b) Establish objectives | (e) Take action      |
| (c) Get the facts        | (f) Evaluate action  |

## VI. TRAINING FOR RESULTS

1. Participants respond best when they feel training is important to them.
2. The supervisor has responsibility for the training and development of those who report to him.
3. When training is delegated to others, great care must be exercised to insure the trainer has knowledge, aptitude, and interest for his work as a trainer.
4. Training (learning) of some type goes on continually. The most successful supervisor makes certain the learning contributes in a productive manner to operational goals.
5. New employees are particularly susceptible to training. Older employees facing new job situations require specific training, as well as having need for development and growth opportunities.
6. Training needs require continuous monitoring.
7. The training officer of an agency is a professional with a responsibility to assist supervisors in solving training problems.
8. Many of the self-development steps important to the supervisor's own growth are equally important to the development of peers and subordinates. Knowledge of these is important when the supervisor consults with others on development and growth opportunities.

## VII. HEALTH, SAFETY, AND ACCIDENT PREVENTION

1. Management-minded supervisors take appropriate measures to assist employees in maintaining health and in assuring safe practices in the work environment.
2. Effective safety training and practices help to avoid injury and accidents.
3. Safety should be a management goal. All infractions of safety which are observed should be corrected without exception.
4. Employees' safety attitude, training and instruction, provision of safe tools and equipment, supervision, and leadership are considered highly important factors which contribute to safety and which can be influenced directly by supervisors.
5. When accidents do occur they should be investigated promptly for very important reasons, including the fact that information which is gained can be used to prevent accidents in the future.

## VIII. EQUAL EMPLOYMENT OPPORTUNITY

1. The supervisor should endeavor to treat all employees fairly, without regard to religion, race, sex, or national origin.
2. Groups tend to reflect the attitude of the leader. Prejudice can be detected even in very subtle form. Supervisors must strive to create a feeling of mutual respect and confidence in every employee.
3. Complete utilization of all human resources is a national goal. Equitable consideration should be accorded women in the work force, minority-group members, the physically and mentally handicapped, and the older employee. The important question is: "Who can do the job?"
4. Training opportunities, recognition for performance, overtime assignments, promotional opportunities, and all other personnel actions are to be handled on an equitable basis.

## IX. IMPROVING COMMUNICATIONS

1. Communications is achieving understanding between the sender and the receiver of a message. It also means sharing information -- the creation of understanding.
2. Communication is basic to all human activity. Words are means of conveying meanings; however, real meanings are in people.
3. There are very practical differences in the effectiveness of one-way, impersonal, and two-way communications. Words spoken face-to-face are better understood. Telephone conversations are effective, but lack the rapport of person-to-person exchanges. The whole person communicates.
4. Cooperation and communication in an organization go hand in hand. When there is a mutual respect between people, spelling out rules and procedures for communicating is unnecessary.
5. There are several barriers to effective communications. These include failure to listen with respect and understanding, lack of skill in feedback, and misinterpreting the meanings of words used by the speaker. It is also common practice to listen to what we want to hear, and tune out things we do not want to hear.
6. Communication is management's chief problem. The supervisor should accept the challenge to communicate more effectively and to improve interagency and intra-agency communications.
7. The supervisor may often plan for and conduct meetings. The planning phase is critical and may determine the success or the failure of a meeting.
8. Speaking before groups usually requires extra effort. Stage fright may never disappear completely, but it can be controlled.

## X. SELF-DEVELOPMENT

1. Every employee is responsible for his own self-development.
2. Toastmaster and toastmistress clubs offer opportunities to improve skills in oral communications.
3. Planning for one's own self-development is of vital importance. Supervisors know their own strengths and limitations better than anyone else.
4. Many opportunities are open to aid the supervisor in his developmental efforts, including job assignments; training opportunities, both governmental and non-governmental -- to include universities and professional conferences and seminars.
5. Programmed instruction offers a means of studying at one's own rate.
6. Where difficulties may arise from a supervisor's being away from his work for training, he may participate in televised home study or correspondence courses to meet his self-develop- ment needs.

## XI. TEACHING AND TRAINING

### A. The Teaching Process

Teaching is encouraging and guiding the learning activities of students toward established goals. In most cases this process consists in five steps: preparation, presentation, summarization, evaluation, and application.

1. Preparation

Preparation is twofold in nature; that of the supervisor and the employee.
Preparation by the supervisor is absolutely essential to success. He must know what, when, where, how, and whom he will teach. Some of the factors that should be considered are:

| | |
|---|---|
| (1) The objectives | (5) Employee interest |
| (2) The materials needed | (6) Training aids |
| (3) The methods to be used | (7) Evaluation |
| (4) Employee participation | (8) Summarization |

Employee preparation consists in preparing the employee to receive the material. Probably the most important single factor in the preparation of the employee is arousing and maintaining his interest. He must know the objectives of the training, why he is there, how the material can be used, and its importance to him.

## 2. Presentation

In presentation, have a carefully designed plan and follow it.
The plan should be accurate and complete, yet flexible enough to meet situations as they arise. The method of presentation will be determined by the particular situation and objectives.

## 3. Summary

A summary should be made at the end of every training unit and program. In addition, there may be internal summaries depending on the nature of the material being taught. The important thing is that the trainee must always be able to understand how each part of the new material relates to the whole.

## 4. Application

The supervisor must arrange work so the employee will be given a chance to apply new knowledge or skills while the material is still clear in his mind and interest is high. The trainee does not really know whether he has learned the material until he has been given a chance to apply it. If the material is not applied, it loses most of its value.

## 5. Evaluation

The purpose of all training is to promote learning. To determine whether the training has been a success or failure, the supervisor must evaluate this learning.

In the broadest sense evaluation includes all the devices, methods, skills, and techniques used by the supervisor to keep him self and the employees informed as to their progress toward the objectives they are pursuing. The extent to which the employee has mastered the knowledge, skills, and abilities, or changed his attitudes, as determined by the program objectives, is the extent to which instruction has succeeded or failed.

Evaluation should not be confined to the end of the lesson, day, or program but should be used continuously. We shall note later the way this relates to the rest of the teaching process.

## B. Teaching Methods

A teaching method is a pattern of identifiable student and instructor activity used in presenting training material.

All supervisors are faced with the problem of deciding which method should be used at a given time.

As with all methods, there are certain advantages and disadvantages to each method.

## 1. Lecture

The lecture is direct oral presentation of material by the supervisor. The present trend is to place less emphasis on the trainer's activity and more on that of the trainee.

## 2. Discussion

Teaching by discussion or conference involves using questions and other techniques to arouse interest and focus attention upon certain areas, and by doing so creating a learning situation. This can be one of the most valuable methods because it gives the employees 'an opportunity to express their ideas and pool their knowledge.

3. Demonstration

The demonstration is used to teach how something works or how to do something. It can be used to show a principle or what the results of a series of actions will be. A well-staged demonstration is particularly effective because it shows proper methods of performance in a realistic manner.

4. Performance

Performance is one of the most fundamental of all learning techniques or teaching methods. The trainee may be able to tell how a specific operation should be performed but he cannot be sure he knows how to perform the operation until he has done so.

5. Which Method to Use

Moreover, there are other methods and techniques of teaching. It is difficult to use any method without other methods entering into it. In any learning situation a combination of methods is usually more effective than anyone method alone.

Finally, evaluation must be integrated into the other aspects of the teaching-learning process. It must be used in the motivation of the trainees; it must be used to assist in developing understanding during the training; and it must be related to employee application of the results of training.

This is distinctly the role of the supervisor.

———

# ANSWER SHEET

TEST NO. _____ PART _____ TITLE OF POSITION _____
(AS GIVEN IN EXAMINATION ANNOUNCEMENT - INCLUDE OPTION, IF ANY)

PLACE OF EXAMINATION _____ DATE _____
(CITY OR TOWN)                                (STATE)

RATING

## USE THE SPECIAL PENCIL.    MAKE GLOSSY BLACK MARKS.

| # | A B C D E | # | A B C D E | # | A B C D E | # | A B C D E | # | A B C D E |
|---|---|---|---|---|---|---|---|---|---|
| 1 | :: :: :: :: :: | 26 | :: :: :: :: :: | 51 | :: :: :: :: :: | 76 | :: :: :: :: :: | 101 | :: :: :: :: :: |
| 2 | :: :: :: :: :: | 27 | :: :: :: :: :: | 52 | :: :: :: :: :: | 77 | :: :: :: :: :: | 102 | :: :: :: :: :: |
| 3 | :: :: :: :: :: | 28 | :: :: :: :: :: | 53 | :: :: :: :: :: | 78 | :: :: :: :: :: | 103 | :: :: :: :: :: |
| 4 | :: :: :: :: :: | 29 | :: :: :: :: :: | 54 | :: :: :: :: :: | 79 | :: :: :: :: :: | 104 | :: :: :: :: :: |
| 5 | :: :: :: :: :: | 30 | :: :: :: :: :: | 55 | :: :: :: :: :: | 80 | :: :: :: :: :: | 105 | :: :: :: :: :: |
| 6 | :: :: :: :: :: | 31 | :: :: :: :: :: | 56 | :: :: :: :: :: | 81 | :: :: :: :: :: | 106 | :: :: :: :: :: |
| 7 | :: :: :: :: :: | 32 | :: :: :: :: :: | 57 | :: :: :: :: :: | 82 | :: :: :: :: :: | 107 | :: :: :: :: :: |
| 8 | :: :: :: :: :: | 33 | :: :: :: :: :: | 58 | :: :: :: :: :: | 83 | :: :: :: :: :: | 108 | :: :: :: :: :: |
| 9 | :: :: :: :: :: | 34 | :: :: :: :: :: | 59 | :: :: :: :: :: | 84 | :: :: :: :: :: | 109 | :: :: :: :: :: |
| 10 | :: :: :: :: :: | 35 | :: :: :: :: :: | 60 | :: :: :: :: :: | 85 | :: :: :: :: :: | 110 | :: :: :: :: :: |

### Make only ONE mark for each answer.    Additional and stray marks may be counted as mistakes.    In making corrections, erase errors COMPLETELY.

| # | A B C D E | # | A B C D E | # | A B C D E | # | A B C D E | # | A B C D E |
|---|---|---|---|---|---|---|---|---|---|
| 11 | :: :: :: :: :: | 36 | :: :: :: :: :: | 61 | :: :: :: :: :: | 86 | :: :: :: :: :: | 111 | :: :: :: :: :: |
| 12 | :: :: :: :: :: | 37 | :: :: :: :: :: | 62 | :: :: :: :: :: | 87 | :: :: :: :: :: | 112 | :: :: :: :: :: |
| 13 | :: :: :: :: :: | 38 | :: :: :: :: :: | 63 | :: :: :: :: :: | 88 | :: :: :: :: :: | 113 | :: :: :: :: :: |
| 14 | :: :: :: :: :: | 39 | :: :: :: :: :: | 64 | :: :: :: :: :: | 89 | :: :: :: :: :: | 114 | :: :: :: :: :: |
| 15 | :: :: :: :: :: | 40 | :: :: :: :: :: | 65 | :: :: :: :: :: | 90 | :: :: :: :: :: | 115 | :: :: :: :: :: |
| 16 | :: :: :: :: :: | 41 | :: :: :: :: :: | 66 | :: :: :: :: :: | 91 | :: :: :: :: :: | 116 | :: :: :: :: :: |
| 17 | :: :: :: :: :: | 42 | :: :: :: :: :: | 67 | :: :: :: :: :: | 92 | :: :: :: :: :: | 117 | :: :: :: :: :: |
| 18 | :: :: :: :: :: | 43 | :: :: :: :: :: | 68 | :: :: :: :: :: | 93 | :: :: :: :: :: | 118 | :: :: :: :: :: |
| 19 | :: :: :: :: :: | 44 | :: :: :: :: :: | 69 | :: :: :: :: :: | 94 | :: :: :: :: :: | 119 | :: :: :: :: :: |
| 20 | :: :: :: :: :: | 45 | :: :: :: :: :: | 70 | :: :: :: :: :: | 95 | :: :: :: :: :: | 120 | :: :: :: :: :: |
| 21 | :: :: :: :: :: | 46 | :: :: :: :: :: | 71 | :: :: :: :: :: | 96 | :: :: :: :: :: | 121 | :: :: :: :: :: |
| 22 | :: :: :: :: :: | 47 | :: :: :: :: :: | 72 | :: :: :: :: :: | 97 | :: :: :: :: :: | 122 | :: :: :: :: :: |
| 23 | :: :: :: :: :: | 48 | :: :: :: :: :: | 73 | :: :: :: :: :: | 98 | :: :: :: :: :: | 123 | :: :: :: :: :: |
| 24 | :: :: :: :: :: | 49 | :: :: :: :: :: | 74 | :: :: :: :: :: | 99 | :: :: :: :: :: | 124 | :: :: :: :: :: |
| 25 | :: :: :: :: :: | 50 | :: :: :: :: :: | 75 | :: :: :: :: :: | 100 | :: :: :: :: :: | 125 | :: :: :: :: :: |

34 85

# ANSWER SHEET

RECEIVED MAY 8 2014

TEST NO. _____ PART _____ TITLE OF POSITION _____

(AS GIVEN IN EXAMINATION ANNOUNCEMENT - INCLUDE OPTION, IF ANY)

PLACE OF EXAMINATION _____ DATE _____

(CITY OR TOWN) (STATE)

RATING

## USE THE SPECIAL PENCIL.    MAKE GLOSSY BLACK MARKS.

Make only ONE mark for each answer.   Additional and stray marks may be counted as mistakes.   In making corrections, erase errors COMPLETELY.